MORE PRAISE FOR
Michele Borba

"12 *Simple Secrets Real Moms Know* is a godsend for all the anxious, stressed-out mothers who worry that they're not 'doing enough' (and that's pretty much everyone!)."

—Christiane Northrup, M.D., author, *Mother-Daughter
Wisdom* and *Women's Bodies, Women's Wisdom*

"As a member of Congress, I am faced daily with the challenge of balancing my work in Washington, D.C., with the most important job that I will ever have—being a mother to my two children. I am a firm believer in the importance of parental involvement and the tremendous influence mothers can have on their child's development. I appreciate the message that this book champions and the guidance it provides to mothers struggling to foster a brighter future for their children."

—Mary Bono, member of Congress,
California's 45th District, and mother of two

"Michele Borba has done it again. She's given mothers a book full to the brim with wisdom, stories, and tips on how to raise happy, well-adjusted children."

—Mimi Doe, author, *Busy but Balanced;* founder,
SpiritualParenting.com; and mother of two

"Michele infuses you with the wisdom and warmth of her more than twenty years of teaching, shares the savvy of her in-depth research of over 5,000 parents, and helps return you to the heart of successful parenting."

—Stacy Debroff, author, *The Mom Book,* and
founder of momscentral.com

"A practical, easy-to-read guide, full of great examples to help mothers teach their children the skills that will eventually be invaluable for greater success and happiness in college."

—Richard Kadison, M.D., chief of the Mental Health
Service, Harvard University Health Services

12 Simple Secrets
Real Moms Know

THE 12 SIMPLE SECRETS
OF REAL MOTHERING

1. A mother who loves teaches worth.

2. A mother who is firm and fair gives her children a moral code to live by.

3. A mother who listens shows her children they matter.

4. A mother who is a good role model gives her children an example worth copying.

5. A mother who teaches values inspires character.

6. A mother who supports her children's strengths builds their confidence.

7. A mother who encourages independence cultivates self-reliance.

8. A mother who applauds effort nurtures perseverance.

9. A mother who accepts her children's shortcomings nurtures resilience.

10. A mother who takes time for her children helps them build strong relationships.

11. A mother who laughs teaches joy.

12. A mother who takes care of herself holds together her happy family.

—Michele Borba

12 Simple Secrets Real Moms Know

GETTING BACK TO BASICS
AND RAISING HAPPY KIDS

Michele Borba, Ed.D.

JOSSEY-BASS
A Wiley Imprint
www.josseybass.com

Published by Jossey-Bass
A Wiley Imprint
989 Market Street, San Francisco, CA 94103-1741   www.josseybass.com

Jossey-Bass books and products are available through most bookstores. To contact Jossey-Bass directly call our Customer Care Department within the U.S. at 800-956-7739, outside the U.S. at 317-572-3986, or fax 317-572-4002.

Jossey-Bass also publishes its books in a variety of electronic formats. Some content that appears in print may not be available in electronic books.

Library of Congress Cataloging-in-Publication Data
Borba, Michele.
12 simple secrets real moms know : getting back to basics and raising happy kids / Michele Borba.
    p. cm.
Includes bibliographical references.
ISBN-13: 978-0-7879-8096-2 (pbk.)
ISBN-10: 0-7879-8096-X (pbk.)
1. Motherhood. 2. Mother and child. 3. Parenting. I. Title.
II. Title: Twelve simple secrets real moms know.
HQ759.B653 2006
306.874'3—dc22   2005033966

Printed in the United States of America
FIRST EDITION
PB Printing   10 9 8 7 6 5 4 3 2 1

contents

With love to the most extraordinary example of
real mothering: My mother, Treva Ungaro

acknowLedqments

One of my favorite quotes is by François Rabelais: "A child is not a vase to be filled, but a fire to be lit." This book could not have been written without the remarkable mothers who told me their stories. They are the ones who inspired in me the notion of "real mothering." In particular, special love goes to George and Bonnie Englund, Don and Marilyn Perlyn, and Jim and Anamarie Anthony for sharing their parenting secrets and touching my own life in more ways than they can ever know.

Special appreciation is extended to the following women who offered personal insights, wise perspective, and just plain great tips on real mothering: Kappy Tobin Armstrong, Catherine Ayala, Judy Baggott, Joan Baker, Andrea Bauman, Aubria Becker, Kathy Been, Lorayne Borba, Jane Mills, Marion Card, Marj Casagrande, Daisy Chan, Bernadette DeFontes, Karen Dischner, Margaret Dwyer, Maureen Ferriter, Andrea Funk, Debbie Gibson, JoAnne Gill, Louise Hampton, Lana Hannas, Anne Kalisek, Barbara Keane, Anne Leedom, Kathryn Livingston, Lenore Markowitz, Gaye McCabe, Carole Morgan, Susie Morrison, Cindy Morse, Barbara Namian, Kim Plumley, Michelle Price, Cheryl Rinzler, Murf Ryan, Joan Saunders, Jane Schneider, Patty Service, Lottie Shivers, Margie Sims, Julie Snyder, Shellie Spradlin, Sue Summit, Cathy Tippett, Barbara Turvett, Treva Ungaro, Bong Ying, and Winnie Yiu. Appreciation also goes to Bob Worswick for telling me the story about the boy and the dog and tracking down various facts for story authenticity.

There is also an incredible group of moms who years ago first helped me learn about the power and love of mothering. They were the mothers of my first special education students. I watched them in absolute awe and have never forgotten their influence on their children. A few who could have written the true manual for mothering include Judy Bartee, Mary Grace Galvin, Diane Long, Laurie Mobilio, Rita Pacheco, Mrs. Speciale, and Bindy Wood.

Every book is a group effort, and there are a number of people whom I gratefully acknowledge for helping me make this book possible. I thank Jossey-Bass/Wiley executive editor Alan Rinzler for his friendship, superb insights, exemplary skill, passion, and guidance through every possible step. At Jossey-Bass and Wiley, Alan is surrounded by the finest publishing staff around, whom I thank for their support on all six of the books we've now worked on together: Jennifer Wenzel, Catherine Craddock, Erik Thrasher, Meghan Brousseau, P. J. Campbell, Paula Goldstein, Carol Hartland, Michele Jones, Sophia Ho, Lori Sayde-Mehrtens, Jennifer Smith, and Karen Warner. In particular, I thank my publishers, Debra Hunter and Paul Foster, for the privilege of writing for them over these many years together.

To Joelle DelBourgo, my agent, for her stellar competence and warm friendship, and for lending an ear at always just the right time. Believe me, every writer should have this woman in her corner.

To the staff of *Parents* magazine, especially Diane Debrover, for the honor of serving on their advisory board and the opportunity of speaking with many of their writers about several of the parenting issues in this book. To Rose Carrano, publicist extraordinaire, it's just been a privilege to work together. To Anne Leedom, president of netconnectpublicity.com, for continuing to be the best backseat cheerleader, and to Steve Leedom, president of nowimagine.com, for creating and updating my Web sites www.behaviormakeovers.com. and www.micheleborba.com.

Once again, no writer could have a better support system than her own family. To my husband, perpetual supporter and best friend, Craig, and the three greatest sons, Jason, Adam, and Zach, thank you once again for putting up with me. This is the twenty-first book we've written "together," and I would never have been able to do this without you.

And finally to the memory of Max Englund: a child whose life was far too short, but who still taught me so much about the power of love and resilience. I swore I'd someday write about this remarkable boy. So Max, here's to you! I hope I told it right.

Michele Borba
Palm Springs, California

note to the reader

All stories in this book are about children and their mothers whom I have interviewed, known, or worked with over the last twenty years. A few stories are composite cases of children I have treated. Actual children's and mothers' names are included, except in those instances where a parent asked that her name be changed to protect her privacy. The exceptions are mothers interviewed for newspapers or written about in books, and those are noted in the References.

Unless otherwise noted in the References, stories and tips are based on interviews I conducted face-to-face, by phone, or through email exchanges with 150 mothers while writing this book. I also surveyed over five thousand additional parents in my workshops about what they felt mattered most in real mothering. Many of their responses are included in boxed tips. A sample of the U.S. cities where these interviews took place includes Albany, Aspen, Atherton, Berkeley, Chattanooga, Chicago, Coco Beach, Dallas, Diamond Bar, Essex Falls, Hays, Kalispel, Las Vegas, Little Rock, Los Angeles, Memphis, Milwaukee, Minneapolis, Nashville, New York City, Oakland, Oklahoma City, Orlando, Palm Springs, Reno, Sacramento, Salt Lake City, San Diego, San Jose, Santa Clarita, Seattle, Tulsa, and Palm Springs. Canadian cities include Bonnyville, Brandon, Calgary, Cold Lake, Edmonton, Kelowna, Lac la Biche, Ottawa, Saskatoon, Simcoe County, Toronto, Vancouver, Westminster, and Winnipeg.

What Is a Real Mom?

"What is REAL?" asked the Rabbit one day. . . .
    "Real isn't how you are made," said the Skin Horse.
"It's a thing that happens to you. When a child loves you
for a long, long time, not just to play with but REALLY
loves you, then you become Real. . . . It doesn't happen all
at once . . . , but once you are Real you can't become unreal
again. It lasts for always."
                    —Margery Williams, *The Velveteen Rabbit*

Hey, Mom: Are you real? Is what you're doing as a mother going to "last for always"?

Sure, that may sound like a silly question, but the answer is going to tell you a lot about just how effective you are as a mother, how influential you will be on your children's lives, and whether they will grow up to be happy adults with character and confidence. It will also make a big difference in just how happy your family is now, today, every day.

But you may ask, "Isn't everyone real? Isn't whatever I do as a mother automatically real?"

Well . . . no. Not necessarily. A lot of us moms are wondering these days if all the incredible amount of "stuff" we're

1

doing for our kids really matters in the long run and if what we're doing is really the best thing for our families. Of course we love our kids to pieces and would do anything in the world for them. That's never been in doubt. But many of us feel torn, pushed, and pulled in different directions. Whether we work full time or part time or are stay-at-home moms seems to make no difference. Most mothers are feeling the same. There are so many parenting choices and opportunities these days, so many new mothering options and strategies, so many new products that are supposed to make our kids brilliant and successful. And all that new research keeps hitting us in the face with what we must do pronto or else. And then there's the pressure of trying to keep up with all the other moms and all that they do for their kids that could give them the edge over ours.

So we're running around making all these appointments— the test prep classes, the soccer practices, the recitals, the Chinese lessons, the gymnastic meets, the camps, the Suzuki drills, the tutors and coaches. And we're trying to play all these different roles: we're the limo driver, the party planner, the wardrobe mistress, the volunteer car washer, the super-organized woman with the longest to-do list on the block. The more we do, the more there is to do. The more we try to keep up with the latest parenting trends and competition for status and achievement, the more pressure and anxiety we experience. The more we wish we could keep it simple, the more complicated and difficult it seems to become.

Is it any wonder that we moms have major doubts about what our role should be? Are you at all concerned that the complicated and demanding roles we're playing, however unintentionally, are being dictated to us from somewhere else, by some expert or guru or lady down the block? Do other feelings bubble up? Is there a little voice in the back of your head that's asking, "What are you doing? Do you really think this is right? So what if everyone else is doing it—why are you doing it too?

Does mothering have to be so difficult?" Do these "mothering" roles and frantic activities represent our authentic selves, our core beliefs, our basic maternal instincts and intuition, what we know is right for our unique and special kids? Are these roles real?

"I Stopped Trying to Be Perfect"　🖉 REAL MOM TALK

I'm often guilty of trying to be all things to my child, only to find myself living in a manic world of to-do lists, high-intensity parenting, and guilt. So I've been working on a new strategy. *Instead of being a perfect mom, I'm giving myself permission to be a "good-enough" mom.* This winter, one of the volunteer leaders of an extracurricular activity my son enjoys had stepped down, and they needed another parent to take his place. My son was eager for me to volunteer. I was tempted. Of course, the perfect mom would have made time and relegated her needs to the bottom of the list. But after giving it some thought, I decided I needed to say no. My son was a bit disappointed initially, but my absence hasn't diminished his enjoyment of the program, and it means he sees his mother in a calmer state. I think that's a fair trade-off. I'm not the perfect mom, but I'm beginning to feel okay about that, and I am learning that good-enough works too.

–Jane Schneider, editor of
Memphis Parent magazine,
single mom of a ten-year-old son

Okay, have I got your attention? Do you agree that all the stresses and pressures of being a mother today can wrench us away from being real and sticking to our intuition of what's best for our kids? So how do we get back in touch with what really matters to our kids? How do we know what is real?

I'll tell you.

Defining Real

Real is one of those words that everybody uses but whose meaning nobody really knows. So here's what I believe.

- Real comes from deep inside.
- Real is instinctive and intuitive.
- Real is authentic and genuine. There's just no faking it.
- Real is never borrowed. It's staying true to you.
- Real has no pretense, fabrication, phoniness.
- Real is simple. It's not complicated or difficult.
- Real comes naturally.

So what does a real mom look like?

- A real mom doesn't worry about what other moms are doing or saying.
- A real mom knows her children so well that she makes her parenting decisions based on their unique needs.
- A real mom is clear about her personal values and code of behavior, and sticks to them.
- A real mom knows what's important for her family and keeps those priorities straight.
- A real mom has confidence in her maternal instinct and isn't pushed around by the latest pressures and trends.
- A real mom knows that what matters most is a close connection with her children so that her influence lasts for always.

And what does a real mom do? Above all, she stays true to herself and connected to her kids, and she doesn't deviate from what she knows is best for her family.

- Real moms have a life of their own.
- Real moms break the rules for their family.

- Real moms let their kids wear the same clothes two days in a row.
- Real moms go on a date with their husbands and aren't afraid to miss the PTA meeting.
- Real moms give their kids pots and pans to play with.
- Real moms leave their food on the tray and head for the parking lot when their kid has a meltdown at McDonalds.
- Real moms make their kids do their own homework.
- Real moms aren't afraid to say no.
- Real moms give themselves time-outs.
- Real moms tell their kids they don't have to play Beethoven's "Für Elise" at the family reunion.
- Real moms know it's not personal when their kids say, "You're the meanest mother in the whole world."
- Real moms say "Good job" when their kids get an A but hold off on the brand-new Lexus.
- Real moms make their sixteen-year-olds set their own alarm clocks.
- Real moms tell their kids to pay their own library fines.
- Real moms ask Uncle Harry to put on the lampshade and do his juggling act on the kitchen table as the birthday party clown.
- Real moms let their kids be bored.
- Real moms say, "Not in our family" when their kids complain that "But everyone else does."
- Real moms say, "I'm not an ATM machine" and tell their kids to save money.
- Real moms admit they're wrong.
- Real moms know they're not perfect.
- Real moms leave the dust when the playgroup comes over.
- Real moms admit when they're grouchy.

- Real moms send their kid to canoe paddling camp when the other mothers enroll theirs in intensive Chinese language immersion.

Getting Back to Real Mothering

Does this sound like you? Do you recognize or identify with the traits of a real mom I've listed here? Of course we all want to be real, to stay true to ourselves and be a positive influence on our kids. But we're living in a high-pressure, fast-paced, competitive world. It's not hard to get swept away and lose sight of reality, of what we know in our hearts to be true.

Mothering is probably the most important job we'll ever have in our lives. Nothing, absolutely nothing, has as much influence and power over our families and future generations in years to come. Yet there's general agreement among all the hundreds of mothers I've spoken to that something isn't working: our kids aren't thriving as well as we'd hoped, and we are too often suffering from guilt, anxiety, and exhaustion. That's why there's been so much national talk lately and so many books written about the epidemic of Motherhood Mania. Far too many of us are responding to the pressure of this modern myth of mothering as a 24/7 sprint to the finish line. Instead of reconsidering what works and what doesn't, we're trying harder to be perfect. And that isn't working either.

The only solution is to be real, to be simple, to get back to the natural and authentic kind of mothering that isn't based on the latest TV show, educational video game, or hot new parenting product. The good news is, you don't have to go back to school, get a license or academic credential, or drive yourself nuts working hard on it every day. Remember: if it's real, it's simple. It's not complicated or difficult. It's easy to do, and you already have the skills.

Not only that, the benefits of real mothering are enormous.

When I Stopped Trying to Be the Ideal Mom

I was twenty-six years old when I married, and instantly became a mom to five stepchildren: four boys and a girl, ages three to eleven. I wanted desperately to be a good mom, but frankly I was overwhelmed. This job didn't come with a set of rules. I read every available parenting book and tried every technique. I even took parenting classes at night. I was stressed and really feeling uncomfortable in my new role as stepmother. I even tried to dress differently to present the ideal image of a more traditional-looking mom, but nothing was working.

One day I went for a long walk to think things through. "You're smart," I kept telling myself. "This should be easier." I asked myself, "Is something wrong with me, or is it how I'm parenting the kids?" Then it suddenly dawned on me what was wrong: I was trying to be someone who wasn't me. I was trying to be this image of what I thought a perfect mother should be, and the kids saw right through it. That was my "ah-ha" moment: I knew I had to be true to myself.

From then on things started to get better in my interactions with the children, because they perceived my relationship with them to be genuine. I didn't have to be perfect with my kids or try so hard to be someone I wasn't naturally—the ideal model depicted of mothering. I didn't have to put on some "ideal role of motherhood" to be accepted by them. I can't tell you what a difference it made in gaining their respect. The gift that my children gave to me was my newfound self-confidence that I could be myself and also their mother.

—Bernadette DeFontes, stepmom of five,
Gaithersburg, Maryland

The Benefits of Being a Real Mother

Some of the long-term dividends of being a real mother are obvious and easy to appreciate; others are more subtle, yet no less important. Here is my list of seven reasons we need to get real:

1. Real moms can help their kids buck peer pressure because the certainty and firmness of their conviction strengthens their influence on their kids.

2. Real moms' children are more likely to adopt their mother's values because their mother hasn't watered down her beliefs with the latest trends or moral compromises.

3. Real moms are likely to be better models of patience and self-control because they're being themselves and are at peace with who they are.

4. Real moms are happier and have more joy in their families because there is so much less pretense and putting on to keep up.

5. Real moms are less guilty and anxious because they're not trying to be perfect by other people's standards.

6. Real moms are more appreciated because their kids have had a chance to know their interests and passions.

7. Real moms have more energy for their families because they don't waste time doing things that don't match their priorities and beliefs.

The result of all these wonderful benefits is that real moms enjoy a powerful connection with their children that lasts for always. If your kids are two, three, twenty, or older, the bond remains as strong and important as ever. You could even say that your model and the lessons you've learned are carried with them in their own lives and families. It's the most important legacy that you can ever provide.

Like a Hamster on a Wheel

Just this week I asked a mom how her family life was going.
"Exhausting," was the first word out of her mouth. Then she
added, "I'm starting to feel like a hamster on one of those
wheels—going around and around and never getting off."

Is that what modern mothering has come to: being a hamster on a wheel? It's that crazed feeling that Judith Warner describes in her best-selling book *Perfect Madness*. But it's that same
notion (the "continual busyness" or "always doing") that seems
symptomatic of mothering these days. It was the same underlying theme of so many of the moms I interviewed.

I've come to realize that real mothering, the stuff that
makes up the true natural essence of being a mother, hasn't
changed and never will. Most every woman I spoke to still had
that basic instinct; that unconditional love, tenderness, empathy, patience, perseverance; the willingness to listen, to devote
themselves, to take joy and pleasure in their children. But the
society we're living in here in the good old twenty-first-century
United States does have a new and different expectation of
what it is to be a good, responsible, conscientious mother.

These days the central expectation of a good mom is for her to be a "doer" (volunteer, home tutor, home coach, carpool driver, PTA enthusiast, social secretary, hostess, and on and on—very complicated).

A decade ago, the main expectation was that she be a "nurturer" (supporter, listener, guider—simpler, and real). And that little switch has had a dramatic impact on our lives as well as on the lives of our children. It's also weakened our influence with our children, zapped our energy, and boosted our guilt. As so many mothers told me, to be a good mom these days you have to "keep up" and "keep doing"; if not, you feel you're cheating your children and flunking motherhood. Bear with me a minute. Read on, and see if you don't agree.

Ask a woman to describe a good mother, and you get a résumé: "A room mother." "The play group coordinator." "A soccer coach." "A scout leader." "The PTA president." "A booster club officer." "An after-school volunteer." The list of roles goes on and on and on. Mothering is a to-do list. And we're exhausted just trying to keep up and keep our family's schedule straight. The more a mom does, the better her chances of making the "Mommy Hall of Fame" (at least in the eyes of the other moms).

Interestingly enough, the kids describe their moms as "always involved" and "busy"—though teens would more likely say that their moms don't have a life. The same kids also describe their moms as "usually tired" and "impatient," and they "wish their moms could spend more time with them." But how could they, when their schedules are so filled?

Fond Memories of Real Moms

Now ask someone to describe what they remember most about their own mothers, the "real moms" they grew up with, and you hear quite a different list of traits: "My mother was such a great listener." "She was always there." "My mom was so patient!" "All my friends used to tell me how nice my mother was." "Mom was so funny, we just laughed and laughed."

I realized from these interviews and surveys that what we all remembered was not what our moms *did*, but who they *were* and how strong (or not) was the connection between mother and child. We remembered the woman herself, or simply "my mother."

These women influenced us by being real: with their own lives, their personal example, and their genuine selves—not with all the things they did for us. They knew instinctively how to connect with us and form a lasting attachment. These moms didn't rely on parenting gurus, use flash cards, learn the latest discipline gimmicks, and read child development charts. They used their natural-born instincts to mother their children, and because they did, their mothering was more authentic, far simpler, and more effective in influencing their kids' lives for the better, because they set their children a terrific example. They were really real.

Six Core Principles of Real Mothering

Having traveled around a lot talking, interviewing, and surveying mothers across the United States and throughout the world these past few years, I can tell you with confidence that being a real mother is founded on just six core principles that these women knew all along. A responsible, caring woman

1. Loves her children deeply and is committed to raising them to the best of her ability
2. Knows the essential and proven parenting principles
3. Maintains a strong belief that no one understands or knows better what's best for her child than herself
4. Recognizes her child's and her own unique strengths and temperament, and customizes her parenting to fit
5. Has the confidence to act on these beliefs

6. Knows, above all else, that it's the connection with her child that matters most

The true essence of real mothering lies in who you really are and how you connect with your child—and that's what we've so often forgotten.

We need to get back to real mothering. The benefits of doing so are profound for you, your child, and your family—they last for always. And the sooner we return to basic, instinctive, natural, authentic mothering, the stronger our families will be.

What About Fathers?

Of course dads make a huge difference in their kids' lives. Yes, their role in how kids turn out is immensely significant. And sure, they're very important, after all, they are half of the "nurture" factor in your kids' development. So you may wonder why they're not part of this book. The truth is, it's more moms than dads who are caught up in this frenzy of hyperactive parenting. Research has shown that in general moms spend more time with their kids and usually have more responsibility for the dropping off, shuttling, arranging, and just being with kids all day.

The catalyst for writing this book has been moms who have come up to me at my workshops and written emails to tell me about their anguish and struggle in raising happy kids. I know that fathers have the same concerns, but my primary experience has been as a mother with other mothers. I believe that ideally every mother has a caring and committed partner to help her raise children. But this book is written heart to heart, mother to mother.

How Do You Want to Be Remembered?

So I have a question. Imagine that your children are grown and now have families of their own. Your children are describing you to their children—your grandchildren. How do you want to be described or even remembered by your children? I would be willing to bet it would be as the type of woman who influenced your life: "A mother who loved and taught me worth." "A mother who listened and showed me I mattered." "A mother who laughed and taught me joy."

If that's the kind of mother you want to become for your children, read on. It will be the woman your children describe years from now if you follow the plan in this book. The core reason I wrote 12 Simple Secrets Real Moms Know is as a call for all of us to get back to what really matters most in raising happy children who have confidence, resilience, and character. A call to redefine a real mother in terms of who she is to her children, not just all that she does. A mother's connection with her child is what matters most. It's time we get back to basic, real mothering.

Your children really do grow up all too quickly, but your connection to them will last an eternity if you learn to use the twelve secrets in this book, follow your instincts, and keep true to yourself. Enjoy! The journey of love is worth every step.

How to Use This Book

The goal of this book is to learn the 12 Simple Secrets of Real Mothering and achieve the critical qualities your child needs for a life that's happy ever after. Part One will give you an understanding of why becoming a real mom is important and why continuing on this fast-paced track of overextended parenting and the quest for Supermom status will get neither us nor our kids anywhere.

Part Two presents twelve true stories about real moms and their children. Each of them introduces one of the twelve simple secrets of being a real mom and how to use the secret yourself. I've used these stories with parents and teachers in hundreds of presentations, keynote talks, and workshops on four continents. Time and time again, I've seen the audience laugh and cry as I told them. They seem to strike a chord. Over the years I've realized that each of them depicts an essential secret of real mothering. In addition, these stories seem to inspire people to use the central message and insights with their own families. They've become tools for teaching, core lessons that motivate parents to make changes and do better with their kids. And years later, people tell me how much these stories have influenced their lives.

In addition to these twelve stories, I've included specific steps, tips, techniques, and guidelines to help you apply the core secret of real mothering in a way that leads to specific success with your kid. For example, how does being firm and fair and setting consistent limits and standards of behavior lead to a young adult who is more secure, confident, and willing to form lasting attachments? How does applauding your child's every effort and not just going for the trophy instill a stronger work ethic and nurture internal motivation?

This is not a simplistic, 1-2-3 method of parenting. This is about creating a life mission. This is about creating A Mother's Promise that you will use forever. Your Mother's Promise will be your personal lesson plan, and, as you would any good lesson plan, you'll need to adapt, modify, and change it as the years go by. After all, real mothering never ends, even when your own kids become parents.

How to Get the Most Out of This Book

There are a few techniques I strongly recommend to get the most out of this book:

- **Create your own Mother's Promise.** A special form is provided for you on pages 54–57 to use after you read each real mom's secret in this book. I explain how to use this form on page 53, but for now, please know that I strongly suggest you complete these pages. Doing so will help you customize the tips, strategies, and advice in *12 Simple Secrets Real Moms Know* to fit your own beliefs and family.

- **Form a book club.** Find a handful of other moms who have similar parenting concerns and the same passion for raising good kids. Read the book together and each week discuss one of the 12 Simple Secrets of Real Mothering and how you can apply it to your own family.

- **Start a journal.** This could be an expensive leather-bound book, a stenographer pad, or even a tape recorder. The point is to express your thoughts about parenting and your concerns about your own kids and to keep track of specific ideas, strategies, and stories you want to remember.

- **Find a buddy.** Don't try to go this alone: find someone with whom you can share your concerns and joys and the progress of your efforts to change and create a stronger attachment with your children.

- **Go one secret at a time.** Please don't overwhelm yourself by trying to take on too much. You're more likely to be successful in creating the change you hope for if you take on only one new goal at a time.

Get ready. Gear up. It's time to make that change happen for yourself and your kids. It's time to stick to what really matters when it comes to creating and strengthening the connection with your children and raising happy, confident kids with good character.

Be not afraid of moving slowly;

Be afraid only of standing still

—Ancient Chinese proverb

part one

How Can a
Real Mom
Give Her Children
Love That Lasts for
Always?

chapter one

From the Sacrificial Mom to the Child Who Can Thrive Without You

I was sitting in front of my computer with a phone pressed to my ear, ready to do an online chat for pregnancy.org. For about an hour each month I serve as a parent expert to several mother Web sites and answer an array of questions from mothers all over the country about child development.

Julie Snyder, the site's chat master, was on the other end of the line to help me through the process and make sure I could get into the chat room. Apparently she coordinates about twelve different chats each month. So, figuring she had a darn good sense about what was on mothers' minds these days, I asked her, "What's the biggest thing these moms really want to know?"

She knew the answer instantly (I must admit it caught me off guard): "The one thing most moms want to know is how to change. They know they're doing too much and are stressing, but they don't know what to do to get on another track. You could really help them by telling them what to do to start simplifying their lives."

"Why simplify?" I asked.

"Because their kids aren't growing up as well as they'd hoped," she said.

"What's wrong?"

"Well, the kids are so stressed, and their moms are just doing so much. They just want their children to be happy so that one day they'll survive and thrive on their own. But they need to get back to just being their real selves and not always trying to copy what all the other moms do."

So let me ask you something: Just how satisfied are you right now with your own parenting? Seriously. Are you content with the way things are going for your children and your family? Are you worried about their future?

Here's another thing to consider: Have you ever said to yourself, "I wish I knew how to be a mom who raises kids who have what it takes to be happy and successful. I feel like I'm always spinning my wheels and knocking myself out trying to do so much for my kids. What really matters when it comes to being a good mom? What do my kids really need from me, and can I really make a difference in their lives?"

Well, you can and do make a difference in your children's lives. Sixty years of research have proven that "parents have a profound effect on their children's emotional, social and intellectual development." The problem is that we mothers have been trying to do so much and be such perfect moms that we've gone way overboard. Many of us have reached the point where we're tired and anxious but still trying to do more and more for our kids.

Real mothering doesn't have to be this hard. We really don't have to exhaust our energy and our finances, and our kids don't have to be this scheduled and stressed. Being a mom should be fun and rewarding and joyous. You just have to admit you want to change.

Are You Ready to Make a Change?

Here are a few more questions to help you realize it's time to get your family out of the fast lane—to slow down and make a few different parenting choices so that your kids will be happier and more confident, develop stronger values, and become self-reliant. Do any of these ring true for you or your family?

- Do you feel guilty about not living up to your own image of the perfect mom? Do you second-guess your mothering or think you're not doing a good-enough job?
- Do you worry about your child—about whether the workload and schedule is too much?
- At your parent-teacher conference, do you find yourself asking more about your kid's grade and how he's competing with the rest of the class than about whether he is happy and how he gets along?
- Are you frequently stressed or exhausted or impatient with your family? Does the littlest, tiniest thing get under your skin? Are you quick to anger? Are you yelling more?
- Are you on the coach's case complaining that your child isn't getting enough game time or respect on the team?
- Has success become such a huge commodity in your family that your kids are afraid to let you down or disappoint you with a poor grade?
- Do you worry that your kid seems really anxious or depressed? That she's not having any fun?
- Do you worry when your kid seems to have nothing to do, and feel as though you have to educate or entertain him every second of the day?
- Do you always compare yourself frequently to other mothers and worry that they're doing a better job than you are?

If you answered yes to any of the questions, it's time to you make some changes for your kids, yourself, and your family. And this book will help you. We'll work on simple changes so that you stop trying to do it all and instead focus on what really matters in giving your kid what she needs to be happy and successful on her own.

Yes, it will involve a little work—but we're talking about simple changes. I'll show you how to make easy adjustments that can have a dramatic impact on your family. And if you stick to your commitment and do make those changes, you will be happier and more content in your mothering, and your children will have a much better chance of being successful not only in school but also in life. And that's because you'll be raising your kids so they can survive and thrive without you.

chapter two

What *Is* a Real Mom These Days?

I don't know what's happened to motherhood, but something is very different about it from the days I was a young mother. I watch my daughter and her friends, and they do so much for their kids. They're exhausted from trying to keep up. It's like they're keeping score with each other. I keep telling her, "Enjoy your kids. They don't need all this stuff. They'll turn out fine not because of all this stuff, but because of who you are." She just tells me I'm out of touch, but deep down I think she's starting to realize this frantic pace isn't good for her family. When did mothering get so complicated? How did women get so far away from just doing what they know is best for their kids and just plain real mothering? What ever happened to lullabies and pat-a-cake?

*—Lenore Jacobson, grandmother of nine
and mother of four, Austin, Texas*

Have you stopped to notice lately just how much mothering has changed since your mom raised you? It's almost as though the definition of a "real mother" has been replaced with a new meaning. My sons are college age now, and I've seen a subtle change just since raising them and, of course, a much more pronounced difference since my mom raised me. I always felt there was a difference, but it wasn't until I spoke to countless moms and had a few pivotal experiences of my own that I was certain that the popular view of good mothering has shifted these days, and it's not all for the best.

What Happened to Pat-a-Cake and Peek-a-Boo?

My first big "ah-ha" moment was at a luncheon where one of my friends announced that her daughter was pregnant. Those next minutes were a blur of cheers, tears of joy, hugs, and then endless toasts to Louise and her grandchild-to-be. The conversation then turned to what the mother would need: a bassinet, crib, changing table, car seat, stroller. Louise admitted that she'd already thought of all those "usual" necessities. What was at the top of her "must-have" list was a new book that taught sign language to babies.

"Is the baby going to be deaf?" I asked.

"Oh no," Louise assured us. "It's a new mothering method that lets us communicate with our babies even before they can talk. It's all the rage with new moms these days."

Her comment caught me off guard. Why spend so much energy teaching a young baby sign language? That has to take a lot of time. And after all, few things are more precious than a mother bonding with her child, so why not spend those moments singing lullabies or playing peek-a-boo? Or making those funny faces to her little one or just cooing and giggling? Teaching your baby sign language seems a little more complicated than just doing the natural stuff moms do. Research has shown that maybe there's some value to this, but jeez, it's just one more complex thing for moms to do on an already crowded plate. Whatever happened to those unrehearsed moments with your baby—singing nursery rhymes, giggling, playing pat-a-cake, or just cuddling up in a rocking chair?

When Did Mothering Become a Billion-Dollar Profit Center?

A few months later, I went to buy a present for Louise's new grandchild and began to get a sense that something had really shifted. My clue came when I walked into a baby store and realized that mothering had become a billion-dollar enterprise. Baby paraphernalia was everywhere; there were so many new products I didn't know where to start looking. And greeting me front and center was a colorful display of Mozart tapes promising to "stimulate brain development" if played to an unborn child. "Wow," I thought to myself, "a mother's first educational purchasing decision comes up even before the baby's born." This seemed a lot more complicated and difficult than choosing between diaper bags or strollers.

Next aisle: magnetic numbers, memory games, phonic kits, electronic vocabulary programs, and gadgets galore to motivate your budding little genius. In fact, almost every product pledged to give your kid that all-important jump-start toward academic success. Just when did mothering a baby or a toddler become so focused on achievement? What the heck happened to the days of sandboxes, blocks, and tree forts?

I felt a tad guilty asking the salesclerk for something as old-fashioned as a copy of *Goodnight Moon* (which I finally bought at the bookstore next door). But I was also struck with just how many choices moms have to make for their kids these days, how many products that appeal to parental anxiety about learning quickly, preparing for tests, competing, and striving ahead—and how much responsibility they must feel about making the right choices.

That same week, on a plane to visit my youngest son at college, I sat next to a lovely young mom and her adorable daughter. We greeted one another and then, for the duration of the just-under three-hour flight, I watched this mom entertain her six-year-old daughter nonstop. As soon as the seat belt sign went off, the mom pulled out a bag packed to the brim with items: from flash cards to workbooks to beginning phonic books to markers and paper—she even had a DVD player with a National Geographic movie about zoo animals. Heaven forbid an unplanned spare moment for the child, but what about her mother? I was exhausted from watching her try to make sure her child was never bored. Just when did mothering get so difficult? So draining?

But I didn't rely on just my experiences to conclude that something was quite different about mothering today. Being a teacher, writer, researcher, and mom myself, I wanted to get some real evidence, proof that this change in attitude was actually happening. So I started interviewing dozens of moms from coast to coast and surveyed hundreds more. And their stories and insights confirmed my theory. One mom shared a feeling that I'd heard from so many other mothers: "I'm just constantly on the go and feel like I'm being graded for doing all this stuff. I keep comparing myself to other moms and think I'll flunk mothering if I don't keep up."

How Did We Get from June Cleaver to Motherhood Mania?

The most important thing she'd learned over the years was that there was no way to be a perfect mother and a million ways to be a good one.

—J. Churchill

Once upon a time, Mom and apple pie were synonymous. What better association could there be for the warmth and love and comfort of idealized motherhood than the delectable sweetness, aroma, and scrumptious taste of apple pie?

It wasn't too long ago that the ideal mother, at least in the world of TV, was June Cleaver, the mom in *Leave It to Beaver*. She was always calm, neat as a pin, never without her pearls, smiling, loving, and always available. When Beaver came bouncing down the stairs for breakfast, Mrs. Cleaver was always in the kitchen in her spotless sparkling white apron, busily making bacon and eggs. And when Beaver came home from school, she was always at the door, still smiling with her pearl necklace on, greeting him with a freshly baked batch of homemade chocolate chip cookies. Okay, it's corny, but the thing about it that I'm remembering fondly is the feeling of warmth, of being always welcomed, and the strong connection between the mother, her children, and their friends.

Fast forward. What is our image of motherhood today? How times have changed! On TV, in movies, in magazine cover stories, in countless syndicated articles, on morning talk shows, on *Oprah*, and on evening network news, the current image of motherhood assaults us with one clear message: motherhood has changed dramatically and not all for the best.

Calm? Neat as a pin? Smiling? Always available? Homemade chocolate chip cookies? Get real!

A typical twenty-four hours in the life of a mother today includes an intense schedule of constant activity, stress, and pressure. Feeding and dressing 2.3 kids. Carpooling to school. Shuffling countless after-school activities—skating, gymnastics, music lessons, special academic coaching, soccer practice, scouting, dance class, play rehearsals, Odyssey of the Mind, playgroups. Then there's helping with homework, science fair projects, PTA meetings, school events, making and cleaning up from dinner, then dashing off to another crazy activity, not to mention mending, cleaning, dusting, picking up after everyone, vacuuming, scrubbing, mopping, and madly trying to find the darn missing library book. If there's by any miracle thirty minutes of unscheduled time at any point during the day, Mom is likely to hop on a home exercise bicycle or dash off to a quick Pilates class. And that's just a weekday. If you think

Saturday or Sunday is going to be any different, forget it. With soccer games, dance recitals, school debates, theatrical and musical performances, slumber and birthday parties, and a host of other frenzied activities, it's a nonstop mad dash with never a moment to spare.

Of course, that's just the tip of the iceberg. Now add all the rest of the stuff we do and it's a wonder we still can move at all by the end of the day. There's juggling things like a full- or part-time career, the relatives, medical and dental appointments, banking, shopping, and social engagements. Now go jump on that treadmill and lift those weights each day. How are you doing? Okay, now find time for your love life: throw on the negligee, light the candles, uncork the bubbly, and look seductive for your honey at the end of the day. Sure you do. Chances are you're more likely to want to pass out from shear exhaustion.

There's more. And in many ways it's the most difficult part of being a mother today. We love our children so intensely and ache so much for them to be happy and successful. The pressure and stress to prepare our children for success in life are enormous. We read and hear so much about how hard it is for our kids to get into the right schools, how hard it is to get a good job. Often from the first days of preschool, mothers are expected to do whatever it takes to help their children succeed. Never mind that many moms have to work outside the home. Never mind that many moms are single. Never mind that we're all exhausted and burned out. All moms are expected to be responsible for their children's education and skill building. All moms are supposed to get their kids on the path to success. And all moms are expected to ensure that their children are happy and secure little creatures.

In addition to all this pressure, a million ads and commercials are blasting us with the message that we'd better look good, stay thin, keep smiling, and moisturize—and it's all because we're worth it!

The Urge to Be Supermom

The result is that many moms today are suffering from what can only be described as a kind of frenzy—an abnormally high level of busyness, tension, stress, speediness, anxiety, heightened awareness, and even panic. Many moms can't get enough sleep; they can never keep up or do enough for their kids and are feeling guilty and inadequate about it. They're overwhelmed trying to be Supermom, to fulfill the expectations placed on them. They overcompensate by taking on more and more until you might as well admit that they're in a state of Motherhood Mania. Of course, we accept those expectations. Isn't that what a good mother does?

You don't believe it? You want some proof? Here are some disturbing statistics:

- Of the American moms surveyed, 70 percent reported finding motherhood "incredibly stressful."
- Depression affects 30 percent of mothers of young children.
- One-third of parents in one survey said that if they were to do it all over again, they would *not* start a family.
- In the same survey, 53 percent admitted they felt significant resentment in making sacrifices as a parent.
- In a Texas survey, 909 women said they found taking care of their kids about as much fun as cleaning their house, slightly less pleasurable than cooking, and a whole lot less enjoyable than watching TV.
- Of the 1,306 moms in one survey, 95 percent said they experienced guilt feelings associated with parenting, and almost half said that the guilt only increased as their kids grew older.
- Two out of three adults say that parents are doing a worse job than twenty years ago.

So how did things get this bad? How did we morph from apple pie and June Cleaver to Motherhood Mania? We know it's not for a lack of love and good intentions. Yet it's painfully obvious that things are bad, and we've got to find the reason. There's no one easy answer, but here are eleven issues to consider:

1. **New knowledge about child development.** We know a lot more about child development than we used to, and everyone agrees that parents do make a difference. What we say and do and how we behave with our children have a huge impact on their development. It's not just nature, its nurture.

2. **Competition.** Parents today want their children to excel—to do better than they did. There's a feeling that kids have to win and do better than other kids, and there's a big fear of failure, as if only the strong or successful can flourish in this age of anxiety. Moms find themselves fighting ruthlessly with other moms for slots in nursery schools or ice time on the hockey team.

3. **More options.** Entrepreneurs have created so many attractive choices and opportunities for kids today. Parents find themselves bombarded with seductive appeals for everything from music, athletic, and academic training to adventure camps in foreign locales that are guaranteed to enrich their children's lives or teach them a second language.

4. **More media.** Here is just a one-week sampling of some of the cover stories in national magazines: *Atlantic Monthly:* "Stop Being a Slacker Mom"; *New York Times Magazine:* "Mommy Madness"; *U.S. News & World Report:* "Mysteries of the Teen Years"; *Newsweek:* "Babies and Autism"; *Time:* "What Teachers Hate About Parents: Pushy Dads. Hovering Moms. Parents Who Don't Show Up at All. Are Kids Paying the Price?" During that same week, many TV and radio talk shows focused on parent-child crisis issues. Over eight hundred books on the concept of motherhood were published between 1970 and 2000; of those, only twenty-seven

were published between 1970 and 1980. My mom had just one parenting "guru": Benjamin Spock. These days it's as though a new study comes out almost daily advising parents how to optimize their children's potential.

5. **Financial pressures.** It's more and more expensive to be a parent. School materials, sports equipment and tournament travel, special lessons, tutoring, computer equipment—the demand for cash seems never ending. Then there's just the "normal" stuff—clothing, food, books. With downsizing and layoffs in our roller coaster economy, parents are also concerned that their kids won't be able to find a job unless they go to the very best schools and have better skills than anyone else. It all adds to the stress and mania.

6. **Guilt.** We're working. We're striving. We're often away from home more than we'd like. We're trying to do the best for our kids, but it also means that sometimes we're tired and cranky and don't do everything we think we ought to be doing for our families. So we're wracked with guilt, shame, remorse, and more guilt.

7. **Wanting to be liked.** Many moms want to be their children's best friend. They can't stand the idea of making an unpopular decision, saying no, or (heaven forbid) disciplining their kids if doing so might cause their kids to resent them or say, "You're mean, Mom."

8. **Outdoing their own moms.** And then there are some moms who are still dealing with unresolved conflicts from their own childhood. The last thing they want to do is repeat the same mistakes their mother made. "I'm going to be a much better mom than she was and show her how it really should be done."

9. **Lack of confidence.** Some mothers feel as though they're being graded every day and may be flunking the Motherhood Test. They lack confidence in their judgment and are constantly second-guessing themselves.

10. **Wanting a trophy child.** Have you ever seen a mother whose child is just her favorite possession—a living representation of her own worth, an accessory? Her kid's achievements give this mom "bragging rights." This type of mother is so self-centered that she thinks of her child only as a reflection of her own achievements.

11. **The test craze.** These days there is no child left untested. Standardized tests. Achievement tests. Aptitude tests. PSATs. SATs. A child's current worth and potential for success are coming to be dictated by a portfolio of numbers. From the preschool admission tests to LSATs—they're making us crazy worrying that our kids aren't going to be good enough.

And is Motherhood Mania worth it? Is it worth all the time and energy and money we're spending? Do our kids really benefit from all these splendid extracurricular activities and stimulating experiences?

chapter three

Why Being a "Sacrificial Mom" Is Bad for Your Kids

Dear Dr. Borba,

I'm the mom of three darling daughters: they're precious, healthy, well-behaved, and happy young ladies. I know I'm lucky—I have a nice house, and my husband has a great job, I work part time, and I also make space in every day for my own stuff, the things I really care about, like photography, exercising, my best friends. But I just don't seem to fit in with the other moms. They spend virtually all day and night working on their kids. They've got their kids enrolled in all these activities, music lessons, and dance, arranging personal tutors for them and sending them to exclusive camps in the summer. They spend all day driving them around, dropping them off, waiting for them, taking them to the next thing, 24/7. And they tell me I'm crazy not to be doing the same thing for my girls. If I don't, they say, my girls will never be able to keep up with the other kids and be left in the shuffle. I don't want to be like them, but the truth is I also don't want to do the wrong thing and jeopardize my girls' chances for success. But I also want to make sure they turn out to be happy, caring human beings. I guess I really do want to do what's right but not if it means sacrificing my own life and my family's peace of mind. Can you help me?

—Jenny L., a mom from Atherton, California

All our obsessive and hyper mothering is not helping our kids become happy and mature young adults and may in fact be doing them more harm than good. Let's take a hard look at some more disturbing statistics, this time about our kids.

- The U.S. surgeon general warns us that 13 percent of kids between nine and seventeen years old experience anxiety disorders.

- In one survey, 43 percent of thirteen- to fourteen-year-olds say they feel stressed every day; by ages fifteen to seventeen, that number increases to 59 percent. The parents of these kids said the primary culprit was too many activities, and pressure to get good grades. When the researcher asked the kids, they said it was their parents pushing them to excel and do better academically.

- Of the parents responding to one survey, 46 percent said that their children's biggest emotional issues were coping with stress and dealing with depression.

- One-third of adolescents say they "worry a lot" about school, family, and world events, and nearly half say they have trouble sleeping due to stress.

- In the same poll, 83 percent of kids say they are stressed about homework and pressure to excel; of those kids, 57 percent say their relationships with their parents is what's causing them stress.

- The suicide rate among American teens ages fifteen to nineteen has increased 30 percent since 1970. In fact, suicide rates for children and teens tripled from 1962 to 1995.

- In a recent national survey, college students reported feeling so depressed that it was difficult for them to function over the past academic year. College counselors tell us that there are more students than ever before on their campuses who are suffering from not only depression but sleep disorders, substance abuse, anxiety disorders, eating disorders, impulsive behaviors, and suicidal thoughts.

What Do the Kids Say?

If these statistics aren't a wake-up call, let's look at what our kids are telling us they really want from us. Do they really appreciate the frantic pace and all the classes and tutoring? Are all of our efforts really making them happy, confident, and self-sufficient? Not if you read the research, Mom. It tells a different story:

- In one poll, 60 percent of kids ages twelve to fourteen said they'd like to spend more time with their parents.

- Kids *do* want time with us—more time—but they're picky about the kind of time—not just this "quality time" stuff. But you get a higher grade from them in your mothering if the time you spend together is not "rushed, but focused and rich in shared activities."

- Regardless of whether we're full- or part-time working moms or stay-at-home moms, kids tell researchers that our interactions with them make them feel rushed and harried. More than two in five kids feel that their time with us is rushed. And, just as we'd expect, our kids rate us more positively if their time with us is less rushed and hurried and calmer. In fact, almost 90 percent of the kids who rate their time with their mom as very calm give them an A for making them feel important and loved compared to 63 percent of those who rate their time with their mom as rushed.

- A survey of eighty-four thousand children in grades 6–12 told researchers they do appreciate all that we do. They do enjoy spending time with us. But what they really would like is for the time that they do spend with us to be *more relaxed time.*

Of course, all our accelerated parenting and overextended efforts to be such perfect moms didn't crop up just overnight. The fact is, researchers and child development experts have told us for years to *slow down.* They cautioned us that this overscheduled, overactive parenting isn't healthy and isn't getting the results we want. We've been warned repeatedly that unless we put on the brakes and check out of this "autopilot mother mode," our kids' emotional state would suffer. But over the years we've actually speeded up our pace and become *more* involved. We're no longer just managing our kids' lives: we're micromanaging their existence, right down to the very last detail. In doing so, we're moving even further away from what *really* matters when it comes to good mothering.

So let's just put on the brakes, at least long enough to review what these experts have warned us about all along: the impact that all this sacrificial, accelerated parenting has on our kids. It just might help us do something we may not be doing nearly enough: seriously thinking about whether all this micromanaging and the almost-smothering approach to "Mommying" are best for our children and families.

The Impact of Stress

Experts now estimate that one in three American children currently suffers from stress-related symptoms, such as headaches or stomachaches, and between 8 and 10 percent of American children are seriously troubled by anxiety. Pediatricians tell us that stress symptoms are now showing up in kids as young as three years of age. Childhood depression and suicide rates continue to escalate: more teenagers and young adults now die from suicide than from all medical illnesses combined.

Other experts in past years were concerned that a growing number of kids would suffer from burnout unless the pace and pressure decelerated. But we accelerated our parenting and hurried the pace even more. To succeed, our kids needed *more* activities and *more* schoolwork. What was cut? Any so-called unstructured time. Here's some more evidence about how our children's and our family's lives have changed over the past two decades:

- Children's homework increased almost 50 percent.
- Unstructured children's activities declined by 50 percent.
- Family dinners decreased by 33 percent.
- Family vacations decreased by 28 percent.
- Children's free time decreased by twelve hours per week.
- Playtime decreased by three hours per week.
- Many school systems these days have abolished recess.

The Birth of Hyperparenting

There is no sign that kids' hectic pace is slowing down or that their parents are stepping back.

Elisabeth Krents, admissions director to a top Manhattan preschool, realized that micromanaging had reached a new height when she received a call from a parent inquiring about the school's age cutoff for their kindergarten program. When Krents asked for the child's age, the parent rather uncomfortably admitted, "Well, we don't have a child yet. We're trying to figure out when to conceive a child so that the birthday is not a problem."

Educators have a new, not so flattering term for parents who are just "always available and forever hovering": helicopter parents. Teachers readily admit they love working with kids—it's the parents who drive them crazy: the eager moms who push too hard, the protective moms who defend the cheater or bully, the rescuers who pay for the missing library book or bring forgotten homework, and the helicopter mom who is always, always there to make sure everything goes smoothly for her child. Their children's high grade-point average and honor roll membership are assured, but lessons in self-reliance have to take a backseat. A survey of U.S. teachers found "parent management to be a bigger struggle for teachers than finding enough funding or maintaining discipline or even enduring the toils of testing."

What about the impact on our kids? Well, they clearly feel pressure from their parents to achieve, please, and not fail. So they're doing whatever they can—and at any cost—to succeed. A recent national survey of almost twenty-five thousand U.S. high school students found that two-thirds cheated on their exams. Interestingly, 93 percent of the same surveyed kids agreed with the statement, "It's important for me to be a person with good character." But don't let a teacher ever accuse a child of "deceit" (that is, cheating). Doing so it seems almost certain to bring his parent armed with a lawyer to the school doorstep in a heartbeat, threatening to sue. That lowered grade, you know, all but destroys their son's Ivy League chances, for which his parents have been planning so long and hard. (Curiously, the detriment to the kid's character seems to get lost in the shuffle, but I guess that's something parents assume can be worked on once he's at Harvard?) Teachers have received so many parental lawsuit threats lately that the number of teachers buying liability insurance has jumped 25 percent in the past five years.

Accelerated, smothering parenting isn't contained at the schoolyard: parents realize that college admissions officials are looking for the "all-around perfect kid," so extracurricular activities are an absolute must for their résumés. That's where parent micromanaging takes on a whole new dimension, and where moms and dads begin behaving very, *very* badly. Umpires were the first to spot the disturbing new trend at their children's athletic events. The National Association of Sports Officials told the Associated Press that it was receiving two to three calls a week from an umpire or referee who had been assaulted by a parent or spectator. The issues were almost always the same: "My kid didn't get enough play time. . . . The umpire was unfair."

The complaints range from verbal abuse to an official's having his car run off the road by an irate parent. Youth sports programs in at least 163 cities were so concerned about the trend of parental overinvolvement and blatant incivility that they began requiring parents to sign a pledge of proper conduct in order to be allowed to attend their kids' games. Some have asked parents to watch a thirty-minute video on sportsmanship, and others have gone so far as to have a silence day, when any parent who even opens his or her mouth at the game is ejected.

Are the kids really better off with all our hands-on parenting? Do they really appreciate all the sacrifices of both our time and finances? Did you know that 70 percent of children who participate in sports drop out by age thirteen? And the principal reason kids give is that "it's just not fun."

What About Responsibility and Character?

We need to prepare our kids for the time when they will be responsible for themselves. We need to help them develop habits of character to equip them to face adult challenges.
—Dan Kindlon, *Too Much of a Good Thing*

Many moms are more than willing to help lighten their kids' heavy workloads. We know how hectic and jammed-packed our sons' and daughters' lifestyles are these days, so we've gotten darn good at doing science projects, finding misplaced library books, rushing forgotten homework papers or school forms back to school just in the nick of time. Our typing and computer skills have even improved from typing our kids' papers. And if by chance our kids don't do as well as we would hope, good ol' mom is right there to conference with the teacher or coach or tutor or music master. To make sure our children never think of themselves as failures, we've even gotten into the practice of giving out trophies at the end of every sports season whether the kids win or lose. By the time our kids graduate, their closets are filled with ribbons and plaques and medals.

Some of us consider all this indulging, rescuing, and smothering as spoiling our kids. Interestingly enough, some even admit their kids are spoiled. For example:

- Nearly two out of three parents surveyed by a *Time/ CNN* poll said that their kids measure self-worth more by possessions than their parents did at the same age.

- More than 80 percent of people now think kids are more spoiled than kids of ten or fifteen years ago.

- Two-thirds of parents say that their own kids are spoiled and that they are to blame.

- In a *Newsweek* survey, 75 percent of parents said their kids do fewer chores than children did ten or fifteen years ago.

- The same survey reported that 73 percent of parents say today's kids are too focused on buying and consuming things.

But it is almost as though parents think that responsibility and character are not priorities. "Kids can't be perfect in everything," parents explain. "They work so hard and are getting great grades, so we should cut them a little slack." And slack is exactly what our kids are getting.

Forget those household chores: "There's not enough time." If the child wants a cell phone, credit card, computer, car, or new outfit: "She works hard and deserves it." After all, "The kids don't have time for other things" (such as building a sense of responsibility or skills that would enhance self-sufficiency). The grade-point average, the high test scores, and exemplary résumé that will meet the stamp of approval of college admissions officials are what matter most.

After all, the Sacrificial Mom will do anything to make sure that the kids have whatever it takes to get ahead in life. Their lives revolve around these children, who are given everything they could possibly ever want or need. Harvard psychologist Dan Kindlon, who wrote both *Raising Cain* and *Too Much of a Good Thing*, contends that all this parental indulgence is actually smothering the development of our children's character and sense of responsibility.

"The body," explains Kindlon, "cannot learn to adapt to stress unless it experiences it. Indulged children are often less able to cope with stress because their parents have created an atmosphere where their whims are indulged, where they have always assumed . . . that they're entitled and that life should be a bed of roses." By always rescuing, caving into their every whim, and not allowing kids to experience frustration or failure, these parents are actually setting their kids up for even bigger troubles: not knowing how to handle life when they are finally on their own.

A national study of U.S. high school students confirms that all this best-intended parental indulging may well be backfiring. Consider these statistics from the Josephson Institution of Ethics about today's "best and brightest":

- Nearly 62 percent of American high school students admitted to cheating on exams.
- More than one in four (27 percent) stole from a store within the past twelve months; 22 percent stole something from a parent or relative.

- Forty percent admitted they "sometimes lie to save money."

But most interesting might be the fact that nearly 92 percent said they were "satisfied with their own ethics and character." A bit strange, wouldn't you say, Mom? Something seems a bit awry.

What Happens When Our Kids Get to College?

What these parents don't realize is that despite this appearance of comfortable status, secure environment, and a pleasant social world, a multitude of hidden problems have caused a steady and alarming rise in the severity of students' mental health problems across the nation in college and universities large and small, public and private.

—Richard D. Kadison and Theresa Foy DiGeronimo,
College of the Overwhelmed

Our frantic, ever involved, hands-on, micromanaging parent mode remains strong even as our kids go off to college. The same helicopter parents from the preschool, elementary, and high school years are still hovering, this time trying to ensure that their kids have the perfect college experience. In fact, parents are *so* active right now in the college admissions process that many universities are concerned that their constant presence (and interference) isn't so helpful for sons and daughters needing (finally!) to sever the umbilical cord. From refusing to let their kids apply to schools that don't achieve a lofty enough rank in the *U.S. News & World Report* list of prominent colleges to completely rewriting their children's application essays (or hiring someone to do it instead—the hottest newer trend), parental micromanaging continues. And when it comes to the actual college orientation visit: parents are right there hovering and asking officials the majority of questions—even filling out their kids' forms. In fact, parents are so involved that many universities are looking for ways to free students so that they can tour campuses away from their parents' perpetual presence. And it doesn't stop once the kids go.

University officials complain that parents are making huge amounts of noise whenever or whatever difficulty arises at school, even dialing the university president directly. Counselors joke that college kids today need "parentectomies." In fact, their continued micromanaging has been so acute that many public universities are creating programs and hiring staff just to deal with problem parents.

But what message does all that nonstop parental activism really send our now twenty-something-year-olds? Sure it says, "I love you." But it can also transmit another, not quite so positive meaning: *"You can't do this on your own."* That may not be the message we want our kids to hear, but chances are it will be their interpretation. And it's the exact same message we've been sending with all our overinvolved ways all along: "Your homework isn't quite right, let me help." "Your science project could use more data, I'll get it." "This letter won't make the admissions cut, I'll rewrite it."

So what happens when our hurried kids do leave home sweet home for college after working so long and hard? How do they do without us right there to pick up the pieces? Admissions directors admit they've never seen freshmen with such superlative grade-point averages. It's their limited "coping" capacities that concern college counselors in particular. In fact, reports about our college-age kids' mental health are troubling—*very troubling*. It appears that the "hurried child" is now stressed to the max in college. Richard D. Kadison, M.D., one of the top mental health experts in the country, chief of the Mental Health Services at Harvard University Health Services and author of a must-read book, *College of the Overwhelmed*, paints quite a picture that we just may not be prepared for: "If your son or daughter is in college, the chances are almost one in two that he or she will become depressed to the point of being unable to function; one in two that he or she will have regular episodes of binge drinking (with the resulting significant risk of dangerous consequences such as sexual assault and car accidents); and one in ten that he or she will seriously consider suicide. In fact, since 1988, the likelihood of a college student's suffering depression has doubled, suicidal ideation has tripled, and sexual assaults have quadrupled."

Kadison calls these smart, much-loved college kids "overwhelmed"—and it's probably not how we dreamed our twenty-something-year-olds would be immortalized. What possibly could be overwhelming them? After all, don't these kids have it made? They've been admitted, for the most part, to the college of their choice. They've worked most of their lives to get to this point. Most have few if any financial concerns. They certainly have the study skills and the academic abilities to get through their course loads. (In fact, the admissions directors admit they doing so with flying colors.) So what is there to be so upset about?

Dr. Kadison tells us what is fueling these kids' stress loads: "powerful parental pressure and cultural expectations." All those pressures to please, achieve, and succeed have been building up over the years, and now that these kids are on their own—really on their own—the one person who usually picks up the pieces, soothes the worries, fixes the schedules, and organizes daily life is missing: the parent. The very person Kadison (and Elkind, Rosenfeld, Kindlon, and scores of others) has said all along was the major stress inducer.

Can Our Kids Make It on Their Own?

These parents are trying to create a really terrific statue of a child rather than a child.

—Mel Levine, *Ready or Not, Here Life Comes*

Scores of anthropologists, sociologists, and psychologists are currently studying our college grads (or yesterday's hurried children) to see just how well they do out there in the real world. It's far from reassuring. It appears that all too many of our expensively well educated, enormously pampered, and extremely loved sons and daughters are having trouble settling down. They hop from job to job, put off buying homes or marrying let alone starting families, and (here's the real clincher) come back to live at home. Make no mistake: our offsprings' social lives may be booming, but as for their growing up "successfully" and being "self-sufficient"—well, that part is still debatable.

The plain and simple truth is that this breed of "twenty-something-plus" seems to be living out the Peter Pan fantasy of not growing up. *Time* magazine recently labeled them "twixters" because they appeared stuck in the "betwixt and between" phase of life with no sign of wanting to get beyond it. There is some bit of good news: almost half of those ages eighteen to twenty-nine talk to their parents *every* day, and 70 percent spent time with their families the previous week. (They like us!) But there's a flip side: they like us so much, they don't want to leave home. (Or could it be that they enjoy being taken care of as they were in the past?) The percentage of twenty-six-year-olds coming back to live at home has nearly doubled in the past three decades (from 11 percent up to 20 percent). Now seriously: Is that really the future you had in mind for your kids as you spent all those hours and hours schlepping them between all those activities?

What's the reason so many of these young adults don't want to be adults? Dr. Mel Levine, a professor of pediatrics at the University of North Carolina Medical School in Chapel Hill and author of *Ready or Not, Here Life Comes,* has studied this group extensively and has a theory. These hurried or over-scheduled kids have been so micromanaged, so coddled and so protected by loving, overinvolved parents for most of their lives that now their ability to strike off on their own, form healthy relationships, and have proper job skills is threatened. Levine sends a clear warning: we cannot continue parenting the same way, for when these kids get out in the real world, they may very well "shatter."

So what went wrong? Could all that immediate gratification have backfired? Too many unearned trophies? Too many carpools? Did we raise our kids with such high expectations that now it's hard for them to get things just right? Did we micromanage their lives so well that now they can't live life on their own? We can hypothesize and theorize ourselves to death, but the fact remains that a whopping 36 percent of today's college graduates readily admit they're not ready for careers. Levine finds so many of today's graduates unprepared for life that he calls the problem "work-life unreadiness" and warns parents that presently we're doing quite a poor job of preparing our adolescents for a successful transition to adult life. Is this what you'd expected? Is it really how you thought life would turn out for your child?

So Do Our Kids Live Happily Ever After, or What?

If you bungle raising your children, nothing else much matters in life.

—Jacqueline Kennedy Onassis

So the hurried children grew up. There's no denying that they're much loved and adored by us. Yes, they admire us and even enjoy our company, and they're the best-educated generation we've ever had. But research also paints a picture that shows another, more troubling aspect—of how these kids turned out. Many appear to have immature coping skills; they're often stressed, anxious, or depressed, and may even lack a "spirit" or tough inner moral core. Researchers point out that the critical piece called character—integrity and ethics—seems also to be somehow amiss in this breed. And self-reliance—a quiet, inner confidence, the skills to bounce back and or make those tough decisions alone—appears weak as well.

The reality is that too many of these hurried children are struggling as adults. They're smart, but many are also sad, anxious, and unfulfilled. Too many can't form lasting relationships and live on their own. Of course, there are many who are doing well and are thriving. But for many others, the "happily ever after" part that we'd all hoped for just isn't happening.

But it doesn't have to be like this. In fact, our kids will be the first to tell us that our current frenzied and competitive mode of compulsive parenting is not working and that something has to change. Obviously we need to get rid of this Motherhood Mania and zero in on what really matters for our kids.

So what do we do? We're all in this together. In fact, there's one thing that all of us share no matter what our income, number of children, education, or location: we want happy kids who will someday be able to thrive without us.

That's where I can help you. And why me? Who am I? I'm a mom with three kids, one of those parenting experts who's written twenty books you've never read. But also over the past two decades I've done hundreds of workshops in front of over a million parents, teachers, and counselors. After seeing all the stress and guilt brought on by the need to be this Sacrificial Mom over the years, I began to ask each group systematically the following question: "If you could give one piece of parenting advice that would help moms raise happy, confident, self-reliant kids, what would it be?"

I collected over five thousand answers and discovered that many of them kept repeating themselves. The fascinating thing was that these parents' responses were almost identical to what child development researchers and clinicians have being telling us for years.

These answers were a wonderful gift: the collective wisdom of hundreds of real moms about what matters most when it comes to raising good kids.

Their answers have provided us all with twelve simple secrets that produce kids of solid character, caring hearts, and the strength to make it in our tough world today. The good news is that we can use these secrets to make our lives much simpler, easier, and more fun. The best news is that once we start using these secrets of real mothering, our children and our families are going to enjoy terrific benefits. So here is the list of twelve simple secrets that will us make us happier, more confident mothers.

THE 12 SIMPLE SECRETS
OF REAL MOTHERING

REAL MOM'S SECRET 1

A Mother Who Loves Teaches Worth

What Real Mothers Know: If Your Children Have Unconditional Love, They'll Be More Likely to Thrive

What Really Matters Most for Mothering: Be Loving with No Strings Attached

The Real Benefit for Kids: Authentic Self-Esteem

REAL MOM'S SECRET 2

A Mother Who Is Firm and Fair Gives Her Children a Moral Code to Live By

What Real Mothers Know: Set Consistent Limits and Standards of Behavior So Your Child Learns to Act Right Without You

What Really Matters Most for Mothering: Be Consistent and Just in Your Discipline

The Real Benefit for Kids: Stability, a Sense of Responsibility, and Inner Direction

REAL MOM'S SECRET 3

A Mother Who Listens Shows Her Children They Matter

What Real Mothers Know: Give Your Children Complete Attention and They'll Carry You with Them Forever

What Really Matters Most for Mothering: Pay Attention

The Real Benefit for Kids: A Feeling of Significance and Self-Acceptance

REAL MOM'S SECRET 4

A Mother Who Is a Good Role Model Gives Her Children an Example Worth Copying

What Real Mothers Know: Model the Behavior You Want Your Children to Copy

What Really Matters Most for Mothering: Be Conscious of Your Example

The Real Benefit for Kids: Character, Values, and Love

REAL MOM'S SECRET 5

A Mother Who Teaches Values Inspires Character

What Real Mothers Know: Understand Your Family's Values So Your Children Can Live Them

What Really Matters Most for Mothering: Be Intentional

The Real Benefit for Kids: Empathy, Strong Character, and a Moral Compass

REAL MOM'S SECRET 6

A Mother Who Supports Her Children's Strengths Builds Their Confidence

What Real Mothers Know: Let Your Parenting Fit Your Child's Personality

What Really Matters for Mothering: Know Your Child's Unique Temperament

The Real Benefit for Kids: Confidence About Identity and Strengths

REAL MOM'S SECRET 7

A Mother Who Encourages Independence Cultivates Self-Reliance

What Real Mothers Know: Let Go of Rescuing Your Kids Every Time, So They Can Thrive Without You

What Really Matters Most for Mothering: Plan for the Future

The Real Benefit for Kids: Self-Reliance and Resourcefulness

REAL MOM'S SECRET 8

A Mother Who Applauds Effort Nurtures Perseverance

What Real Mothers Know: It's Not Just Winning But Never Giving Up

What Really Matters for Mothering: Be Affirmative

The Real Benefit for Kids: Internal Motivation and Stick-to-Itiveness

REAL MOM'S SECRET 9
A Mother Who Accepts Her Children's Shortcomings Nurtures Resilience
What Real Mothers Know: Support Your Children's Natural Abilities and Don't Stress Their Weaknesses
What Really Matters Most for Mothering: Be Accepting
The Real Benefit for Kids: Optimism and a Bounce-Back Attitude

REAL MOM'S SECRET 10
A Mother Who Takes Time for Her Children Helps Them Build Strong Relationships
What Real Mothers Know: Do Whatever It Takes to Maintain a Connection with Your Children
What Really Matters Most for Mothering: Stay Engaged
The Real Benefit for Kids: Healthy and Loving Attachments

REAL MOM'S SECRET 11
A Mother Who Laughs Teaches Joy
What Real Mothers Know: Take Time to Enjoy Your Family Life
What Really Matters Most for Mothering: Be Lighthearted
The Real Benefit for Kids: Happiness and Joy

REAL MOM'S SECRET 12
A Mother Who Takes Care of Herself Holds Together Her Happy Family
What Real Mothers Know: The Best Thing for Your Family Is a Happy, Healthy You
What Really Matters Most for Mothering: Stay Balanced
The Real Benefit for Kids: Happiness, Optimism, and Security

And here's the bottom line: you won't have to work so hard to get your kid ready for a life that's happily ever after.

But what is the connection between these 12 Simple Secrets of Real Mothering and your child's future as a successful adult? How can one lead to the other? How can this book help every mother create her own plan for giving her kids the critical skills, qualities, and characteristics they need to make it in the real world? And what are these skills, qualities, and characteristics?

The Twelve Qualities Your Child Needs for a Life That's Happily Ever After

Look at your child and try to picture him or her in twenty-five years as a grown-up. What do you see? Does your son or daughter have these twelve essential qualities:

1. Is he happy, optimistic, and secure? Does he have authentic self-esteem?
2. Is she in a healthy, loving relationship? Does she have good friends and loyal allies?
3. Does he have a strong moral compass? Does he have good values and strong character?
4. Does she have empathy and compassion for all people? Is she kind, unselfish, and humane?
5. Does he have self-control and patience? Can he delay gratification?
6. Is she able to make good decisions on her own?
7. Is he self-reliant?
8. Is she responsible and internally motivated? Does she have a good work ethic?
9. Is he practical and resourceful in handling day-to-day living?
10. Is she resilient? If life throws her a curve, can she bounce back?
11. Is he confident and positive about his identity and strengths?
12. Does she have fun? Does she laugh? Is her life balanced between work and love, self and others?

Yes, each of our kids is born with a certain temperament and genetic predisposition. Certainly there are some things about our kids' development that are not under our control—but many are. And that's why you can use the 12 Simple Secrets of Real Mothering to foster the qualities your child needs for a life that's happily ever after.

Creating Your Own Custom Mothering Plan

What I promise to give you in this book is a way to create your own individual, custom-made, best-possible, state-of-the-art plan, called A Mother's Promise, for raising good kids. This Mother's Promise is based not only on what academic and clinical research has proven but also on what hundreds of real moms say matters most and really works. Best yet, if you follow the promise you make to yourself and your children—your very own personalized mothering plan—you get off the Sacrificial Motherhood Mania bandwagon, become the real mother you know you should be, and raise kids who will not only survive but thrive without you.

My greatest hope is that you will apply the simple secrets in this book to your own family. So here are my suggestions: Read each story and then take a few minutes to reflect on whether the secret is one you would like to use with your children. If so, continue reading the tips, strategies, and advice other moms give as to how they've incorporated the secret into their lives. Then ask yourself the most important question: How would I use the secret in my own parenting? But don't just think about it—if you really want to use the habit, then plan exactly how you will use it with your children. After all, the more you think through what you want to do, the greater the chances you will succeed. Finally, I urge you to write your plan on a special form I've created for you called A Mother's Promise, found on pages 54–57. If you take just a few minutes to jot down your promise at the end of each chapter, you will have created your own unique mothering plan for your family.

A MOTHER'S PROMISE

REAL MOM'S SECRET 1: A Mother Who Loves Teaches Worth

The one thing I'll promise to do over the next 21 days to use this secret in my mothering to help enhance my child's self-esteem is _____

_____

_____

_____

REAL MOM'S SECRET 2: A Mother Who Is Firm and Fair Gives Her Children a Moral Code to Live By

The one thing I'll promise to do over the next 21 days to use this secret in my mothering to cultivate in my child a feeling of stability, personal responsibility, and inner direction is

_____

_____

_____

REAL MOM'S SECRET 3: A Mother Who Listens Shows Her Children They Matter

The one thing I'll promise to do over the next 21 days to use this secret in my mothering to help my child develop confidence about his identity and a feeling of significance and acceptance is _____

_____

_____

_____

REAL MOM'S SECRET 4: A Mother Who Is a Good Role Model Gives Her Children an Example Worth Copying
The one thing I'll promise to do over the next 21 days to use this secret in my mothering to help my child acquire patience, self-control, and strong values is _____

_____

_____

_____

REAL MOM'S SECRET 5: A Mother Who Teaches Values Inspires Character
The one thing I'll promise to do over the next 21 days to use this secret in my mothering to help nurture in my child empathy, strong character, and a moral compass is _____

_____

_____

_____

REAL MOM'S SECRET 6: A Mother Who Supports Her Children's Strengths Builds Their Confidence
The one thing I'll promise to do over the next 21 days to use this secret in my mothering to help my child develop confidence about her unique identity and natural strengths is

_____

_____

_____

REAL MOM'S SECRET 7: A Mother Who Encourages Independence Cultivates Self-Reliance
The one thing I'll promise to do over the next 21 days to use this secret in my mothering to help build in my child self-reliance and resourcefulness is _____

_____

_____

_____

REAL MOM'S SECRET 8: A Mother Who Applauds Effort Nurtures Perseverance
The one thing I'll promise to do over the next 21 days to use this secret in my mothering to help my child develop internal motivation and stick-to-itiveness is _____

_____

_____

_____

REAL MOM'S SECRET 9: A Mother Who Accepts Her Children's Shortcomings Nurtures Resilience
The one thing I'll promise to do over the next 21 days to use this secret in my mothering to help my child develop optimism and a bounce-back attitude is _____

_____

_____

_____

REAL MOM'S SECRET 10: A Mother Who Takes Time for Her Children Helps Them Build Strong Relationships
The one thing I'll promise to do over the next 21 days to use this secret in my mothering to nurture a healthy and loving relationship with my child is _____

_____

_____

_____

REAL MOM'S SECRET 11: A Mother Who Laughs Teaches Joy
The one thing I'll promise to do over the next 21 days to use this secret in my mothering to help me develop happiness and joy with my child is _____

_____

_____

_____

REAL MOM'S SECRET 12: A Mother Who Takes Care of Herself Holds Together Her Happy Family
The one thing I'll promise to do over the next 21 days to use this secret in my mothering to give my child a stronger feeling of security, happiness, and optimism is _____

_____

_____

_____

Trust yourself.

You know more than you think you do.

Dr. Benjamin Spock

The 12
Simple Secrets
of Real Mothering

A Mother Who Loves Teaches Worth

What Real Mothers Know: If Your Children Have Unconditional Love, They'll Be More Likely to Thrive

What Really Matters Most for Mothering: Be Loving with No Strings Attached

The Real Benefit for Kids: Authentic Self-Esteem

The Lesson a Real Mom Teaches: Of course mothers love their children, but unconditional love goes deeper and is far more complicated. This is about our complete, unequivocal acceptance of our children's true selves—including all their little quirks, bad decisions, tantrums, weaknesses, and flaws. The lesson our love teaches is profound: "You are a person of worth." "I believe in you, so you should believe in yourself." We convey our feelings through our everyday words and gestures: our excited voice, wide-open arms, eyes lit up just because our child is in our presence. This doesn't mean doing more, trying harder, being self-conscious. No, it just means staying in touch with our deepest instinctive feelings for our own flesh and blood. You don't plan these reactions: they just bubble over spontaneously in the natural ways we respond to our kids in the moment. Make no mistake—we do influence our children's opinions of themselves.

The lesson our children learn from how they are loved by us will last long after we're gone.

"She Learned to Show Her Unconditional Love"

I do not love him because he is good. I love him because he is my child."

—Rabindrath Tagore

Everyone assumed that thirteen-year-old Michael Wong was going to be a big success.

"That kid is going to make it!"

"You just know he's going to make his parents proud someday."

"Keep an eye on that boy—we'll be reading about him a few years from now."

That was the verdict a small community in Northern California had bestowed proudly on one of its young citizens, this bright and popular ninth grade boy who was always at the top of his class.

Most of the townspeople already knew Michael personally—the rest had certainly heard about him—and all were positive that this boy had the makings of greatness. And they surely had legitimate reasons for their predictions: kids' parents in the town described Michael as "so nice and well-mannered" and "just a born leader"; his soccer coach declared he was the best player he'd had in years; his music teacher was certain that Michael's talent on the oboe could earn him a music scholarship. And if that wasn't enough, the kid was smart: always on the honor roll with exemplary test scores. His teachers unanimously agreed that this child could do anything he set his mind to. And he was so lucky to have a mother who coached and supported his every success.

"He works so hard," they said, "and always wants to make his mom happy."

Michael Wong was just one of those special kids who everyone felt "just seemed to have it all."

Both of Michael's parents were hard-working professionals who always wanted the best for their child. His father was in the import-export business and traveled away from home frequently. His mother was a local pediatric surgeon well-known for her dedication to her patients and for the long hours she spent at the hospital. She never liked to talk about herself, but everyone knew she'd been a Rhodes Scholar and top in her class at Harvard Medical School. She was so pleased that Michael wanted to follow in her footsteps that she had even hired a personal academic trainer to make sure her son would get into an Ivy League school so that he could become a successful doctor, too.

"Every kid should have a mother like that," the townspeople concurred. "No wonder he tries so hard to please her— she loves him so."

But everyone was to learn that Michael was not as fortunate or happy as had been assumed.

One afternoon early in April, the police dispatcher received a 911 cell call from a woman who had been jogging in a remote area just outside of town.

"There's a boy here sitting on a rock down the Cripple Creek Gulch with a rifle pointed to his head," she exclaimed.

Detective Sergeant Henry Weiss heard the call coming in and was closest to the scene. He and his partner, Officer Sheila Covington, were a canine unit who happened to be training their German shepherd, Eddy, in the nearby park. So they immediately jumped back into their patrol car and headed to the spot on the double. Spotting a distraught woman with a cell phone to her ear on the side of the road, they pulled off, jumped out with their dog, and headed off quickly in the direction she pointed.

After a five-minute sprint through the underbrush, they came to a small clearing and stopped dead. About twenty-five yards away, a young boy was slumped down on the ground, leaning on a big rock with a hunting rifle stock clutched between his feet and the pointy muzzle dug into his breastbone.

"I know that boy," Sergeant Weiss tried to whisper, gasping for breath. "It's Dr. Wong's son, Michael. I can't believe it!"

"Stay cool. Let's not startle him," Sheila said. "That gun could go off with the slightest movement."

The two officers crouched down behind a bush, commanding Eddy to lie down behind them.

"I don't get it," Henry said as quietly as he could in his partner's ear. "Michael's a great kid—he's a real star in school—such great parents. What's going on?"

"I know his dad is out of town," Sheila replied. "I'll call dispatch to contact his mom."

There was a crackle of static as Sheila turned on her portable radio, and the boy suddenly looked up.

"Don't come any closer, whoever you are," he cried, jerking the rifle muzzle up to his head.

"Michael, it's Sergeant Weiss and Officer Covington." The two officers rose slowly to their feet. "Put down the rifle, son."

"Leave me alone."

"Take it easy, Michael. We're calling your mom, Michael."

"Don't bother. She'll be too busy."

Michael was right. Dispatch called back to say Dr. Wong was in surgery and couldn't be disturbed.

The partners noticed Michael fingering the rifle's trigger and appearing more and more agitated. His whole body began rocking back and forth, and they heard little whimpering sounds.

"Go away," he cried. "If you come any closer, I'll shoot."

They could see his hands trembling and his finger on the trigger as he slammed the muzzle into his forehead. The officers froze, fearing the worst, as the boy continued to quietly moan and whimper.

Eddy's ears shot up, and he rose to an alert stance. He responded instinctively to the sound of a child's distress. The two officers exchanged glances and had the same sudden thought. If the two of them couldn't get near the boy, maybe sending their big German shepherd might be safer. It might distract Michael and could buy them the time they needed to calm him down. At this point they figured they didn't have anything to lose. If they didn't do something soon, the partners had a gut feeling that they'd have a real tragedy on their hands.

Officer Covington signaled Eddy permission to go forward, and the dog, sniffing the air and with ears alert, started cautiously toward the boy. Michael looked up, wide-eyed, and saw the German shepherd coming, but didn't say a word. The two officers held their breath: those next seconds seemed like an eternity. Would the dog scare the boy? Would the gun go off intentionally or not? The next minutes would remain etched in their minds forever.

Eddy went straight to Michael and stopped. It was almost as though the dog was trying to size up the situation and feel out what the boy needed. Eddy cocked his head, looked back at his masters for a split second, looked back to the boy, and then seemed to know exactly what to do. He jumped into the kid's lap and started licking him. And within minutes Michael surrendered to the dog's affectionate assault and lay the rifle to the ground. As tears streamed down his cheeks, the boy grabbed onto Eddy's thick coat for dear life, hugged him close to his chest, and began stroking the dog's back over and over again.

Stunned by the quick change in the course of events, the officers at first hesitated, then slowly walked toward the scene. As they got closer they saw Eddy still licking the boy's face and wagging his tail nonstop. Michael clearly wasn't about to let go of their dog as he continued to sob.

Sergeant Weiss removed the gun, put his hand gently on the boy's shoulder, and asked, "Are you okay, Son?"

For the next few minutes the boy cried and trembled with emotion. Eddy sat closely beside his new friend, watching him attentively. He was very tuned into Michael and obviously wasn't going to move an inch until he was sure everything was okay. And the whole while, Michael never stopped petting Eddy's head and stroking the dog's fur down his big, strong back. The two officers stood by silently, enormously relieved but still terribly confused as to how this could have happened to Michael Wong of all kids.

Finally, Officer Covington asked softly, "What happened, Michael?"

Slowly, Michael looked up, his eyes red and swollen, and shook his head.

"I'm such a loser."

"Are you kidding? How can you say that?"

"It's true. I'm just one big disappointment to my mom. Didn't you ever feel that life would be better off without you?"

The officer was shocked. How could a wonderful kid like Michael ever think he was a disappointment to his mother?

Gradually the boy told his sad story. He'd studied for weeks for the PSATs, tests that usually aren't taken until the eleventh grade. But his mom was adamant that he take them earlier so it would "look" better on his school transcripts. Apparently the boy had gotten "only" in the ninety-eighth percentile.

"But that doesn't count for anything; you get the real SATs later and besides that's an incredible score," Officer Covington, who was a mom herself, interrupted.

"Oh, you don't know my mother," he said shaking his head sadly. "When I told her my score she asked me why I didn't get a hundred and then she said what she always says, 'You've got to do better.' I studied harder than I've ever studied in my life. It was the best I could do. I couldn't have done any better," he sobbed.

"She says that because she loves you so much," the Officer Covington responded.

"But she doesn't love me the way I am. She wants me smarter. I'll never be good enough for my mom. What's the point of trying anymore?"

Eddy started licking Michael's cheek.

"So today I decided to do her a favor."

Knowing the "favor" would have been to end his life, the shocked officer asked, "What changed your mind?"

"It was your dog.

"Eddy? But how did Eddy have anything to do with this?"

The boy shook his head slowly. "Don't you know that as soon as he saw me, he jumped in my lap and started to lick me. I didn't have to do a thing. He was happy just to be with me," Michael said. He paused to hug the dog and then continued. "It's like I always have to prove myself with my mom. Why can't she just love me the way I am?"

Both officers remained silent as Eddy nuzzled Michael lovingly behind his ear.

"I just needed somebody to feel that way about me."

The officers, fighting back tears themselves, glanced at one another and almost could read each other's thoughts: How could such a wonderful kid like Michael feel so worthless and unloved? And for God's sake, why was it that a dog could figure out what this young boy so desperately needed, when everyone else—especially his own mother—had missed it?

It wasn't until the next day that the two officers were able to sit down again with Michael and his mother, Dr. Wong, in the living room of their home. The officers made sure they brought along Eddy who lay attentively at Michael's feet. His mother was clearly upset and looked as though she hadn't slept all night.

"How could I have missed this? I'm so sorry. I had no idea," she said sadly to her son. "You know I would do anything for you. I work night and day because I want things to be easier for you than it was for me. I love you so much that I just want everything for you—the whole world."

"But Dr. Wong, Michael seemed so terribly unhappy and was feeling so worthless," Officer Covington said. "Our dog, Eddy, picked up on it right away."

"I know," she said sadly. "And his own mother missed it."
She turned to face her son. "I've been so insensitive to what you
need and how you've been feeling, Michael. I'm just so glad I
have a second chance to show you that I love you. I don't know
how I'd live without you. Please forgive me for ever giving you
the idea that you had to do anything to earn my love. You don't
have to do a thing. You're my son, and everything about you is
perfect already. I'm just so glad you're mine."

Dr. Wong looked at the big German shepherd who continued to sit protectively next to her son. The mother gently
patted the dog, and whispered softly in his ear, "Thanks, Eddy.
You saved my son's life. I really promise I'll be more sensitive
and love him better from now on."

What Real Moms Can Learn from This Story

Jennifer Wong loved her son as much as any mom could; that
was never in doubt. The problem was that Michael didn't know
it, because his mother was so wrapped up in her dreams of his
future that she was insensitive to what was really going on with
him in his present day-to-day struggles to please her. Sure his
test scores and grades were important, but in Michael's mind
they had become the only way to earn his mother's love. What
she missed was how much Michael needed her unqualified affection and approval, regardless of how he did in school.

The essential secret for real mothering here is that unconditional love doesn't depend on performance (or anything else,
for that matter). Unconditional love is your total, absolute
commitment, devotion, and tender affection for your children
exactly as they arrived to you and have developed so beauti-
fully over the years. The basic foundation for all good parenting is the ability to convey this unconditional love and
sensitivity to your child's needs.

Being Sensitive to Your Child's Real Needs

Sue Summit of Minneapolis noticed something amiss one blistering January morning when William, her first-grader, declined to get on the school bus. Worried that something had happened at school, she queried her child as to what might have happened. A bully? A bad grade? William assured her that none of those were the cause, and simply told her the real reason: "I haven't had enough playtime." A bit of soul searching and a review of her seven-year-old's schedule were enough to tell Sue her kid was right. Soccer, hockey, and violin lessons left little free time for what kids like to do best—just hang around, goof off, and play. As Sue said, "Sometimes things get out of whack, and you have to pull back and determine why it's not working. We've made different adjustments over the years." Their new family rule: schoolwork always comes first, and then William takes on no more than one extra activity at a time.

So how are you doing in your home? Better yet: How would you think your children would respond if they were asked the same question? Hmmm. Might a tune-up or a bit of rethinking be something you want to commit to? If so, when will you start?

Is This Real Mom's Secret Part of Your Parenting?

Here are some questions to ask yourself:

1. How well do you really know your child?

   - What are your child's real passions, the things he loves to do? What are his interests, his hobbies? What does he tune in to or seem fascinated about?
   - What are her true talents? For instance, does she draw well? Does she have great rhythm, incredible grace, endurance, a kind heart? Does she think in numbers, have an amazing vocabulary?

- What are his academic abilities? For instance, does he remember things quickly, enjoy reading or listening, like to write, have a knack for numbers, have a long attention span?
- How does she handle social settings? Is she more of a watcher or a joiner? Does she lead or follow? Does she buckle to peer pressure or stand up to it? Does she prefer to be around lots of people, a few, or none at all? Does she make friends easily or need guidance? Is she more of an extrovert or an introvert?
- How well does he handle pressure or criticism? Do deadlines stimulate or paralyze him? Does he need reminders, or is he self-motivated? When he fails, does he need encouragement, or does he pick himself right back up? Does criticism shrivel him or help him? Does he welcome competition or wither? Is he laid back or intense? Does he have positive or negative self-esteem?

2. Thinking now about the profile you've just created for your child, you need to ask yourself whether your hopes and dreams for her are based on who she really is or on who you want her to be. Are your current expectations—the ones you've more recently crafted for your child's life—matching your kid so that they enhance his self-esteem? Are your dreams in line with your kid? What would need altering? Here are some things to consider: Would you say for the most part that your child is thriving or barely surviving? Loving the competitive pace or dreading it? Jumping out of bed each morning with an "I can't wait" attitude for practice or playgroup or violin, or using excuses to get out of it? Is she talking excitedly about gymnastics or that new chess club you've enrolled her in, or is she feigning headaches? Is your kid really capable of taking the accelerated class, doing the chore, participating in soccer or the playgroup? Are some of the tasks above his level of ability? Is he mature

enough? Is this something he really wants to do, or is this *your* dream? Does he have the skills needed to succeed? Write a list of your concerns. Doing so will help you develop a plan to deal with them.

3. Has your kid or someone else ever wondered out loud if you're being sensitive to who your kid really is?

4. If you're sitting in a room and your child walks in unexpectedly, do your eyes light up with joy no matter what's the latest mishap?

5. If there is one thing you could do to be more sensitive to your child and show your unconditional love, what would it be? Write it on the lines here. Then get ready to learn the secret and use it with your family. _____

_____

_____

The Rubber Band Test ◌ REAL MOM WISDOM

Pick up a good, strong rubber band. Hold it firmly at both ends with two hands. Now consider your own list of expectations for your child. For everything that doesn't appear to be a good fit (such as your expecting him to be a great defensive cornerback, and he's more into playing chess), pull the band more tightly. For everything that seems more natural (for example, your daughter loves to sing, so you bought her a guitar), let the band relax a little. Think of every expectation you're placing on your child. If the band gets so taut that it's in danger of snapping, you and your kid are in trouble. Your goal is to be sensitive to ensuring the necessary match of who your kid really is to what you want him to be. A good measure of your sensitivity as a mother is for you to be able to set expectations that gently stretch your children to become their best without snapping their spirit.

Five Steps to Boosting Your Sensitivity

Step One: Match Your Expectations to Your Child's True Self. To make sure that the expectations you set for your child are ones that stretch her potential without unintentionally zapping her self-worth, ask yourself this: Are my expectations

1. **Developmentally appropriate.** *Is my child developmentally ready for the tasks I'm requiring, or am I pushing him beyond the limits of his internal timetable?* Learn what's appropriate for your child's age, but still keep in mind that developmental guidelines are not etched in stone. It's always best to start from where your child is.

2. **Realistic.** *Is my expectation fair and reasonable, or am I expecting too much?* Realistic expectations stretch kids to aim higher, without pushing them beyond their capabilities. Be careful of setting standards too high. Putting your child in situations that are too difficult puts her at risk of failing and lowering her feelings of competence.

3. **Child oriented.** *Is what I'm expecting something my child wants, or is it something I want more for myself?* We all want our kids to be successful, but we have to be constantly wary of setting goals for our kids that are attempts to fulfill our dreams and not those of our kids.

4. **Success oriented.** *Am I setting the kind of expectations that tell my child I believe he's responsible, reliable, and worthy?* Effective expectations encourage kids to be their best so that they can develop a solid belief in themselves.

Don't get so wrapped up in your hopes and dreams for your child's future that you lose sight of what matters most in the here and now. After all, what could be more important than your child's knowing that you love and cherish her for who she is—not for what you want her to be and what you hope she will become?

Step Two: Tune In to What's Really Going On with Your Kid. Put down that cell phone. Don't worry about the dust. Be intentional. Take time every day—I'm not talking hours, just a few minutes—to take a good look at your child's life and how things are going.

Step Three: Check Your Kid's Vital Signs. First the face: Are his eyes sparkling or flat? Is he scowling or smiling? Next the body language: Is she relaxed or stiff? Slumped down or coiled up? Finally, the voice: Is it tense and edgy or warm and resonant? Are you hearing whines or laughter? Any sudden changes in behavior: Clinginess? Anger or temper tantrums? Avoidance of situations? Negativity? Loss or big increase of appetite? Too little or too much sleep? Remember, your child isn't going to come up and say outright, "You're making demands on me I can't fulfill," but there are many ways, if you're sensitive, that you can see it for yourself.

Step Four: Identify the Specific Misfit Between Expectation and Reality. Is that accelerated class too hard? Is the coach too demanding? Are you too critical of your kid's grades? Is that clique you've encouraged her to join too upscale? Talk to your spouse, the teacher, or your best friend.

Step Five: Take Action to Remove the Mismatch Between Your Expectation and Reality. Find a better class. Take a break from soccer. Back off from stressing over grade-point average. Let your child choose her own friends. Remain vigilante and sensitive to your kid's needs. Never stop checking for stress and overload, identifying the potential causes and taking action to provide the remedy.

Happy Kids Are Loved with No Strings Attached

Dr. Stanley Coopersmith, author of *The Antecedents of Self-Esteem*, conducted a famous study to determine the kinds of conditions that enhance self-esteem; he discovered three critical factors. First, he found that children with high self-esteem clearly felt they were loved unconditionally with no strings attached. Second, contrary to "conventional wisdom," the high-self-esteem children were raised with clear, fair rules that were consistently enforced by their parents, so they knew what was expected. Finally, because their parents took time to listen and paid attention to their ideas, they grew up believing that their opinions mattered and were respected. Coopersmith found that parents who provide the kind of love that conveys acceptance, fair and clear expectations, and respect produce children who believe in themselves.

How would you describe the three esteem conditions in your family? Are your words and actions conveying to your child, "I believe in you," or are they in need of repair?

Making a Promise to Yourself

1. Did you identify with or were you inspired by the story of Michael and his mom, Jennifer Wong? Is this one of the secrets you want to focus on and tune up in your family? How would applying what matters most about being loving with no strings attached benefit your child?

2. How would you apply the five steps to boosting your sensitivity to your child? Review all the boxes, guides, tips, and stories in this chapter.

3. Go to A Mother's Promise on page 54 and write in the one thing you will do over the next 21 days to practice being sensitive by tuning into your kid's needs, not yours.

A Real Mom's Resource Guide

College of the Overwhelmed: The Campus Mental Health Crisis and What to Do About It, by Richard D. Kadison and Theresa Foy Di-Geronimo (San Francisco: Jossey-Bass, 2004). Sure, your kids may still be toddlers, but every parent should be aware of this book, and the sooner you read it the better. Written by the chief of the Mental Health Service at Harvard University Health Services, the book warns us of a mental health crisis in college students today. With the rising numbers of stressed-out, depressed, suicidal students who cannot cope with failure (that is, their first B grade), parents need to understand the crisis now to better prepare their kids for life later.

The Heart of Parenting: Raising an Emotionally Intelligent Child, by John Gottman, with Joan deClaire (New York: Simon & Schuster, 1997). A renowned psychologist teaches you the five steps of Emotion Coaching not only to help you tune in to your children's emotional needs but also to help kids become better at soothing themselves when they are upset.

"Help Me, I'm Sad," by David G. Fassler and Lynne S. Dumas (New York: Viking, 1997). This book is full of solid advice for parents on recognizing, treating, and preventing childhood and adolescent depression.

The Hurried Child: Growing Up Too Fast Too Soon, by David Elkind (New York: Perseus, 2001). The title says it all. Now in its third edition, this classic is still pertinent today.

KidStress, by Georgia Witkin (New York: Viking, 1999). This book talks about what causes kids' stress and offers practical ideas to alleviate it.

The Over-Scheduled Child, by Alvin Rosenfeld and Nicole Wise (New York: St. Martin's Griffin, 2001). The authors make a compelling argument against what they consider "hyperparenting" and the impact it has on kids. Put this book on your "must-read" list, Mom.

Parenting by Heart: How to Stay Connected to Your Child in a Disconnected World, by Ron Taffel, with Melinda Blau (Cambridge, Mass.: Perseus, 2002). In this book based around a long-standing series of parenting workshops, Taffel aims to debunk the most damaging myths of parenthood and replace them with a flexible set of solutions that can be easily adapted to different situations. This book presents a variety of innovative ideas that can boost our sensitivity to our children's needs. Taffel, as always, is practical and affirming.

Positive Pushing: How to Raise a Successful and Happy Child, by Jim Taylor (New York: Hyperion, 2005). Dr. Taylor shows that achievement and happiness can be mutually inclusive. By providing active guidance and positive support, parents free their children to seek out and pursue true success and happiness in life.

The Pressured Child: Helping Your Child Find Success in School and Life, by Michael Thompson, with Teresa Barker (New York: Ballantine, 2004). This book helps sensitize parents to the real pressures that new cultural norms impose on kids at school these days and offers advice to parents and educators on how to help children cope. It is based on interviews with children, parents, and teachers and—most revealing—shadowing students at school.

What Do You Really Want for Your Children? by Wayne W. Dyer (New York: Avon, 1985). This book offers straightforward advice about raising children and increasing their self-esteem.

Your Anxious Child: How Parents and Teachers Can Relieve Anxiety in Children, by John S. Dacey and Lisa B. Fiore (San Francisco: Jossey-Bass, 2000). This book describes proven ways to help kids handle stress and cope with difficulties more confidently.

A Mother Who Is Firm and Fair Gives Her Children a Moral Code to Live By

What Real Mothers Know: Set Consistent Limits and Standards of Behavior So Your Child Learns to Act Right Without You

What Really Matters Most for Mothering: Be Consistent and Just in Your Discipline

The Real Benefit for Kids: Stability, a Sense of Responsibility, and Inner Direction

The Lesson a Real Mother Teaches: No mother wants to reprimand her child. The very word *discipline* seems to go against the concepts of motherhood and love. But does it? After all, we moms have one overriding goal: to raise our kids to be happy, well-behaved, good and decent human beings. So anytime you are worried that your child is getting on the wrong track and is learning some behaviors that aren't right, then it's time to apply some limits. That's exactly what real moms do. They know that by being consistent and using the right discipline, their relationship with their kid will improve, their family life will be more harmonious, mothering will be more enjoyable, *and* their kid will behave the way they hope he will. Sure it will take work, and of course this isn't easy, but these are exactly the benefits you'll experience when you step into Real Mom Mode and act on your gut instinct that tells you that consistent limits really are best for your kids. There's even an added lesson: your setting firm limits will help your kid learn good behaviors and strong moral habits. And those are what will ultimately form your kid's reputation as a human being. That's how critical this second secret of real mothering is! But your clear and consistent behavior expectations also give your child inner discipline so that he knows how to act right even when you're not around. After all, raising your kids in a loving, secure, stable home and teaching them how to act right with or without you are two of the greatest legacies you can give.

"She Knew She Needed to Be a Parent, Not Her Kid's Best Friend"

Parents who are afraid to put their foot down usually have
children who step on their toes.
—Vern McLellan

Genevieve's mother was really strict. What she remembers most about growing up was when all the rest of her friends could stay out late, pierce their ears, and wear mascara, she had to be home by nine and wait until she left home for college to wear makeup. It had seemed as though her mom wasn't like the rest of the mothers, who were more tuned in to their daughter's wants and desires and let them do what they wanted.

So when Genevieve's daughter, Emily, was born, she resolved to be a different kind of mom, a "cool mom" who kept up with the latest trends and made sure her daughter could do everything the other girls did. She also wanted Emily to have all the advantages she felt she'd been denied. Most important, Genevieve was determined not to be the Wicked Witch of the West but instead to be her daughter's close pal and confidant.

At first, being this kind of mother was fun. Genevieve enjoyed buying Emily the fanciest dresses and prettiest dolls and enrolling her in the most popular dance classes and Gymboree. Sure it meant she had to work longer hours to pay for all these luxuries, but it was worth every dime. She was giving her daughter more privileges and pleasures than she had ever had as a child.

By the time Emily was five, there was hardly any room in her closet for all the pretty outfits and dance costumes. But overnight, the little girl decided she hated dance class and wanted to be a figure skater.

"But Emily, you're such a graceful dancer. And we've spent so much money on your lessons. Don't you want to be in the big recital next week?"

"Noooooo, Mommy! I don't like Miss Parsons. She never lets me just dance the way I want to or talk in class. She just wants us to practice, practice, practice. And besides, Mommy, Kelly just went to skating. Her mom let her."

Genevieve tried to talk her daughter out of quitting. The teacher had told her that Emily had exceptional talent and that if she continued to study, she might have a real future in dance. But when Emily started to cry, then scream and hold her breath, Genevieve gave in and took her to buy a brand-new pair of expensive figure skates.

"You're spoiling the child," Genevieve's mother told her on the phone the next day.

"Oh Mom, you just don't understand. All of Emily's friends are skating now, and none of their mothers would think of saying no."

Then one evening Genevieve went with Emily to visit her second-grade class for a parent-child school night. Her teacher, Miss Takeda, wanted the parents to appreciate all the good work her students had accomplished that year and review their children's work folders. Genevieve was enjoying sitting with her daughter leafing through pages of math, writing, and art, when suddenly Emily jumped up.

"Mom! This is boring. I'm going to find Kelly and the other girls."

"Emily, you're supposed to stay with me. Your teacher wanted us to talk about your work."

"This is dumb, Mom. I've seen all this stuff already."

"No, Emily. I don't want you running off. I had to change my schedule around to get here tonight."

"Oh, Mom," Emily whined loudly.

"Sit down, Emily. Miss Takeda is coming over. You can play with your friends later."

"You're so mean. You're the worst mom in the world. I hate you!" she yelled as she jumped up and bolted from the room.

"Hello, Mrs. Trudeau. I'm so glad you were able to make it. What happened with Emily?"

"Oh, nothing, Miss Takeda. You know how kids can get a little sassy now and then. It's just one of those phases."

"Be careful it doesn't become a habit. If they start acting out at this age, think about what they could be like when they get older."

Genevieve listened carefully. What Miss Takeda said made a lot of sense. She'd been noticing that for some time now Emily had been sassing her more and more. Not only that, she'd been so demanding and hard to satisfy. Instead of the idyllic mother-daughter friendship Genevieve had hoped for, their relationship had become tense and stressful.

Over the next few years, things between them went from bad to worse. Emily hung up her skates forever and demanded riding lessons at a stable that was almost an hour away. Genevieve's paychecks were all going for expensive, brand-name clothing her daughter just "had to have" that Genevieve later found thrown all over the floor in Emily's room. The second-grader's whine went up one hundred decibels and was accompanied by some pretty shocking four-letter words that Genevieve would never use in her life. Worse yet, Emily wasn't being disrespectful only in the privacy of her home, but frequently in public— even, to her mother's dismay, in front of her grandmother.

"Genevieve, why are you letting your daughter talk to you like that? It's appalling," her mother announced. "And not only that, you're going to ruin your relationship with her if you continue to put up with that behavior."

"Mother, this is *my* daughter. Things have changed. Parenting is not the same as when you brought me up."

"No, Genevieve, some things never change. Kids will always need to have a strong moral compass. And firm limits help them learn that. They're actually happier with rules and structure in their lives."

Genevieve didn't want to admit it, but she was beginning to wonder if her mother was right. Emily seemed increasingly unpleasant, not the "best friend" Genevieve had hoped for but rather a defiant, unsatisfied, and basically unhappy kid—the exact opposite of the child in her old dreams of perfect motherhood.

The turning point came as Emily approached her thirteenth birthday, when she began to insist on a coed slumber party.

"All the other kids do it, Mom. Don't be so out of it. What's the big deal?"

"Boys and girls sleeping together? Come on! Don't you remember the problems those boys caused at Kelly's party?"

"Get real, Mom. That was nothing. You get so worked up about . . ."

"Wait a minute, young lady," Genevieve interrupted. "What about the beer bottles Kelly's mom found in their backyard?"

Suddenly Emily put her head in her hands and, to Genevieve's great surprise, began to sob. "Oh . . . Mom . . . You never do anything for me. Don't you want me to be happy? You just make my life miserable."

Genevieve was stunned. "Miserable? I never had half of what you have. How can you possibly be unhappy, Emily? I've given you everything in the world you've ever wanted, and haven't I always been your best friend?"

Emily looked up in surprise, wiping the tears from her eyes. "What do you mean, best friend? You're my mother. You should know what I need. That's what parents are for—they're supposed to know what makes their kids happy."

Yes, Emily was right, and so was her grandmother. Genevieve knew in her heart that Emily would be much better off if her mother started to act more like a parent and less like one of the gang. Her daughter's tears had really shocked her. Emily really was not a happy camper. And their relationship had disintegrated.

It was time for Genevieve to put her foot down. A coed slumber party was just asking for trouble.

"Emily, you're not having a coed slumber party. You can invite the girls, but that's the limit."

Her daughter looked up at her, surprised at her mom's new tone of voice.

"And not only that," Genevieve went on, "from now on I'm not going to take any more of your bad attitude and disrespect. You need to start appreciating what you have, and maybe the best way to do that is by my not giving you so much—more than you really need."

Is This Real Mom's Secret Part of **Your** Parenting?

Diana Baumrind, a psychology professor at the University of California at Berkeley, extensively studied parenting styles by observing families firsthand. She identified three different styles of parenting and also determined that one is more effective in raising confident children.

1. *Use the rewind method.* To be absolutely sure your child knows what you want, state your request and then ask her to "rewind" (repeat) what you just said back to you. It takes only a few seconds and eliminates any chance of misunderstanding.

2. *Try the "Ten-Second Rule."* Limit your words to exactly what you want your child to do. If you can't state your request in ten seconds, you're saying too much.

3. *Lower your voice.* Sometimes the fastest way to get kids to comply is by lowering your voice tone. Nothing turns a kid off faster than yelling. Teachers have used this strategy for years because it works.

4. *Keep it short.* Kids are more receptive when they know they don't have to hear a lecture, so keep your request short and to the point: "Please make your bed before you go outside." Sometimes saying one word does the trick: "Homework!" "Chores!" Or just write the word on a Post-it and stick it on the TV while your kid is still watching: "BED!" "GARBAGE!" He'll get the hint. (If not, push the power button off.)

- **Permissive.** You dish out a lot of affection, but you make few demands on your kid and wouldn't consider yourself a strong disciplinarian. You'd rather be your kid's best friend than her parent.

- **Authoritarian.** You use a lot of commands and threats based on an absolute standard of conduct and higher authority. You rarely ask your child what he thinks or consider compromising or negotiating. You believe in indoctrinating your child with respect for work, authority, and tradition. There's no give-and-take.

- **Authoritative.** Your parenting combines confident authority with reasoning, fairness, and love. You encourage your child's input and acknowledge your own responsibility as an adult but also your child's individual needs and desires.

If you think you're too permissive, see if any of these statements reflect your attitude:

☐ I want to raise my child differently from how I was raised. My parents were too strict, and I don't have a good relationship with them.

☐ My schedule takes me away from my family a lot. This is my way of making up for not being there for my kids.

☐ Everyone gives their kids things. Why should I be any different?

☐ I'm trying to be a friend to my kids. I think that's a big part of raising children and being a good parent.

☐ I want my child to be happy and have a happy childhood. Always being on his case for his behavior isn't going to help develop that outcome.

☐ I'm afraid to say no to my child. He might not love or approve of me.

☐ My child has had some tough breaks, and I'm just trying to make things easier.

☐ I don't believe in punishment.

☐ I'm afraid that if I say no I might crush my child's self-esteem or spirit.

☐ Bad behaviors just go away on their own. They're really just a phase.

If you think you're too authoritarian, see if any of these statements fit you:

- [ ] I'm exhausted. I really don't have time to listen to my kids' opinions.
- [ ] I believe kids should be seen, not heard.
- [ ] This is how I was raised, and it's how I plan to raise my kids.
- [ ] Deep down this isn't my philosophy, but my spouse is authoritarian. I'm copying my parenting partner's style of discipline.
- [ ] I think kids today are spoiled and need a firm hand, or they will never respect authority.
- [ ] I don't know another way to discipline my kids.
- [ ] I'm afraid to lose control.
- [ ] I believe in a family culture where you respect your elders and there is a clear hierarchy.

Which parenting style do you think produces kids who are more confident as well as more respectful? You're right if you guessed "authoritative." Consistently using this style of parenting greatly improves the chances that you will raise a more respectful, confident, happier child who also has a healthy relationship with you. What will make you decide to change your current style of discipline? What is the first step you need to take to make that change happen? Write it on the lines here. Then get ready to learn the secret and use it with your family.

Being Firm and Fair Builds Character

Temple University psychologist Laurence Steinberg and his research team studied twenty thousand adolescents and their families in nine different communities in the United States. Like Baumrind, Steinberg found that teens with authoritative parents were more likely to have solid character and to be confident and successful in school than those adolescents whose parents were permissive or authoritarian. The teens were also less likely to use alcohol or drugs. Steinberg reminds us that "The most important thing that children need from their parents is love, but a close second is structure."

Nine Steps to Squelching Bad Behaviors Firmly and Fairly

Step One: Establish Your Rules. Think through what you stand for and what you won't tolerate in your kids. Pick your battles and stick to what you think matters most, then let your child know what that is. Keep in mind that your expectations will vary as your child matures, so don't be afraid to change and bend your rules.

Step Two: Deal with One Behavior at a Time. Suppose your child is repeatedly displaying the same misbehavior. Zero in on it. Granted, your child may be displaying a number of behaviors that need fixing, but it's really best to work on improving only one—and never more than two—behaviors at a time. That way, you will be much more likely to stop the bad behavior permanently. So narrow your focus and target the specific behavior you want to eliminate that is getting in the way of your relationship or your kid's character: Is it your child's whiney voice? Those temper tantrums? That staying out late?

Step Three: Connect Calmly with Your Child. If your child breaks your rule or displays that bad behavior, it's time to be firm. Always take a deep breath and calm down before you address your child. If *you* need a time-out, take it. Then get eye to eye and make sure you have your child's attention. Remember, your goal is to discipline in love—never in anger.

Step Four: Clarify Your Concerns. Don't assume that your child knows what she's doing wrong. Using a firm and calm tone, review your rules or why the behavior is wrong. You might start by asking the child, "What are our house rules?" "Why do you think your friend is upset?" or "Why do you think I'm upset?" If your child isn't certain, then review why the behavior was wrong. (With little ones, just plainly explain your rule: "We don't pull kitty's fur. We pat." "You may not hit.") Just be clear and brief. "If you leave your bike outside, it will be stolen." "Your tone is disrespectful." To be fair, listen carefully to your child's side so that you get all the facts. If you discover in your fact-finding that you were wrong (it does happen, you know), admit you were mistaken. Apologize.

Step Five: Suggest a Positive Alternative. What specific new behavior do you want your child to display? Give a child a positive option or two. "Please talk nicely to me." "You must come home immediately after the game." Ask a younger child to display the alternative behavior so you're sure he understands your request. "Show me how to ask for a turn nicely." Don't be shy about asking your child for suggestions: "What could you do next time so you don't use that same behavior [or break the rule] again?"

Step Six: Explain the Consequence If the Misbehavior or Rule Infraction Continues. "If you can't talk nicely to me, you will not be able to use the phone." "If you can't stop yelling at your sister, you will go to time-out." Be specific, be brief, be firm.

You might consider asking your child what a fair consequence would be if he displays the behavior again. Generally the ones kids choose are not only tougher than ones adults choose but also fairer and more likely to "fit their crime." To make sure he understands, have him repeat what you said. For more egregious behaviors with older kids, it's sometimes a good idea to put your agreement in writing and have both of you sign it. A young child can draw the contract. Put it in a safe place so you can rely on it later if needed.

Step Seven: Correct the Misbehavior on the Spot and Carry Out the Agreed Consequence. If the behavior continues, follow through with your consequence. You must be consistent and act ASAP so that your child knows you mean business. The moment your child uses any inappropriate behavior is the time to correct it.

Step Eight: Be Fair. Your goal is not to turn every little problem into a world war with your kids, so try to keep a balance between being *firm and fair.* When it comes to conflicts over rules, take in mind the circumstance. Here are a few fair discipline options to use in settling disputes:

- **Compromise.** "You're supposed to do your homework now, but you're working so hard on your dribbling. Do you agree to do your homework in half an hour?" Don't ever let your kid force you into a compromise you don't think is fair or appropriate.

- **Offer choices.** "Your chores need to be done today. Would you like to finish them before dinner or after?"

- **Joint problem solving.** See if you and your child can create an alternative that you both can agree to. This would mean finding a way to change the rule so that it satisfies both of you.

- **Give in.** When the issue you're battling over is trivial, then you might decide it's easier simply to agree to your child's request. Just make sure he can give you a sound reason, then tell him why you agree to bend the rule this time. By the way, always do give in whenever you're mistaken, and remember to admit your mistake to your child.

Step Nine: Congratulate Good Efforts. Don't overlook the simplest and often most effective way to change behavior: "That was a respectful voice. That's the kind I listen to." Change is hard—especially for kids—so acknowledge your child's efforts and improvements.

Carole Tobias, a mother of three from White Plains, New York, had a problem with her youngest son, Sean, when he started hitting other children in his neighborhood. Mom targeted the hitting behavior and told him that he was going to time-out any time he used his hands instead of his words. Things were working fine at home, but when she got a note from his preschool teacher, she realized they needed to form an alliance to ensure a consistent approach to the problem. She called Mrs. Simmons and set up a conference, where she explained her time-out policy and gave the teacher permission to use the same approach at school. And because the two women cooperated on this together, Sean learned to stop hitting whether he was at home or at school.

Whatever behavior you're trying to change, tell your plan to at least one other adult who spends time with your kid. Even if the other caregiver sees your child only five minutes once a week, she'll be reinforcing your policy, so you're more likely to see the change you want and in less time.

Making a Promise to Yourself

1. Did you identify with or were you inspired by the story of Emily and her mother, Genevieve? Is this one of the secrets you want to focus on and tune up in your family? How would applying what matters most about being firm and fair benefit your child?

2. How would you apply the nine steps to ending bad behaviors firmly and fairly in your family? Review all the boxes, guides, tips, and stories in this chapter.

3. Go to A Mother's Promise on page 54 and write in the one thing you will do over the next 21 days to practice being firm and fair with your kids.

A Real Mom's Resource Guide

The Discipline Book: How to Have a Better-Behaved Child from Birth to Age Ten, by William Sears and Martha Sears (New York: Little, Brown, 1995). A foremost husband-and-wife team (a pediatrician and a registered nurse and childbirth educator, respectively) tells you everything you need to know about discipline to raise a happy, well-adjusted, and well-behaved child.

Discipline: The Brazelton Way, by T. Berry Brazelton and Joshua D. Sparrow (Cambridge, Mass.: Perseus, 2003). This renowned pediatrician has written a short book filled with wonderful wisdom on how to discipline your child using what really matters: love and limits.

8 Weeks to a Well-Behaved Child: A Failsafe Program for Toddlers Through Teens, by James Windell (Old Tappan, N.J.: MacMillan, 1994). From "fair" and "unfair" punishment to how to use reprimands, time-out, and removal of privileges, Windell offers tools to give parents the confidence to transform children's behavior problems.

The Happiest Toddler on the Block: The New Way to Stop the Daily Battle of Wills and Raise a Secure and Well-Behaved One- to Four-Year-Old, by Harvey Karp and Paula Spencer (New York: Bantam Books, 2004). This book describes a unique and sensitive approach that helps you gain perspective on why your little one is acting up, and offers sensible ways to discipline.

How to Behave So Your Children Will, Too! by Sal Severe (New York: Penguin, 2002). This book provides a wealth of valuable advice on how parents need to behave in order to raise well-behaved children.

Kids Are Worth It: Giving Your Child the Gift of Inner Discipline, by Barbara Coloroso (New York: HarperResource, 2002). Using a combination of compassion and respect when disciplining a child will teach limits without damaging the child's or the parent's self-esteem. Coloroso tackles some of the most difficult topics, from how to teach a toddler the meaning of *no* to handling a troublesome teen. Good, comforting advice from a fabulous parent educator.

Kids, Parents, and Power Struggles, by Mary Sheedy Kurcinka (New York: HarperCollins, 2000). A noted family educator helps you cope with the everyday challenges of disciplining your child while understanding the issues behind his or her behavior. The author offers sound strategies to end those power struggles and begin connecting with your child.

No More Misbehavin': 38 Difficult Behaviors and How to Stop Them, by Michele Borba (San Francisco: Jossey-Bass, 2003). You're right. I wrote it. But it's also my favorite. Fighting, biting, homework battles, tantrums, talking back, being mean, rude, or selfish— I'll give you a customized makeover plan and simple-to-use guide for each of the thirty-eight most troublesome behaviors and how to change them once and for all.

Parenting with Love and Logic: Teaching Children Responsibility, by Foster W. Cline and Jim Fay (Colorado Springs, Colo.: Piñon Press, 1990). This book is filled with good, solid, practical parenting advice that helps you raise a responsibly behaved kid who can make good decisions. You'll also discover great tips on how to change your behavior so as to reduce the number of battles with your kids and address the issues that really matter.

Raising Good Children: From Birth Through the Teenage Years, by Thomas Lickona (New York: Bantam Books, 1994). Based on solid child development theory, this is a practical guide to helping your child develop a lifelong sense of honesty, decency, and respect for others, and to *act right*.

A Mother Who Listens Shows Her Children They Matter

What Real Mothers Know: Give Your Children Complete Attention and They'll Carry You with Them Forever

What Really Matters Most for Mothering: Pay Attention

The Real Benefit for Kids: A Feeling of Significance and Self-Acceptance

The Lesson a Real Mother Teaches: A child whose mother knows the secret of attentive listening is truly blessed. When a mother stops what she's doing to focus totally on her child, she's conveying her love and acceptance. This isn't about doing more, but about doing less. It's like the old Zen saying, "Don't just do something, sit there." Sit and listen. When you do this, you're teaching your child that at that moment absolutely nothing matters more than hearing what he or she has to say. And that is exactly why listening with full presence is one of the most precious gifts a mother can give. It is also one of the simplest of all maternal secrets to use. It requires only split-second choices—clicking off a cell phone, setting down the paper, closing a book—and then a total willingness to let your child know you're there. It requires only such small intentional actions as looking at your child, nodding gently, leaning in slightly to appear interested—all of which your child will perceive as "My mom cares"; "I can tell my mom anything"; "She wants to hear what I say." There is also a hidden benefit: attentive listening is the foundation of a deep and enduring relationship between mother and child. Make listening a habit now and your child will seek you out as a sounding board, loyal confidante, and patient guide forever.

"She Gave Her Child Complete Presence"

The mother's heart is the child's schoolroom.
—Henry Ward Beecher

Most teachers would admit that there are some students whom they'll never forget. Six-year-old Ricky Anderson was one of those students I still think of fondly years after he left my class. In fact, this child is so special that I can remember the exact moment when I first laid eyes on him.

It was the first day of school in my second year of teaching. My classroom was at the end of a short hallway, and that's where I stood waiting to greet my first-graders. I spotted Ricky the moment he stepped off the bus. (Actually, it would have been impossible to miss him.) The first reason was that he was one of those "just plain adorable" six-year-olds: he had bright red hair, twinkling blue eyes, a round tummy, and an impish little face that was sprinkled with just the right amount of freckles across his nose. You couldn't help smiling when you saw him—he was that cute. He looked just like Opie from the old *Andy Griffith Show*. The second reason was that he was making such a racket. While the other students walked to their classrooms, Ricky skipped. (In fact, he *always* skipped—it seemed to be his preferred mode of mobility.) And all the while he bar-reled down the hall, he was singing Mr. Rogers's theme song at the top of his lungs (you know: "It's a beautiful day in the neighborhood . . . ," though he seemed to know only the first line, so he repeated it over and over and over). He was a bun-dle of energy and just bursting with excitement.

He screeched to a halt when he arrived at my door and recognized that this was to be his first-grade classroom. He flashed me a big grin, then stuck his head inside to check things out. Both the room and I must have passed inspection, because he turned and exclaimed quite matter-of-factly, "This is going to be the best year of my whole life." He then added excitedly, "This year I'm going to learn to read!"

Well, I was smitten. Frankly I adored him, and I was struck not only by his enthusiasm but also by his confidence. That's because learning to read wasn't going to be easy for Ricky. I was a special education teacher, and Ricky was enrolled in my class-room because of severe learning disabilities and attention deficits. It was difficult for him to remain focused on almost anything for more than a few minutes—on some days even a few seconds was a challenge. In fact, of all the special educa-tion students I'd taught, Ricky's attention span was the shortest.

A few weeks into the school year, I found Ricky at the art center busily cutting out dozens of small paper hearts. (It was Halloween time, so I was a bit concerned that he was working on the wrong holiday symbol.) But I saw a kid who was obvi-ously trying his hardest to make something very special turn out just right. He struggled to attach stickers to the cut-out shapes and painstakingly added crayon scribbles to his project. This was tedious stuff for any young child, but especially for a little boy who had such a hard time concentrating.

"That's lovely, Ricky," I told him, then asked curiously, "Who's it for?"

"It's for my mom," he explained proudly.

"Is it her birthday?"

"Nope!" he said while shaking his head from side to side, clearly elated that I was noticing his efforts.

"Well, what's the special occasion?"

It has been over two decades, but to this day I can still remember his exact words. He looked up, smiled, then explained in a whisper: *"I'm making my mom a card because she always makes my feelings feel so good."*

He smiled and then turned back to finish what he had started: a special card for his mother, whom he so obviously cherished.

Well, I couldn't wait to meet this mother. As far as I was concerned, this lady walked on water when it came to parenting. She was doing something very right to instill such confidence and joy in her child (besides making his feelings "feel so good"). I had to see just what she did to create such adoration in her child, and the sooner the better. My opportunity came the following week.

I scheduled a class field trip and needed a parent volunteer to help out. Ricky's mom was the first person I asked, and she agreed. On the day of the trip, she walked into my classroom, and within seconds I knew exactly what this mother did to make her son's feelings feel so good. It wasn't anything difficult or even mysterious. It was really quite simple and certainly nothing new.

Actually, Ricky spotted his mom before she found him. He'd been anxiously waiting for her by the door, and as soon as this kid saw her he ran straight into her arms. He was so eager to tell her about his class. I must admit, my room was a bit chaotic at the time, with boys running around, someone accidentally knocking over the library cart, and a box of papers crashing to the floor. It was also terrifically noisy, with constant chattering, laughing, and squeals of excitement. But in the midst of all that, this wonderful mom began to use her "little secret" that made her child feel so good.

Now please don't get the wrong idea about what happened: you might be thinking this was a sophisticated and lengthy process. Actually, it was far from it. In fact, their entire encounter was probably no more than two minutes—max. But during that time nothing mattered to that mom except what her child had to say. I watched in fascination, and here's what happened.

Mrs. Anderson walked in and immediately got down on her knees. She settled on the floor with Ricky and looked straight ahead at him, with her eyes riveted to his and her hands gently on his shoulders so that they were in close physical contact. She sat. She smiled. She listened. She obviously had a wonderful knack for being able to block everything out except Ricky (or at least for making her kid feel that only he mattered).

As I watched the two of them in their own little world, Ricky talked—and his mom listened—but the key is that she was listening with such genuine interest in what he was saying that all the noise and action around them seemed to fade away. Occasionally she'd respond with a simple "Uh huh," or "Really?" or just describe his feelings. ("You seem so happy"; "That must have made you proud.") But the effect it had on her child was profound: Ricky's whole being just blossomed.

The mother's "magic" was really very straightforward: she focused intently on only her son and gave him her complete presence when he talked. And because she did, Ricky knew just how much he mattered in her eyes. It was such an easy concept and almost effortless to use, but it produced very powerful results. Mrs. Anderson spent the rest of the day with our class helping everywhere and everyone on our field trip. She was a delight—always pleasant, always smiling, but often focusing only on her son and giving him her full and total presence. But there was absolutely no doubt in my mind that this was what she did to make her son feel that his mom "always made his feelings feel so good." It's a secret we can all learn and use with our children.

What Real Moms Can Learn from This Story

Mrs. Anderson knew that one of the best ways to let children know just how much they really matter to us is by listening when they tell us their thoughts, interests, or concerns. And the easiest way to do so is by giving them our full and complete presence, tuning in not just to what they are saying but to how they are acting and what feelings they are expressing with all of their behavior.

Yes, you may be going ninety miles an hour in fifty different directions, but when it's time to listen to your child, you have to sweep all that aside. We're not talking about lengthy sessions here but just the time it takes, ordinarily three to five minutes per occasion, to stop and focus—really focus—on what your child has to say. Mrs. Anderson wasn't attentive to her son once or just when he was at school. No, she listened to her son with her heart as well as her ears whenever she was with him. Attentiveness had become a maternal habit.

After all, what is more important than helping your child develop a strong sense of self and identity? And what better way to convey just how much you care than by blocking everything else out for those few minutes and devoting your total attention to your child?

Is This Real Mom's Secret Part of Your Parenting?

These next questions will help you assess just how well you are applying this essential maternal secret with your children. As you read each item, do some serious, honest soul searching. If you want to learn this parenting secret, you must be willing to identify your current weaknesses so that you *can* change. Write down your thoughts in your journal so you can review them frequently to help you learn this lesson.

1. In the story, Ricky described his mom as someone who always made his "feelings feel so good." How do you think your kids might describe your listening abilities? (Have you ever thought to ask?)

2. On an average day, how many total minutes do you think you spend attentively listening to your child? Be careful: discussing chores, homework, messy bedrooms, or misplaced library books doesn't count. So add up *only* the number of actual minutes spent attentively hearing your kid discuss things he cares about or is excited about, such as his thoughts, feelings, fears, loves, concerns, hopes, dreams, successes—"the personal stuff." Your goal is to double that current number—or even triple it—by the end of three weeks.

3. Pretend that the last few conversations between you and your child were videotaped. Rewind the tape, push Play, and watch yourself carefully. As your child was talking to you, what were *you* doing?

   ☐ Were your eyes on your child or elsewhere?

   ☐ Did you make assumptions, or did you try to practice letting go of judgments and just listening?

   ☐ Did you reflect back any of the emotions your child might be feeling when she shared something meaningful with you?

   ☐ Did you ask questions to get information instead of trying to prove a point?

   ☐ Did you tell your child you enjoyed or valued what she said, or in any way let her know you found it interesting?

   ☐ Were your hands doing another task, or were they still, so that you could tune in to your kid?

   Now for the moment of truth: If you were the child, would you have wanted to talk to the adult in the video?

4. On a scale of 1 to 10 (1 being the lowest and 10 the highest) how would you rate your listening skills? Why did you choose that rating? What one little thing could you do to improve your score?

5. What is the one thing you recognize in yourself that you know you need to change so you can become a more attentive listener to your child? Write it on the lines here. Then get ready to learn the secret and use it with your family.

Four Steps to Listening with Full Presence

Step One: Stop Everything Else. The very next time your child wants or needs you, put down that cell phone. Turn off the TV. Get off the computer. Let the pasta boil, and give your full attention. Turn and face him. Get eye to eye and at his level. Nod every once in a while. Smile if appropriate and even lean in slightly. Don't interrupt or offer any opinion: just listen! Your silence can be affirming, and besides, the last thing kids want to hear all the time is our advice.

Step Two: Offer Encouragement. To let your child know you're interested, repeat a few key words that you've heard your child say. Offer a nonjudgmental word or two to encourage her continuing, such as, "Oh?" "I see." "Really?" or even "Mmmm." Or you can simply repeat back your child's last phrase:

Child: "I can't stand being around Josh this year."
Adult: "So you can't stand being around him?"
Child: "Yeah! He's so bossy."

Step Three: Acknowledge Feelings. When you recognize how your child is feeling, describe the emotion: "Looks like you're angry." "You seem really frustrated." "Sounds like you're irritated."

What Grade Would Your Kids Give You?

A 2005 nationwide sample of one thousand teens ages twelve to nineteen were asked to assign letter grades to adults in twenty-four categories. Focus groups of teens then met in Washington, Los Angeles, and Chicago to explain the grades. More than 35 percent of teens surveyed gave poor grades (D's or F's) to adults for failing to listen and understand teens. How would your child grade your listening ability?

"You seem unhappy." This simple act helps your child know you are giving her your full attention, really trying to understand her, and interested in what she has to say.

Step Four: Provide Reassurance. End your talk with a response that conveys your support or appreciation: "I hope things work out." "That was really interesting." "I'm so sorry." "I'm here if you need me." "I enjoyed that." Wait to see if your child needs anything else: advice, a hug, reassurance. He'll be more likely to want to share his ideas and feelings with you because he knows you care and are giving him your full presence.

The best way I learned to listen attentively was not from a book but from my son Adam. He taught it to me when he was just two. Whenever we would talk, he had a habit of taking my chin in his hand and pulling my face toward him so that my eyes were directly in front of his face. His actions were crystal clear: Adam wanted my complete attention. The way he knew I was listening was by seeing my eyes exclusively on his eyes. That's what our kids want most—to know we're really listening and interested in what they have to say. Using active listening with our kids conveys that message to them.

To make sure you really master each lesson part, I recommend that you practice one or two—but no more—pieces per week. For instance: During the first week, tackle only the first part: Focus Fully. During the second week, continue practicing Focus Fully but also add the next piece, Offer Encouragement and Repeat Key Ideas. Then continue adding a new piece each week until by the end of the month you will not only have learned the whole lesson but also be more likely to use it in your daily family life.

Giving Your Child "Wait Time"   ✐ REAL MOM WISDOM

Mary Budd Rowe, a noted educator, discovered that children need "wait time"—more time to think about what they hear—before speaking. So whenever you ask a question or give a request, remember to *wait at least three seconds* for your child to think about what she heard. She will absorb more information, be more likely to respond, and probably give you a fuller answer. That also means, Mom, that during those three seconds you need to wait patiently and continue to give your kid your full presence. Just to see how well you're doing, the next time you ask your child a question, time yourself: How many seconds are you waiting until you get impatient for her immediate response? Stretch *your* "wait time."

Seven Simple Ways to Keep Your Kids Talking (So You Can Listen More)

1. **Listen during active times.** Some kids (particularly boys) are more responsive to talking when they are doing something active. So find active things your child likes to do (fishing, kicking around a soccer ball, building with Legos, shooting baskets), and talk together.

2. **Talk about your child's interests.** Try tailoring the conversation around your child's interests: her CD collection, his baseball cards, her Strawberry Shortcake doll, his Power Ranger collection. It might be a great entrée to a discussion about what's really going on in your kid's life.

3. **Go to your kid's zone.** If you want some one-on-one talking time with your kid, then go to a place your kid enjoys: the mall, the batting cage to practice his swing, the golf range to hit a bucket of balls, a favorite parlor for ice cream. Your child will be more relaxed because she's in her territory and just might be more likely to open up.

4. **Ask specific questions.** Kids get turned off by those generic "How was your day?" type questions. If you want to invite conversations, then ask more specific questions: "Who did you sit next to during lunch?" "What story did your teacher read today?" "What game did you play in PE?"

5. **Ask questions that elicit more than one-word responses.** Make skillful use of your questions so that your child must respond with more than a one-word answer: "How would you have ended that book?" "What would you have done differently in the game?" "What are your feelings about . . . ?"

6. **Find the best time and place for listening.** Research finds that parents can learn a lot about their kids en route to school and activities. Here are common topics parents say they either talk about or overhear conversations about that help them find out more about their kids' lives while in the car: school, 91 percent; children's friends, 90 percent; values, 82 percent; extracurricular activities, 81 percent; chores, 69 percent. So now think: Where do you and your kids have those great conversations? Once you identify that sacred spot, make sure you frequent it often so you can use it to get to know your child.

7. **Mandate family dinners.** When my kids were growing up, sports, church group meetings, music lessons, and play practices used to appear on the calendar constantly, taking away from our "together time." So we finally sat down and figured out the times no one had anything scheduled, and those were mandated for family dinners. If your family schedule is equally hectic, you may want to set aside specific weekdays

for your family dinners. Don't let anything interfere with your plan: family dinners still are the greatest place to give your kids your full attention and hear what's going on in their lives.

Making a Promise to Yourself

1. Did you identify with or were you inspired by the story of Ricky and his mom, Mrs. Anderson? Is this one of the secrets you want to focus on and tune up in your family? How would applying what matters most about listening with full presence benefit your child?

2. How would you apply the four steps to listening with full presence in your family? Review all the boxes, guides, tips, and stories in this chapter.

3. Go to A Mother's Promise on page 54 and write in the one thing you will do over the next 21 days to practice listening more attentively to your children.

A Real Mom's Resource Guide

Between Parent and Child, by Haim G. Ginott (New York: Avon, 1972). This classic shows the difference between destructive and constructive communication and is rich with helpful ideas.

Cool Communication, by Andrea Frank Henkart and Journey Henkart (New York: Perigee, 1998). Cowritten by a parent and a teen, this book provides much-needed perspective on how to boost communication and understanding.

How to Talk So Kids Will Listen and Listen So Kids Will Talk, by Adele Faber and Elaine Mazlish (New York: Avon, 1982). This is a practical volume for helping parents learn to communicate more effectively with their kids. It's become a parenting classic.

How to Talk to Your Kids About Really Important Things, by Charles E. Schaefer and Theresa Foy DiGeronimo (San Francisco:

- *Hang a "Do Not Disturb" sign.*
Karen Kleindeist, a mom of three girls from
Reno, Nevada, told me she was so frustrated from always
being interrupted in the middle of conversations with her
kids that she brought a "Do Not Disturb" sign home from
a hotel. Now, whenever a child starts a conversation that
needs tuning in to, Karen and her child go to her bedroom,
hang the sign on her doorknob, and talk uninterrupted
while she gives her daughter her full and complete
presence. Family members know that if the sign is up, no
interruptions are allowed except in extreme emergencies.
(If you have younger children, you may need to schedule
talking appointments when another adult is home
to watch your younger kids.)

- *Turn on the answering machine.* I heard Maria Shriver
from Sacramento, California (yes, that's right, "the" Maria
Shriver), describe on the *Oprah Winfrey* show a strategy
that I love: she enforces a "no-phone policy" from six to
eight in the evening. That's the time her family usually
gathers for family meals and sharing their day, and she let's
them know there's nothing more important than what they
have to say. Sure, the phone may ring, but she just turns on
the answering machine. Set times in your home where
listening to your kids with your full presence matters most.

Jossey-Bass, 1994). This is a great source for helping parents
answer some of their children's most difficult questions.

P.E.T. Parent Effectiveness Training, by Thomas Gordon (New York:
Signet, 1975). Every parent should own this book. It offers a
proven method to help enhance communication between parents and their children.

*Raising Kids Who Can: Using Family Meetings to Nurture Responsible,
Cooperative, Caring, and Happy Children,* by Betty Lou Bettner and
Amy Lew (New York: HarperCollins, 1992). This is a simple

guide to help parents use the principles of family meetings with their children—a great way to practice listening as a family.

What to Say When You Talk to Your Kids, by Shad Helmstetter (New York: Pocket Books, 1989). This book is a wonderful resource full of ways to improve communication with your children.

A Mother Who Is a Good Role Model Gives Her Children an Example Worth Copying

What Real Mothers Know: Model the Behavior You Want Your Children to Copy

What Really Matters Most for Mothering: Be Conscious of Your Example

The Real Benefit for Kids: Character, Values, and Love

The Lesson a Real Mother Teaches: One of the simplest and most important secrets of real mothering is recognizing that kids learn by watching and listening. So be careful, Mom. Our children see how we react to stress, and they mimic our example. They hear how we speak to (or about) our friends, and they talk the same way to their peers. They tune in to what makes us tear up or become angry or soften, and they mimic. Our kids learn patience or impatience, compassion or indifference, tolerance or prejudice, frugality or materialism through our daily example. It's such a simple secret, but one too often overlooked. We just plain fail to realize how influential we can be in our children's lives. Maybe it's because we're all too caught up in this modern motherhood misconception that the other stuff (the doing, the going, the activities) is what's crucial. Slow down, Mom: *don't undermine your influence.* Your everyday example is a living textbook to your children. What you model to your child in those little everyday unplanned moments can be far more important than all the flash cards, carpools, computer games, and tutoring. Real moms recognize the teaching tool of modeling and know that it has a tremendous influence on their children's lives.

"She Set a Great Example"

What you do speaks so much louder than what you say.
—Native American saying

Four-year-old Ryan O'Shea had never seen such a crowd in his life. Hundreds of people were huddled around the customer service desk where he and his mother stood in a long line with other disgruntled passengers whose flights had been cancelled. It was the day before Christmas, and everyone at the Atlanta airport was trying to get somewhere else to be with their families for the big day.

Ryan and his mom were no exception: Ryan's dad and big sister would be picking them up in San Francisco and whisking them home to Palo Alto just in time to put out the cookies for Santa's arrival. For Ryan it was going to be his best Christmas ever. He hoped Santa would be bringing the big red tricycle and SpongeBob videos he wanted. And he had a surprise for his mom and dad as well: Granny had secretly helped him make a beautiful frame for his preschool photo by gluing macaroni to Popsicle sticks, spraying the whole thing with gold paint, and sprinkling it with glitter.

But now Ryan was hearing a lot of adults crushing around him who seemed to be pretty upset.

"What do you mean, 'computer error'? . . . No crews were scheduled for any of these flights? . . . That's the most outrageous thing I've ever heard! . . . There's only one person behind this counter; at this rate we'll be here for days."

Once passengers got wind of what had happened, there was a mad dash to find out what options—if any—they had: Were any other airline carriers flying? Were any flights available—or trains, rental cars, anything? Hotel rooms filled quickly, so where would they sleep? Would the airline compensate them for their extra expenses? It was getting late, and everyone in line was getting desperately tired, hungry, and impatient. Tempers were flaring, and the whole situation had rapidly turned into a traveler's worst nightmare.

"Honey," Ryan's mom, Abby, said to him, "don't get lost. Stay right next to me."

"But Mom, why aren't we on the plane?" Ryan asked. "We have to get home so we can put out the cookies for Santa."

"Don't worry; we're going to make it, Ryan," Abby assured him. "Nothing can stop us from getting home in time for Christmas."

So the mom and her young son waited. And waited. Seconds, minutes, quarter hours, half hours—time passed very slowly for the mom and her boy.

But despite the endless moments, quarter hours, and half hours—in fact for the next three whole hours—this mom kept her child occupied by talking to him, singing, telling him stories and nursery rhymes, one after the other, with a real persistence and stamina that was wonderful to behold.

"Ryan, do you remember that guessing game we play in the car when we try to name the animals?"

"Sure, I remember, Mom: alligator, bear, cat . . ."

After a while, a grandma in the crowd gave the mom a little relief and played "Eensy, Weensy, Spider" and "Farmer and the Dell" with Ryan. A few other passengers took turns talking to the child—and was this kid ever eager to talk.

"Hey, did you know Santa is coming to my house?" Ryan exclaimed excitedly. "This is going to be my bestest Christmas ever," he told everyone around him.

Finally, after three hours and forty-three minutes of standing in line, it was Abby's turn at the counter to speak to the agent, and those waiting nearby eavesdropped, hoping to learn something about their fate. She began her questions amicably enough: her husband and other child were home, and she needed to get there to be with them.

"I'd be willing to rent a car and drive or take a bus to the nearest airport that has planes still flying. Any way we get there is fine," she explained loud enough so her child could hear. "Santa is coming tomorrow, you know, so we have to make sure my little boy gets home in time for Christmas Eve."

But the harassed, stressed-out, and disgruntled agent's answer was clearly not what the young mother, or anyone behind her in line, wanted to hear—especially after being stranded and waiting almost four hours just to talk to him.

"Sorry," said the agent. "There are no flights available for the next few days. Santa just won't be able to come this year—you're stuck."

Everyone uttered a collective gasp. For the first time, Ryan began to feel discouraged. It was like the wind had been knocked out of him. He'd never even considered that he might miss Santa's special visit to his house. Abby looked as though she were going to explode: her face turned beet red, her hands clenched into fists, and she began taking short, shallow breaths. She was going to have a massive stroke or break into tears.

But then another surprising thing happened. Abby glanced down at her small son, which seemed to stop her momentarily. Then she turned to the agent, stuck her face within inches of the man's face, and said quite brusquely: "Excuse me. I need a second so I won't do something I may regret."

Suddenly the line of frustrated and exhausted travelers became dead silent. The ticket agent turned absolutely white.

Several passengers glanced nervously at each other; one appeared ready to go into "duck and cover" mode. Everyone assumed mayhem would break out in the next minutes—and the agent looked as though he thought he was about to take his last breath. All eyes turned tensely on the woman; then, in the next few seconds, they saw the mom do something quite amazing.

Abby pivoted on her heel so that her back was to the agent. Then she froze. She closed her eyes, took a few deep, very slow breaths and let each one out slowly. Then she began quietly counting to ten under her breath. When she reached ten, she opened her eyes, unclenched her fists, and wiped her palms on her pant legs. Slowly the bright red color in her cheeks began to fade, and her breathing returned to normal. The whole process took no more than thirty seconds but seemed like an eternity.

Ryan looked on in awe as his mother turned back to the counter and looked squarely at the agent. Then he heard her say calmly, "Wait a minute, Sir. You've got it all wrong. Of course, Santa is coming. So we're going to figure out how to get Ryan back in time for Santa."

There was a visible sign of relief. The SWAT team wouldn't have to be called in after all. Then the group started applauding! Everyone realized they'd just experienced something quite revolutionary: they'd actually witnessed an incensed, irate passenger display self-control—something very rare at airports these days. This was quite a memorable event.

The agent, of course, reacted a bit differently. He was wiping sweat off his brow, probably grateful to be alive. But the best reaction by far was from Ryan. The little guy had quietly watched the whole episode and was now beaming from ear to ear. And the expression on his face was priceless: he was looking up at his mom with absolute pride and adoration. He was also the person clapping the loudest.

"Way to go, Mom!" the older woman patted Abby on the back.

For the first time, the young mother realized that Ryan had watched the whole thing carefully and had seen how she had acted. She was so relieved to see her son smiling up at her with such respect and delight that she grinned back down at him. She smiled at the older woman and said, "Thanks. You never know when our kids are watching us, do you?"

At that point, something else quite amazing occurred. Without raising his eyes to look at Abby directly, the former Grinch behind the customer service counter muttered under his breath, "Lean forward. I can't say this too loud, but there's a Delta flight leaving for Nashville in twenty-seven minutes. Go straight to Gate 32. I've told them to hold two seats for you, and I made a reservation for you and your son on a flight leaving Nashville for San Francisco ninety minutes later. Don't say a word, just get going, and you'll be home in plenty of time for Santa."

Abby beamed and squeezed Ryan's hand as hard as she could as she said to him, "I told you we'd home in time for Santa."

And just before Ryan dashed off with his mother, his little voice piped up to the man behind the counter, "Merry Christmas, Mister!"

What Real Moms Can Learn from This Story

Patience was not Abby O'Shea's greatest virtue, but somehow she had the good sense to realize that the only way she was going to get her son home in time for Santa was by controlling her temper. She was consciously very controlled and patient at the service counter, but what she didn't realize until she happened to glance at her son and see he was watching her every move. And isn't that always the truth? We just never know when our kids are watching us. But at least one thing is for sure: the lesson in the values of compassion, perseverance, patience, anger management, and optimism the mom modeled that day was one that her four-year-old son wouldn't forget.

From that day on, Abby was infinitely more conscious of how everything she did had a powerful impact on her son. She learned very quickly how her example was one of the best ways for Ryan to learn. After all, our behavior is like a living textbook, so always ask yourself what lessons your children might be learning. We all need to consciously become the model we want our children to copy.

The One Question Every Mother Should Ask

⌕ REAL MOM WISDOM

If you want to ask yourself one question each night that would be the best barometer of how well you've parented that day, use this one: *If my child had only my actions to watch today, what would he have learned?* Your honest answer will be your signal as to what behavior you should consciously tune in to the next day so you are the best role model for your children.

Is This Real Mom's Secret Part of Your Parenting?

Before you take this quiz, let's be clear: the goal here is not to become the perfect mother but to recognize the one or two behaviors you want to change in yourself to become a better role model. So check those areas that concern you, such as any behaviors your kids might copy or ones that could hinder their character, reputation, or health. Also jot down any notes in your journal to remind yourself why you want to change. What kind of role model are you in regard to

- **Health and well-being.** Do you go for regular medical and dental checkups? Are your eating and sleeping habits ones you want your kids to copy? Do you exercise regularly? Do you have any addictive habits, such as smoking, drinking, binge eating, or splurge dieting? Do you recognize your stress signals and respond by finding ways to relax?

- **Character, integrity, and moral choices.** Would your kids be able to identify the virtues—such as kindness, fairness, and tolerance—that matter most to you in your daily actions? For instance, if you want your kids to be honest, would they say *you* are? How are you when it comes to filling out your income tax forms: any bragging about what you got away with? What about buying age-appropriate movie tickets for your kids? Do you try to slip them in under the radar?

- **Spiritual or religious values.** Do you walk your talk when it comes to your religious and spiritual beliefs so that your kids will pick up your example? For instance, do you practice the Golden Rule daily? Pray or meditate regularly? Attend church or synagogue weekly?

- **Self-control.** How are you when it comes to impulsive buying or eating, handling that temper, driving sanely (even if someone cuts in front of you), and curbing your tongue when someone says something vicious? Are you a model of good sportsmanship at your kids' games (even if you're irritated at the coach's call or if he benches your kid)?

- **Work habits.** Do you model the values of self-discipline, perseverance, doing your personal best, meeting deadlines, and following through on what's required?

- **Service and charity.** Do you volunteer, give up time for charity, and practice the values of kindness and generosity to show your kids that it's better to give than to receive?

- **Etiquette and civility.** Would you want your kids to emulate your manners? Do you send thank-you notes, answer RSVPs, and bite your tongue when it comes to swearing and vulgarities?

- **Prejudices, superstitions, and fears.** Do you make sure your kids don't catch any of your racial, economic, religious, or cultural biases? Are you modeling abnormal fears of heights, flying, spiders, or snakes, or belief in superstitions, such as avoiding walking under a ladder, crossing a black cat's path, or staying on the thirteenth floor of a building? **Hint:** to answer this question you'll first have to admit your biases and fears.

- **Relationships.** How are you treating your friends, relatives, and spouse? How do you handle such issues as gossip; loyalty; sticking up for a friend; and taking time for your friendships, your spouse or ex-spouse, and your relationships with relatives?

- **Life outlook.** Are you more positive or negative? Are you more optimistic or pessimistic? Do you sometimes poison your child's outlook with your negative views?

- **Intellectual and cultural stimulation.** Are you curious about things, and do you follow through on making new learning a priority? Do you read in front of your kids; talk about the value of education; take time to go to museums, lectures, classes; talk about the news; strive to learn more about the world; or make an effort to learn a new hobby?

- **Financial issues.** How are you when it comes to saving, financial planning, sticking to a budget, and generally appreciating the value of money?

Now get picky and realistic: What are the one or two things you now recognize need changing in yourself right now so that you will be a better role model for your kids? Write them down and commit to making those changes. The next section will show you how to make them happen. Then get ready to learn the secret and use it with your family.

Four Steps to Becoming a Better Role Model

Step One: Choose What You Want to Change. Review your answers from the earlier quiz and select one behavior, attitude, or belief you want to change in yourself right now. If you're having trouble choosing, then answering these questions will help you decide.

- What negative trait do I see my child copying from my example?
- What behavior do I model that makes me look like a hypocrite to my kid?
- What positive trait do I hope my child copies, but probably won't unless I tune it up?
- What trait does my whole family probably wish I would change?

Now open up your journal to a blank page and write across the top the one thing you want to change in yourself. Here are a few examples: Be more patient. Be less critical of my child. Be calmer when I discipline my son. Emphasize spirituality in our home. Let my kids know I can also be fun.

Step Two: Acknowledge Your Reason to Change. The more you recognize why you need to change, the more committed you will be to making the change. So take a minute to think through and jot down how making this change will affect your family and what they stand to gain.

Careful, Mom: The Kids Really Are Watching Your Behavior

A famous experiment in social psychology that involved kids, an adult, and an inflatable Bobo doll was conducted almost half a century ago by Stanford University psychologist Albert Bandura. Bandura and his research team wanted to find out if kids can learn aggressive behavior by watching adults. Video cameras and two-way mirrors were set up, and kids were sent into the room, where they found an adult and a large plastic blown-up doll (the kind that bounces back to you after you knock it down) named Bobo. There they watched the adult aggressively knocking Bobo around, as well as sometimes verbally abusing the doll. A short while later, the kids were allowed to play with Bobo. It probably comes as little surprise that the kids not only copied the adult—excitedly knocking, smacking, and taunting old Bobo—but also developed their own creative forms of aggression toward the doll. Bandura's classic experiment teaches us a key lesson: kids do mimic what they see.

- What effect does the trait have on my family right now?
- If I make this change, how will things be different for my children and myself?
- What is one small difference this will make in my family?

Step Three: Make a Plan for Change. *Unless you plan exactly what you will do to make the change in yourself happen, there will be no change.* That's a guarantee. So your next step is to create your plan for success. Keep that journal page open and begin brainstorming all the things you could do, then review your ideas until you come up with a plan that fits you and your family. The best plans (of any kind) usually have five characteristics: they are (1) specific, (2) measurable, (3) achievable, (4) realistic, and

(5) time-limited. To help you see what a good plan looks like, here are two samples:

Sample Mother Plan: To be more positive around my kids

My concern: I'm negative, and my kids are starting to catch my pessimism. To become a more positive role model to my kids, I could:

- Think of one positive thing to say each day to my child and say it.
- Read a few books about cultivating optimism (there are lots of them) and find an idea that works for me.
- Learn to catch my negative comments before they leave my lips.

My plan: For the first few days, I will write a positive comment about my child on an index card as I'm drinking my coffee. I'll tape it to my bathroom mirror to remind me to say it.

Sample Mother Plan: To control my temper so I model self-control to my kids

My concern: I get cranky and irritable and lose my temper too quickly. Kara is starting to model my behavior and yell at her friends. To become a better role model, I need to be calmer and catch myself before I lose it. I could:

- Exercise more because I know it calms me down. I could do yoga when Kara is at day care.
- Read up on anger management, find one technique that works for me, and practice it.
- Institute a no-yelling policy at home. (That means the kids could Red Card me.)
- Take three slow, deep breaths at the first sign that I'm getting upset.

Mothers Need Time-Outs, Too

A study of 991 parents by sociologist Murray A. Straus, codirector of the Family Research Lab at the University of New Hampshire, found that half the parents surveyed had screamed, yelled, or shouted at their infants. By the time a kid reaches seven years of age, 98 percent of parents have verbally lashed out at him. The main reason kids yell is that they hear the people they're living with yell. Some families use a time-out hand gesture agreed on by everyone. As soon as any member's voice goes one step above a normal range, family members give the signal reminding him to lower his voice, pronto. It's also fine for anyone—mom, dad, or kids—to take a brief "time-out" and walk away to calm down. Honor it. Believe me, your kids will remind you when you need to take a time-out yourself.

My plan: I will buy a video and exercise thirty minutes each day while Kara is napping. I'll also practice taking deep breaths each day while I'm cooking dinner, because that's when I get the most irritable.

Step Four: Develop a Self-Monitoring System. Let's be very clear: change is *not* easy. So don't kid yourself, this is tough work. Sure, you've identified what you want to change and have even developed your plan, but now you need to create a technique to remind you to keep on with your plan. Here are a few ideas:

- Ask a good friend to be your "nag partner" and to "gently" remind you each day to keep on that plan.
- Wear a specific piece of jewelry such as a necklace, ring, or bracelet so that each time you look at it you'll be reminded of your goal. Even better: don't take it off.

- Tape a sign on your refrigerator, bathroom mirror, computer screen, bedside table, car dashboard (or all the above) to remind you of your goal. It can be a single word, such as "Control," or just a piece of red paper as an image that to you means "temper." No one needs to know what it means, but keep it visible.

- Track your performance on your monthly calendar, paper or electronic organizer, or journal, or just an index card. If you tally your actions at the same time every day, you'll be more likely to keep on with your plan.

- Reward yourself periodically. Everyone needs a pat on the back for hard work, so don't overlook your own efforts. Every once in a while, take yourself out to lunch, rent a favorite movie, or light the candles and take a bubble bath.

Making a Promise to Yourself

1. Did you identify with or were you inspired by the story of Ryan and his mom, Abby? What about the story triggered an "ah-ha" moment for you? Is this one of the secrets you want to focus on and tune up in your family? How would applying what matters most about being a good role model benefit your child?

2. How would you apply the four steps to becoming a better role model? Review all the boxes, guides, tips, and stories in this chapter.

3. Go to A Mother's Promise on page 55 and write in the one thing you'll do differently over the next 21 days to model the behavior you want your children to copy.

- **Be obvious.** Cheryl Little of Reno, Nevada, spends hours volunteering for charitable organizations, but because her kids were in school, they missed seeing her example. "I want my children to think about others and be charitable, so now I make sure I describe what I did and explain the joy I get from volunteering. I also found a pediatric hospital where my children can volunteer with me a few hours each month. Now they see what I'm doing."

- **Explain yourself.** Steffani Walker of Salt Lake City, Utah, recognized that raising well-mannered children was her parenting priority, but wasn't always sure her two young sons were "watching" her example. So now she consciously makes a habit of explaining her actions to her boys: "My napkin goes on my lap." "I'll wait until everyone is seated before eating." She says she is seeing a change.

- **Get the whole family involved.** Carol Harker, mother of two sons ages eleven and thirteen, from Tulsa, Oklahoma, realized that self-control was a trait her whole family needed to tune up. She began by writing "self-control" in huge letters across the top of a monthly calendar and taping it to her refrigerator to remind all family members. But that was just her first step. She consciously looked for family videos, children's literature, and news articles about real people who embodied that trait, and used them as a springboard for describing why the trait is so valuable. The family also developed their personal motto and started saying it with one another: "We stop and think before we act."

Six Fast Ways to Calm Quick Tempers

Anger is normal: how you choose to deal with it can make you the Queen Role Model for your family or the Wicked Witch of the West. There are a number of anger management strategies to cool tempers. The trick is to find the one that works best for you and then to rehearse it again and again until it becomes a habit. And the best way is to practice it together as a family. Here are a few possibilities:

1. *Leave the scene.* Whenever you feel you can't control your temper, walk away. Just explain to your kids, "Mommy needs a time-out for a minute to get calm." If you need to lock yourself in your bathroom to get back in control, do it!

2. *Use self-talk.* Learn to say a simple, positive message to yourself to control your temper. Some ideas: "Stop and calm down." "Stay in control." "I can handle this." Choose a phrase you feel most comfortable saying, then rehearse it a few times each day until you can use it.

3. *Teach "Stop and breathe."* As soon as you feel you're losing your temper, say to yourself, *Stop! Calm down.* Immediately take a deep, slow breath (or two or three if necessary). Getting oxygen into your brain is one of the fastest ways to relax.

4. *Imagine something calming.* Think of a person or place that helps you feel calm and peaceful—for instance, your spouse, the beach, your bed, your backyard. Right before your temper starts to flare and you feel those body warning signs kick in, close your eyes and think of the face or the spot while breathing slowly.

5. *Do elevator breathing.* Close your eyes, inhale deeply, then imagine you're in an elevator on the top of a very tall building. Press the button for the first floor, slowly breathe out three times, and watch the buttons for each level slowly light up as the elevator goes down. As the elevator descends, your stress fades away.

6. Melt away stress. Find the spot in your body where you feel the most tension, perhaps your neck, shoulder muscles, or jaw. Close your eyes, concentrate on the spot, tense it up for three or four seconds, and then let it go. While doing so, imagine the stress slowly melting away.

A Real Mom's Resource Guide

Coach Yourself: Make Real Changes in Your Life, by Anthony M. Grant and Jane Greene (Cambridge, Mass.: Perseus, 2003). This straightforward text packed full of researched-based tips and techniques will help you create the changes you desire in yourself. Highly recommended.

Family First: Your Step-by-Step Plan for Creating a Phenomenal Family, by Phil McGraw (New York: Free Press, 2004). Dr. Phil tells you plainly and simply what you need to stop doing and what you need to start doing to lead your family with a clear purpose.

How to Change Anybody: Proven Techniques to Reshape Anyone's Attitude, Behavior, Feelings, or Beliefs, by David J. Lieberman (New York: St. Martin's Press, 2005). A legendary leader in the study of human behavior provides step-by-step instructions to show you how to make conscious changes in yourself as well as in others.

The Mad Family Gets Their Mads Out: Fifty Things Your Family Can Say and Do to Express Anger Constructively, by Lynne Namka (Charleston, Ill.: Talk, Trust & Feel Press, 1995). This book offers useful ways to help kids who are struggling to express anger constructively, and to help families learn how to deal with anger in nonviolent ways.

ScreamFree Parenting: Raising Your Kids by Keeping Your Cool, by Hal Edward Runkel (Duluth, Ga.: Oakmont, 2005). As the author states, "Every kid wants to have cool parents." We're not talking about being "with it" but about being able to keep one's cool no matter what. The result: cooler kids who are far less anxious and more levelheaded. This is a principle-based relationship approach that urges parents to focus on themselves, grow themselves up and calm themselves down, and still remain connected to their kids. Amen.

When Anger Hurts Your Kids: A Parent's Guide, by Patrick McKay (New York: Fine Communications, 1996). This is a superb guide explaining how parents' anger affects kids and offering ways to regain control.

A Mother Who Teaches Values Inspires Character

What Real Mothers Know: Understand Your Family's Values So Your Children Can Live Them

What Really Matters for Mothering: Be Intentional

The Real Benefit for Kids: Empathy, Strong Character, and a Moral Compass

The Lesson a Real Mother Teaches: There's something about being a mom that makes us want to do everything possible for our kids. Well, why not? Don't we hope that our children will have every opportunity for happiness and success? That's why we're so brilliant at packing in all those special classes, rehearsals, team practices, and private coaching for our budding little geniuses every day. It's a marvel how we're able to multitask from dawn to midnight. But is all this frenzy in our children's best interests? Do they really need so much? Real moms don't think so. They recognize that their influence will be far greater if they center instead on only those things that they feel matter most. So they focus on the real stuff: being clear about their family's values. Real moms know that kids must have a moral code to live by and that they will learn that code through you—but only if you are mindful of that code and live it yourself. Stick to what really matters for your family, Mom, stay true to your beliefs, and you will greatly increase your positive influence.

"She Prioritized Her Values So Her Family Could Have a Code to Live By"

Strong families have something that they believe in together.
—Marilyn Perlyn

Six-year-old Amanda Perlyn was afraid that her new teacher, Dr. Malko, was going to give her an injection on the first day of her new school in Ft. Lauderdale, Florida. But once her teacher explained that she wasn't "that" kind of doctor ("Don't worry, I'm a doctor of education. I won't ask you to stick out your tongues and say 'Ahhh'"), the first-grader warmed up to her right away.

One day, however, Amanda came home from school quite disturbed and upset. She told her mom, Marilyn, that Dr. Malko was trying very hard to put on a smile but that Amanda and all her friends could tell that their teacher was worried about something.

"Dr. Malko told us that her daughter, Elena, was sick and that there might be days when we'd have a substitute teacher in her place."

A week later Elena herself came to visit Amanda's class. She was twenty-seven years old and wearing a large hat that covered the entire top of her head.

"And when she took off her hat, Mom, there wasn't any hair! She was bald. But she let me touch it, and her head felt so smooth."

That's when Dr. Malko told the class that her daughter had cancer and was receiving chemotherapy that made her hair fall out. A few weeks later, Elena stopped coming to visit, and Dr. Malko was absent more, too. Every day it seemed harder and harder for Dr. Malko to smile, until one day Amanda over-heard two teachers in the hallway outside her class talking about how difficult it was getting to be for Dr. Malko to pay for Elena's medical expenses. Her husband had died of cancer, and she had no health insurance.

Amanda came home and asked her mother, "What's insur-ance?" and "Can I have some money to give my teacher so she can help Elena's cancer?"

Marilyn's first reaction was to try to protect her child from the seriousness and potentially fatal outcome of Elena's disease. But Amanda was persistent and continued to ask her mom how she could help.

"Amanda was feeling her teacher's pain and wanted to be a part of the solution to help her. But she was only six! I wanted to shelter her from suffering—she was so young. But she was so insistent. "Mommy, we have to help Dr. Malko," she'd plead. I finally realized that I was the one who didn't have the courage—it was my daughter who taught me that you should act on your feelings because those strong emotions are what mobilize com-passion. My acceptance of my daughter's empathy empowered me to learn, to act, and to teach others that children can make a difference in the lives of others."

Marilyn and her husband, Don, were working very hard at that point in their lives. Beside the fact that their funds were limited, they didn't think that just writing a check would have been the best way to nurture their daughter's empathy. Marilyn began to realize that this was a great opportunity to show her daughter some of the most important things she valued as a mother: service, compassion, selflessness, helping others. But she wasn't sure how to go about doing it.

Marilyn remembered reading a newspaper article about children helping others. It said that children need to be given some ability to fix a corner of their world even at a young age. Though her daughter was only in the first grade, she wasn't too young to make a difference.

So she and her daughter started to brainstorm together. What could they do to earn some money for Dr. Malko that didn't cost them a cent except their time, energy, and creativity? Marilyn knew that her daughter was very artistic and liked to do things with her hands. After talking it over, the family, including Amanda's two older brothers and dad, decided to make reindeer ornaments for both Christmas and Chanukah—some with red noses (Rudolph) and some with blue (Moishe).

"We took the bark from palm trees, and the glue, noses, and eyes were donated, and we spread everything out all over the floor to create our own reindeer assembly line," Marilyn reported. Then Amanda and her family sold them all door to door in one weekend for $10 each.

Amanda counted out the $1,000 they'd earned, put it in a box, and brought it to her astonished teacher.

"I still get goose bumps when I remember the words that Dr. Malko said to Amanda as she embraced her in front of the class. "When children do such acts of kindness," said Dr. Malko, "they are like angels with invisible halos on their heads."

That spring, Dr. Malko's daughter, Elena, died. Amanda was very sad.

"I had the same old instinct, to protect her from pain and sad feelings," Marilyn recalled. "Amanda wanted to go to the funeral, and at first I said no. But she was so insistent that once again I knew I had to trust her heart and give her another opportunity to show other people she cared for and supported them."

Amanda continued to think about Elena and be concerned about Dr. Malko as she entered the second grade. That Christmas, she and her mother were at the shopping center and saw an announcement for a contest to write an essay about someone you wish could be with you for the holidays. But Amanda turned it around and wrote instead that she wanted Dr. Malko to visit her only living child.

"I want to show my first-grade teacher, Dr. Malko, how much I love and care about her. Her daughter died this year. All she has left is her son, Michael, who lives in Idaho. For all her hard work teaching kids her whole life, I think she deserves to have Christmas with her only family. I got a fortune cookie that said, 'An emptiness will soon be filled.' Now I want to give my fortune to Dr. Malko."

Then one day Amanda received a phone call: She'd won the trip for her teacher. Dr. Malko was overjoyed and flew off to Idaho to spend Christmas with her son. But she wasn't the only happy one.

"It was one of the proudest moments of my life," Marilyn said, "that my child had helped someone else. It was an incredible high."

Amanda showed Marilyn the strength of their family's values through her compassion, empathy, selflessness, and willingness to give of herself and work hard to make good things happen for other people. It motivated Marilyn's mothering instinct to cultivate caring for others with her whole family.

"I sat down with my family and said, 'Look, Amanda has just had this experience. She learned something that the rest of us didn't know. No matter how old you are, you're old enough to make a difference in someone else's life. I want you two boys to experience what Amanda has just taught all of us. And Daddy and I need to get involved helping others as well.'"

Marilyn and her husband decided to help each of their three children develop a project that was of personal interest to them and that helped fill a need in the community. Amanda's love of stuffed animals led her to a project called "To Have and to Hug," in which she collected and distributed thousands of new stuffed animals donated by various toy stores to hospitals, foster children, and abused and neglected kids. Eric, their athletic child, started a project he called Stepp'n Up, in which he solicited sneakers from shoe stores and has so far distributed more than fifteen thousand pairs to needy kids. Their oldest son, Chad, who aspired to be and now is a physician, started a project call Doc-Adopt, in which doctors and dentists adopted the medical or dental needs of an underprivileged child.

"Before all the reindeer, the funeral, and the essay contest, we had never really talked about what we stood for as a family and what we expected our kids to do about it. But my husband and I learned something from our six-year-old daughter about what's right and wrong as a parent. She showed us how things can cross your path sometimes, and you have to stop and choose which way you're going to go. We have to recognize those opportunities where we can help our kids use their own strengths, feelings, and skills to make a difference according to our family's values.

"The feeling that Amanda and the rest of us got from helping Dr. Malko's family was incredibly wonderful, so we decided that helping others was going to be a year-round priority in all our children's lives. Over the years our children have received many awards and much recognition for their service to the community. But nothing has made us happier than knowing how their characters have developed into the kind of caring young people who we are proud to say are our children."

What Real Moms Can Learn from This Story

The story of Marilyn and her children shows how important it is for a family not only to have values but to apply them. Marilyn and her husband hadn't really talked about their shared beliefs, hopes, and expectations for their children. They knew instinctively without saying that of course they wanted their children to have compassion and empathy, to be selfless and care for other people, but it wasn't until Amanda showed them how important it was to find a way to express these values, to be helpful to the teacher she loved in a moment of crisis, that

Suppose you were allowed just one wish for your children, and just suppose your wish would be granted. Here is the rule: the wish must be something you personally can control (so it can't be related to things like your kids' health, financial status, or longevity). It has to be something you can inspire or nurture in your kids and family. Once you figure out your one wish, it will become your "one central truth" or your core family motto. It will be what you want to keep true as your central mantra for your day-to-day mothering. What would your wish be? Write it down, then tape it on the fridge, keep a copy in your wallet, key it into your Palm Pilot—and read it often. It will remind you of what you think really counts when it comes to your family and will help you stay focused on what matters.

Marilyn became intentional and developed the maternal secret of guiding her kids in expressing their family values.

Many moms tend to go in too many directions at once and struggle to take on every potential activity and opportunity for achievement. Instead of succumbing to that temptation, Marilyn focused her family's energies and commitment on one major passion. And the outcome? Her approach not only produced great results but also actually made their family life more manageable by not scattering their efforts and by bringing their family closer.

Amanda taught her family what a difference they could make—each of them. Marilyn and Don taught their children how to use their special feelings and unique skills to help other people and fulfill their family's values. What happened to them ultimately was that these caring activities not only defined the purpose of their own lives but inspired other families as well. The Perlyn family, who now live in Boca Raton, received the

R. David Thomas Child Advocate of the Year Award and an award from the Points of Light Foundation. Marilyn's children have appeared on the *Oprah Winfrey Show* and in books, magazines, and other media.

Of course I'm not implying that your ultimate mothering goal should be to end up on *Oprah* or receiving accolades from the White House. But by identifying your family values and tuning in to what matters most and then sticking to it, you'll discover that you will have more quality time together and will be more likely to create a family of purpose. Here is how this secret can help you and your family:

- Every family has values, whether or not they write them down or think them through. If you identify and express these values, they can give your family vision and purpose.

- There are daily opportunities to apply your family's values and beliefs.

- Often your children create chances to express these values and beliefs. Your role is to support and guide them to use their special feelings and skills in ways that are unique to them.

- Defining your vision and purpose as a family will help you prioritize your daily life so that you're not spinning your wheels trying to be the perfect mom.

- Putting your vision and purpose to work will save you energy, time, and money because you'll base your decisions for your family on what really counts.

Is This Real Mom's Secret Part of **Your** Parenting?

How intentional is your day-to-day parenting? How well are you nurturing empathy and compassion in your kids?

Sticking to What Matters Boosts Your Happiness

Researchers find that parents and grandparents who have clearly targeted beliefs and then stick to them as their family purpose helps them feel more satisfied with their lives. In fact, 55 percent of caregivers felt more positive about their role if they stuck to their purpose of what they felt mattered most in raising kids.

1. Have you stopped to identify your top value or belief for your family? For example: economic security; education for career enhancement; spiritual connection to a higher power; good health and nutrition; service and caring for others. What is it?

2. If you turned to your parenting partner right now and asked him if he could identify your values or beliefs, what would he say? Would he share those values?

3. If you sat your kids down on the couch and asked them, "What is the most important thing we all stand for as a family?" how would they respond?

4. During the last week, have you been confused about such "mom stuff" as "Should I let my kid watch that TV show or listen to that CD?" "Should I make my daughter finish her homework alone, or should I help her so she can go to sleep on time?" "Should I let my son buy those really pricey sunglasses so he can look like his friends?" Do you stop and ask yourself, "How are my values and beliefs affecting my children's day-to-day lives?"

5. Think over the last few days. How many times have you discussed or explained your values with your kids? If you do object to that TV show, have you told your child why? If you do insist that your child practice that "stupid violin," do you explain your reason?

6. What is the one thing you recognize in yourself that you need to change to become a more intentional mom? Write it on the lines here. Then get ready to learn the secret and use it with your family. _____

_____

_____

Stopping the Dreaded Three D's

Margie Sims of Essex Junction, Vermont, is a mom of eight kids ages one to eighteen who realized that a big part of her mothering would have to be prioritizing. After all, carting eight kids from piano to French to soccer to violin each day was not only unaffordable but also simply impossible. But Margie also knew that what did matter was raising her kids to have strong character. That goal was at the top of her parenting priority list. A mom in her Bible study class gave her a real mothering tip that she swears was the best advice she's ever heard to help her keep focused on that priority: "Always discipline for just three things: "Disrespect, Deceit, Disobedience." Anytime any of her kids displays one of those "Three D's," they know their mom will not tolerate it. "Sticking to those three rules in my house has helped my family enormously," Margie says. "It's given my kids a code to live by, helped them develop the character I want most for them, and helped me prioritize what matters most."

Four Steps to Boosting Intentionality

Step One: Create a Family Value's List. Turn off the TV, put the kids to bed, and turn on the answering machine. Get yourself focused and leave enough time so you can really think. Take out your laptop or a pad and pencil. Now answer this question:

Aside from good health and security, what traits do you hope your child will possess as an adult? Write down as many as you can think of, but write at least ten traits. Here is a list to help you get started.

altruism	gentleness	politeness
assertiveness	genuineness	prudence
calmness	graciousness	purposefulness
caring	gratitude	reliability
charitableness	helpfulness	resourcefulness
chastity	honesty	respect
citizenship	honor	responsibility
compassion	humility	reverence
compatibility	idealism	self-control
consideration	industriousness	self-discipline
cooperation	initiative	self-motivation
courage	insightfulness	sensitivity
courtesy	integrity	serenity
dependability	joyfulness	simplicity
determination	justness	sincerity
discipline	kindness	steadfastness
empathy	love	tactfulness
excellence	loyalty	temperance
fairness	mercy	tenacity
faithfulness	moderation	thankfulness
fidelity	modesty	tolerance
flexibility	obedience	trustworthiness
forgivingness	optimism	truthfulness
friendliness	patience	understanding
frugality	peacefulness	unselfishness
generosity	perseverance	wisdom

Step Two: Identify Your Top Three Family Values. Now reread your list. Which traits really matter to you the most? Start crossing off ones that aren't as important to you until you finally have your top three to five family values.

Step Three: Choose One Value to Nurture. Now select the one value you want to tune up in your family right now. Use the following five strategies in the acronym TEACH to boost the value.

T—Target the value you want to apply right this minute in your home. Focus on only one at a time so you don't get overwhelmed and spin your wheels trying to do too much. Many moms target a different key value each month. Write down your choice so you don't forget.

E—Exemplify this value in your own everyday behavior. The easiest way for your child to learn any new value is by actually seeing it in action. So intentionally start looking for ways to tune up your chosen value anytime you're with your children. If you think courtesy is important, then intentionally start using more courteous language and behavior. If self-control is your targeted value, then this is the time to start taking those deep breaths and counting to ten.

A—Accentuate the targeted value in simple ways. For example, if respect is your targeted value and a song that abuses women is played on your car radio on the way home from school, seize the opportunity to make a point about treating all people with dignity.

C—Catch your children displaying the value and praise them for it. "Hey, I know it was hard to admit you broke your brother's hockey stick. I appreciate your honesty."

H—Highlight the value of the value. "I loved how you smiled at Grandma. That was being really kind. Did you see how her face lit up? Whenever you're kind, it helps make the world a better place." Whenever you highlight, be sure you name the value and tell your child exactly how it made a difference.

Step Four: Do It Again. Repeat the process for as many values you want to nurture in your children.

Simple Ways to Remind You of Your Core Beliefs

- *Collect inspirational quotes.* Patty Service, a mother of two from Palm Springs, California, has for years collected inspirational quotes that depict her values. She cuts them out or prints them on index cards, then puts them under a piece of glass covering her dresser. She can then read them each morning, and doing so reminds her of what matters most to her and her maternal vision.

- *Create a family intention statement.* Joanne Kleindeinst, a mother of four, felt that conveying her maternal mission statement about perseverance to her children was so important that she had her family spend an afternoon together brainstorming mottoes about their value. Her kids finally chose "Our Family Always Finishes What We Start"; they printed it on colorful pieces of card stock and hung them on their bedroom and kitchen walls. The motto reminds them of their intention.

- *Enforce a two-times-a-day rule.* Judy Baggott, a mom of three from Palm Springs, California, identified kindness as the one value she wanted most for her children to acquire. She emphasized the value by quickly reminding her children before they left for school each day to do two kind things for someone. Her intentionality paid off: her kids are now grown, and a strong trait in each is kindness.

Six Simple Steps to Boosting Empathy and Compassion in Your Kids

Often the most difficult part of getting your child to do kinder deeds for others is knowing where to begin. So tune in to your child's passions and interests and match them with appropriate projects. Here are six steps passed on from other parents on how not only to become a more charitable family but also to get your kids passionate about doing compassionate deeds for others by guiding them toward projects of their choice.

1. **Choose a project based on your child's interests and talents.** The first step is to help your child choose something that he is good at and enjoys doing. Tune in to problems that concern your child and start by looking around your neighborhood—for example, property that needs cleaning up, a park where kids no longer feel safe playing, a homeless shelter that needs sprucing up, or elderly people who are lonely. Look for other service projects in the Yellow Pages under "Social Service Organizations." Help your child analyze the good and bad points of each possibility and then choose the one problem he wants to work on most.

2. **Research the topic.** Next, help your child find out as much information as she can about the problem. A word of caution: don't be discouraged if the organization is not receptive to actual kid involvement and only encourages your child to collect money and donate possessions. Stress to your child that she doesn't need an organization to make a difference. Any small action is a start.

3. **Think of all possible solutions.** Suppose your child is concerned about the homeless living in the park; he might brainstorm and come up with these ideas: build a shelter, get a hotel to house them, put beds in the park, give out blankets, raise money for cots. Now have him choose the ideas he feels are most manageable and that he wants to commit to doing.

4. **Enlist others in the cause.** Some kids like to form clubs, which can include neighborhood kids, classmates, scout or church members, or just friends. The more people in the group, the more energy they have to make a difference.

5. **Plan for success.** The more your child thinks through her plan, the greater the likelihood she will succeed. So help her organize for success by asking her what resources and

people she will need for her cause and then offer age-appropriate help in gathering resources. The older your child is, the more responsibilities she should assume.

6. **Implement the solutions and evaluate progress.** Now encourage your child to carry out her plans. Getting started is often the hardest part for kids, so you might ask, "What is the first thing you need to get started?" Support her efforts so that she carries out her plans. Stress that the best-laid plans never go smoothly, so help your child evaluate her progress and change any areas that need correcting.

REAL MOM ALERT

Doing Good for Others Is a Happiness Booster

Marilyn Perlyn recognized that her daughter felt happier doing good deeds for others. It was a big reason why her purpose for her family was to become more charitable so that her sons could gain the same feelings of satisfaction as Amanda. Research supports Marilyn's gut feeling that performing acts of altruism or kindness boosts your happiness quotient. Sonja Lyubomirsky, a psychologist at the University of California at Riverside, found that people who do five simple kind acts a week, especially all in a single day, experience dramatically magnified feelings of happiness.

Making a Promise to Yourself

1. Did you identify with or were you inspired by the story of Amanda and her mom, Marilyn? What was it that resonated for you and your family? Is this one of the secrets you want to focus on and tune up in your family? How would applying what matters most about intentionality benefit your child?

2. Tough as it may be day after day, being intentional is the best way to teach your family such values as compassion and empathy so that your children can follow them. So check

A Pledge to Stick to What Really Matters

When I was pregnant with my first child, I noticed how my friends always seemed to be rushing about with their children. They'd packed their days with practices, lessons, and appointments, and all the while they complained they were "so busy." I'd sit and wonder: What's the point? Are they really enjoying their kids doing all this stuff? Where's the simple joy of playing, having fun, and creating happy memories? It was at that moment I vowed not to jump on that bandwagon of frantic over-scheduling and manic mothering. I wrote a promise to myself in my journal that day: I would stay true to myself by raising my future children based on my beliefs. I jotted down what I hoped most for my children: that they become respectful, have solid character and kindness of heart. I also knew that I wanted them to love imaginative play and be creative. The journal entry became my mothering plan. The best part was that it was so simple, and it helped me focus on what mattered most. It also kept me guiltless: I wasn't concerned with what other mothers did with their kids. I knew what was right for mine.

It's been eighteen years since I wrote my promise, and now as I look into my children's eyes, I'm so glad I stuck to my plan. My daughter is a happy and confident sophomore in high school. Just last week I hugged my son goodbye as he begins his freshman year at Princeton. I felt assured in knowing he'll be just fine on his own. Realizing that my children have a strong sense of character, respect for others, and kind hearts makes me genuinely happy that I stayed true to the promise I'd made so many years ago.

–Jaynie Neveras, mother of two children
from Atherton, California

out the four steps to boosting intentionality and review all the other boxes, guides, tips, and stories in this chapter.

3. Go to A Mother's Promise on page 55 and write in the one thing you'll do differently over the next 21 days to apply the beliefs you hold dearest to your heart.

A Real Mom's Resource Guide

The Biggest and Brightest Light: A True Story of the Heart, by Marilyn Perlyn and illustrated by Amanda Perlyn (Bandon, Oreg.: Reed, 2004). The wonderful true story of Amanda Perlyn's gift of caring for her teacher is told in this charming picture-book version written for four- to eight-year-olds. It should be required reading for every child.

Family First: Your Step-by-Step Plan for Creating a Phenomenal Family, by Phil McGraw (New York: Free Press, 2004). Dr. Phil provides a plan to help you identify what you need to stop doing and what you need to start doing to lead your family with a sense of purpose. In particular, read and reread the section on how to help you define what you consider to be success and then use the steps to create and claim it.

Life Matters: Creating a Dynamic Balance of Work, Family, Time, and Money, by A. Roger Merrill and Rebecca R. Merrill (New York: McGraw-Hill, 2003). This book offers good advice that might help you recognize what you really want to give high priority in your family, and the strategies to get started.

Mommy Guilt: Learn to Worry Less, Focus on What Matters Most, and Raise Happier Kids, by Julie Bort, Aviva Pflock, and Debra Renner (New York: AMACOM, 2005). If you're caught in the guilt trap of trying to "do it all" for your kids, this book may help you realize it's time to prioritize.

Parenting from the Inside Out: How a Deeper Self-Understanding Can Help You Raise Children Who Thrive, by Daniel J. Siegel and Mary Hartzell (Los Angeles: Tarcher, 2003). The bottom line to great parenting is that we need to understand who we are and what we believe so we can pass those beliefs on to our children. This book will help you recognize what matters most to you.

The 7 Habits of Highly Effective Families, by Stephen R. Covey (New York: Golden Books, 1997). This book offers excellent resources to help you clarify what really matters most to you in your role of mothering and raising great kids, and the tools to achieve it.

Teaching Your Kids to Care: How to Discover and Develop the Spirit of Charity in Your Children, by Deborah Spaide (New York: Carol, 1995). No more excuses! Here are one hundred projects to get your kids involved in doing good for others. It's a practical guide for parents of children from kindergarten to high school, with clearly outlined ways to help your family learn to care about others.

A Mother Who Supports Her Children's Strengths Builds Their Confidence

What Real Mothers Know: Let Your Parenting Fit Your Child's Personality

What Really Matters for Mothering: Know Your Child's Unique Temperament

The Real Benefit for Kids: Confidence About Identity and Strengths

The Lesson a Real Mother Teaches: The more you understand who this child of yours really is—*her* passions, *her* temperament, *her* learning style, *her* interests—the more effective you'll be in your mothering. It is such a simple secret, but one that can have a dramatic impact on how your child turns out. This is also why real moms recognize that discovering their children's unique qualities and strengths is one their most important parenting tasks. After all, each child is different, so we shouldn't expect the same three-step discipline approach to work for each child; we can't assume that each kid will excel with the same teacher; and we shouldn't automatically enroll our child in violin, soccer, or karate just because the other sibling or the neighborhood kids did it. Real moms have learned to tailor their mothering to fit each child's individual needs and temperament. When you do this, you teach your child acceptance in *herself*, confidence in *her* identity, and recognition of *her* strengths. But the lesson can be even more far reaching: because your child is relying on her own natural talents, temperament, and personality, she is also more likely to reach her potential. That's what real mothering is all about.

"She Treats Each of Her Children as Individuals"

> *Children are not things to be molded, but are people to be unfolded.*
>
> —Jess Lair

It was the first day of kindergarten, and Jean Cardinale had to admit she was rather anxious as she waited outside the class door for her youngest son, Matt. Preschool hadn't always gone so smoothly, and she was feeling those "mommy pangs" when you hope things went well for your kid but a part of you is not quite sure they did.

What can you say? Matt was her youngest son, and he was a little pistol. (That's a mom's nice way of saying he could sometimes be a bit of a "challenge.") Boy, was he ever different from her two older sons. Tim was the oldest at nine. He was serious, sensitive, and artistic. The middle son, Daniel, was laid back, athletic, and musical. And then there was Matt.

Let's face it: this child was born full of energy and into everything. "Be careful, Matt!" "Slow down, Honey." "That's going to fall!" "Let's take it easy." He was also curious, fun, and *always* on the move. Jean knew that sitting at a table and meticulously cutting out colored circles and triangles just wasn't going to be this kid's cup of tea. Moving, pushing, riding, exploring, climbing, and running were more Matt's style.

So there were more than a few occasions during Matt's last school year when his preschool teacher and his mother would have the "little talk" about his behavior. Miss Saunders would share her "concerns" that Matt wasn't following her specific learning objectives for the day (at least when it came to the indoor activities of the preschool curriculum). There was even a time or two in their little chats when the dreaded "H word" appeared.

"Have you considered that Matt might be hyperactive, Mrs. Cardinale?" his preschool teacher would suggest. "We may want to explore the idea." More than once, Miss Saunders tried to work the "H word" into her conversation.

In fact, his preschool teacher had pretty much sold herself on the idea that Matt's energy level went beyond the "normal" range, but Jean wasn't buying it. Not one bit.

Come on, she had told herself back then. *The kid is only four. He's a little boy. He's the youngest son. His brothers were ready for paper and pencil at his age, but he's not. He's a different kid.*

Matt may be active and energetic, but he is not hyperactive, Jean said to herself. She was convinced that the label was wrong—dead wrong—but obviously hadn't done such a great job of changing his preschool teacher's opinion.

The bell rang, and the big day was over. As usual, Matt was first out the door and ran full speed to his mom, almost knocking her over with his hug. Always the bundle of joy and energy, he'd never let her down.

"It was fun!" he exclaimed, and Jean sighed with relief.

Matt's mom could see that his teacher, Sally Hunter, was standing a few feet from the door. Jean couldn't help but notice her eyes following Matt as he made his way to her. Mrs. Hunter's "look" told her she'd chosen the label "hyperactive" to apply to her son. It was the last way Jean wanted Matt's school year to start. Somehow she had to change that image in his teacher's mind, but how?

Take it slowly. Keep smiling, she kept telling herself. Then Jean figured she just had to bite the bullet and face Mrs. Hunter. So she walked over to the teacher and introduced herself.

"Hi, I'm Jean Cardinale, Matt's mom!" she said. "I just wanted to introduce myself and tell you how excited Matt is about school. He loves it here, and I'm so glad."

His teacher smiled, but really looked as though she had something else on her mind that she wanted to say. Jean looked at her again and recognized she was ready to give that "little talk" and casually throw in that "H word" Jean never wanted to hear again.

So before his teacher could say a word, his mother blurted out, "Don't you just love Matt's spirit?"

Mrs. Hunter appeared stunned. This clearly wasn't what she was expecting to hear. But now that Jean had the teacher's attention, she figured she might as well keep going and take this as far as she could. Without missing a beat, Jean quickly added, "I just hope nobody ever tries to tame Matt's spirit. We need more people in this world with spunk."

Jean took her son by the hand, and they headed off to the car to drive home. She hadn't planned to be quite so direct with her son's teacher, but the whole idea of categorizing her child really distressed her. She knew how important it was for each of her sons to have an authentic sense of who he really was. She'd never wanted anyone to call her oldest son "the brainy one" or her middle boy "the jock," either. Besides, there was absolutely no redeeming value to sticking a label like that on a five-year-old—or on a child of any age, for that matter. How could anything positive come from it?

But she also drove off wondering if she'd put her foot in her mouth and somehow damaged the relationship with Matt's teacher. And it was only the first day of school! "Great way to start the year," she mumbled to herself. But a few weeks later, Jean was pleasantly surprised to discover that things had turned out far better than she ever could have imagined.

The first teacher conference was held at the end of October. Jean was in weekly contact with Mrs. Hunter during those first weeks, and even worked a few times in her son's classroom. But she'd never gotten around to actually talking to the teacher about Matt. (Maybe there was a part of her that was putting that off.) So Jean had to admit she was a bit nervous when it finally came time to sit down face-to-face. She actually dreaded listening to what she was sure would be the teacher's "concerns" about her kid's "overenergetic nature." What she wasn't prepared for at all were the words Mrs. Hunter used to describe her child. In fact, the teacher didn't beat around the bush— they were almost the first thing that came out of her mouth: "Matt is such a joy," the teacher said. "I just love his spirit and energy!"

Jean breathed a sigh of relief. Matt's teacher was seeing her child as a strong and interesting individual in his own right.

P.S. There's a happy follow-up to this story. Jean reports that fifteen years later, Matt is still the same energetic, self-confident, fun-loving kid who now is finishing up his junior year in college. School hasn't always been easy: to this day Matt still hates cutting, pasting, and sitting quietly at a table doing paper-and-pencil worksheets, but this kid is a "people person" who his mom is convinced will make the world a better place.

Jean also wants us to know that Tim is now graduating from law school, still as serious and sensitive as ever. And his very different brother, Daniel, fresh out of college, majored in sports psychology and is looking for a job and not worrying about it too much. "How different they all are!"

"And whenever there's a sideways glance from an adult questioning Matt's overenergetic nature," Jean goes on to say, "I just smile, look the person square in the eye, and say: 'Don't you just love Matt's spirit?' It's amazing that no one ever says no."

What Real Moms Can Learn from This Story

Jean Cardinale was perceptive enough to realize that each of her three sons was a unique and distinct individual. By the time her youngest came around with his avidly high-spirited personality, she knew to adjust her parenting for his temperament. She also knew how to advocate so that no one would put a label on him that might be harmful or self-defeating.

We can learn from this mother how important it is to treat each of our children as individuals and avoid stereotypes or one-size-fits-all solutions. Many moms try to cram the same activities and opportunities for each kid into the family's pressure-cooker, high-stress schedule. You can't parent using the same cookie cutter because our kids don't fit the same mold. What's crucial is to develop the maternal secret of perception, distinguishing each child from the others and treating them differently so that you can help each of them flourish in their unique way. Here's why:

- Each child has her own unique temperament, personality, intelligences, interests, talents, strengths, and ways of learning, adapting, and relating. One of our most important "mom jobs" is tuning up our perception so that we understand and recognize each child's uniqueness and help others recognize those positive qualities.

- Our role is not to change our children's differences but to nurture their special strengths and talents, understand their unique learning styles and temperaments, and teach them strategies that will help them cope with their weaknesses and drawbacks. We also need to find ways to help others see our children in a positive light.

- There are daily opportunities to help your child recognize and develop his positive traits. Doing so is one of the best ways to nurture your child's self-esteem.

- Often your children create chances to express their uniqueness. Your role is to support and guide them to use their special temperaments, strengths, and skills in ways that are unique to them.

- Identifying your child's unique way of dealing with the world will help you determine the best way to relate to and discipline your child and how to nurture your child's natural talents and make wise choices as to which teachers, extra activities, or even hobbies will be more appropriate.

- Developing the maternal secret of perception will also help you prioritize your child's schedule so that you're not trying to have each child do "everything," but instead putting your efforts (as well as your energy, time, and money) into the kinds of activities that will help each of your children become the best she can be.

Is This Real Mom's Secret Part of Your Parenting?

Here are a few questions to help you reflect on how well you're treating each of your children as separate and unique individuals.

1. Start by thinking about your own childhood. What activities did you do when you were growing up? For instance, did you play an instrument, take art lessons, join a chess club, play football? Next, think about your interests today: What types of music, sports, travel, and hobbies are your favorites? Now ask yourself this: Do you base decisions about your child's academic, extracurricular, and social activities on your perception of her temperament, interests, and talents, or is your view filtered through your own interests and childhood memories?

2. Deep down there are things we don't like about our kids. (I know, I know, our goal is to love our kids unconditionally, but be honest: there are traits in each of our kids that we secretly wish we could change—for instance, your oldest son's

Five Types of Kid Temperaments

Drawing from the best child development research, Stanley I. Greenspan, one of the nation's foremost child psychiatrists and author of *The Challenging Child*, tells us there are five major types of difficult kid temperaments, each with its unique strengths. Greenspan says that by applying the maternal secret of perception and playing to your child's natural strengths, you can help even the most challenging kid turn out right. The trick is to turn challenges into opportunities. Here are the five types of difficult temperaments. Do any fit your child?

1. *Highly sensitive.* These kids feel everything in the world more intensely than most and can make you feel as though you're walking on eggshells. They can be quite demanding and irritable and can resist change. Your best parenting approach is to use a mixture of empathy and clearly established limits, provide structure, and encourage their natural initiative. These children can become creative, insightful, and compassionate.

2. *Self-absorbed.* These kids may seem easy at first because they make few demands and are content to be left alone. Later you'll see that they are slower to warm up and fit in, so your goal is to engage this kid and cultivate social skills so she feels more comfortable in groups.

3. *Defiant.* Is your child stubborn, negative, controlling, and apparently stuck on the word *no?* Can he manage to turn even the simplest activity into a trial? Defiant kids can be exhausting. It helps if you stay calm (I know, I know), set limits, watch those transition times, and try negotiating things you're willing to negotiate.

4. *Inattentive.* "That's the third time!" "Don't you ever listen?" These kids have a difficult time "tuning in to" the world. Your goal is to help your child focus, make decisions, and become more self-observant.

5. *Active or aggressive.* Some kids are just "movers and shakers," but Greenspan points out that they can be "tamed" if you consistently apply firm limits calmly and nurture your child gently and warmly. He'll learn to handle his world better if you teach him anger management and relaxation strategies.

laziness, your daughter's large build, your youngest kid's quick temper.) Just for the heck of it, ask yourself how many of those traits are the same as yours (or vastly different). Having thought about that question, could it be that you've discovered why your kid's annoying trait might be getting in the way of your relationship?

3. How well are you tuning your parenting to your child's differences? For instance, do you expect each of your kids to study the same way, read the same books, explore the same interests, and play the same sports, or do you consider the special skills and unique talents of each child in your decisions?

4. Do you discipline each child the same way (time-out, spanking, or talking it through, using the same consequences for all your kids), or do you use your perception and vary your approach in accordance with what you think works best for each child?

5. What is the one thing you recognize in yourself that you need to change to become a more perceptive mom and help each child develop her own unique strengths and personality? Write it on the lines here. Then get ready to learn the secret and use it with your family. _____

_____

_____

_____

Six Steps to Treating Your Child as an Individual

Commit yourself to making an "identity album" for your child. Instead of including photographs, it will contain "snapshots" of your child made up of words or symbols. For each album you'll need six pieces of 4" x 6" paper (index cards are ideal) and a pen or pencil. Some moms like to get fancy and use colored markers or even print this on a computer. If your style is artsy, go for it, but pencil-and-paper technique is just fine too. Now find a quiet time and place to really think through the steps here. Answer each question on one of the cards; feel free to use drawings or symbols as well as words. This identity album makes a wonderful keepsake not only for you but for your child as well. The easiest way to make the album permanent is to insert the papers or cards in a 4" x 6" size photo album (the kind with the plastic sleeves).

Step One: Describe Your Child. Suppose you ran into an old friend who has never met your child, and she asks you to tell her about him. Close your eyes. Really think about your child. If you have a photograph of your child, put it in front of you to help you really concentrate. On the first card, write all the adjectives—the good as well as the bad—you would use to describe this child of yours. Who is he?

Step Two: Decide What You Like Best About Your Child. What are the special qualities that make this kid so lovable and likeable and charming in your eyes? What are the traits you want to remember most about her right now and never forget for the rest of your life because they are so endearing? Write all of these positive traits on the second card. When you finish, take a moment to ask yourself: How many of those traits are different from mine? The same as mine? How about my parenting partner's traits? Put your initial next to the traits that you share.

Step Three: Identify Your Child's Passions and Interests. What does your kid just love to do? This might be very different from what you love, but think about it. If your child could choose to do anything, what would it be? What does she do most in her free time? Is she doing anything now she says she "hates" (or at least wishes she didn't have to do)? Take a quiet walk into your child's room to remind yourself of who this kid of yours is and what turns her on. Write your thoughts on the third card.

Step Four: Describe Your Child's Temperament. When you get right down to it, what kind of kid is your son or daughter? Aggressive or calm? Social or a loner? Easy or difficult? Laid back or tense? Outgoing or shy? Academic or physical? Self-motivated or externally driven? Flexible or rigid? Sensitive or insensitive? Self-absorbed or concerned about others? Independent or dependent? If he had his choice, would you be more apt to find him outside or indoors? Doing something active or quiet? Would she prefer to be with people or alone? Write your thoughts on the fourth card.

Step Five: Explain Your Child's Learning Style. Howard Gardner, Harvard psychologist and author of *Frames of Mind,* has developed a theory that every child is born with a unique combination of intelligences and learns best when she uses her strongest intelligences. To help you determine your child's strengths, read the descriptions of the eight intelligences Gardner has identified, then check the ones that best describe your child and copy onto the fifth card your discoveries about your kid's unique learning identity. If you're unsure, then observe your child a little closer, ask teachers, and tune in to your child's natural interests.

☐ *Linguistic learners* like to read, write, and tell stories. They learn by hearing and seeing words, and they know unusual amounts of information, have advanced vocabularies, memorize facts verbatim.

☐ *Bodily/kinesthetic learners* handle their bodies with ease and poise for their age, are adept at using their body for sports or artistic expression, and are skilled in fine motor tasks.

☐ *Intrapersonal learners* have strong self-understanding, are original, enjoy working alone to pursue their own interests and goals, and have a strong sense of right and wrong.

☐ *Interpersonal learners* understand people, lead and organize others, have lots of friends, are looked to by others to make decisions and mediate conflicts, and enjoy joining groups.

- [ ] *Musical learners* appreciate rhythm, pitch, and melody, and they respond to music. They remember melodies, keep time well, like to sing and hum tunes, and may play instruments.

- [ ] *Logical/mathematical learners* understand numbers, patterns, and relationships, and they enjoy science and math. They categorize, ask questions, do experiments, and figure things out.

- [ ] *Spatial learners* like to draw, design, and create things, and imagine things and daydream. They remember what they see, read maps and charts, and work well with colors and pictures.

- [ ] *Naturalists* like the out-of-doors, are curious, and classify the features of the environment.

Step Six: Recognize Your Child's Drawbacks. What are your child's weaknesses or "challenging traits" that might dampen his chances for happiness, fulfillment, or success? Displaying these traits might hinder his reputation among teachers, peers, or peers' parents as well as diminish his self-esteem. These drawbacks are most likely your secret concerns or worries about your child. For instance, is she overly sensitive and prone to tears, a poor loser, or selfish? Does she have a short attention span? Is she aggressive or quick tempered? Write your child's drawbacks on your sixth card.

Making a Promise to Yourself

1. Did you identify with or were you inspired by the story of Matt and his mom, Jean? What was it about them that seemed similar to your own family? Is this one of the secrets you want to focus on and tune up in your family? How would applying what matters most about being perceptive benefit your child?

Celebrating Children's Strengths Through Family Rituals

- *Holiday mementos.* Marion Card, a mom of four grown daughters from Saratoga, California, used her Christmas stockings to boost their individuality. Each child's stocking was covered with different little trinkets their mother sewed on representing the girls' interests and strengths. They also were a visible reminder of each daughter's special place in the Card family. Marion passed away just a few years ago, but her legacy lives on in her daughters. The stockings she so painstaking added on to at each holiday are not only alive in each of her daughter's hearts and minds but hanging up on their own mantels each Christmas. You might display each child's special mementos depicting her unique talents or interests in her own special box, on a piece of colored felt, or even glued inside a picture frame.

- *Birthday celebration letter.* Cindy Morse, a mom of two grown children from San Jose, California, found a special way to recognize each of her children's individual positive qualities and strengths. Each year she wrote a Celebration Letter to both of her children on their birthdays. She highlighted their year's special moments and, most important, validated their special strengths and acknowledged any efforts they took to improve their talents and behaviors. Cindy and the children would enjoy the letters together, then she saved all of them to present to her children on their twenty-first birthdays.

2. How would you apply the six steps to treating your child as an individual? Review all the boxes, guides, tips, and stories in this chapter.

3. Go to A Mother's Promise on page 55 and write in the one thing you will do differently over the next 21 days to help your child become more confident in her unique individuality.

Two Simple Steps to Turning Negative Labels into Positives

It's time to use your perception. Identify any current label that could be destructive to your child's self-esteem or reputation (such as *lazy, selfish, dumb, slow, irresponsible, sloppy, unreliable, uncoordinated, inconsiderate, stubborn,* or *rebellious*). Go back to the identity album you just created for your child and review what you wrote for "drawbacks" in step six. Write down the negative term, image, or nickname your perception tells you needs altering.

1. **Create a positive new label to replace the negative one.** Write it down. Here are a few to get you started:

Old Negative Label	New Positive Label
Hyperactive	Spirited
Shy	Cautious
Unpredictable	Flexible
Daydreamer	Creative
Aggressive	Assertive

2. **Substitute the new positive label.** Now tune up that perception: any time you can use that positive new label with your child, do it. That includes using the term in front of your child, his siblings, and his friends, as well as adults. Also remember never to let anyone else label your child. Just as the mother in the story did, immediately turn any negative label into a positive one. Negative label: "Your son is so shy!" Positive label: "Not at all, he's just a great observer." Be very careful of nicknames: unless they build your child up and are respectful, don't allow them!

A Real Mom's Resource Guide

All About Motherhood: "A Mom for All Seasons" and Other Essays, by Kathryn E. Livingston (New York: iUniverse, 2005). Treat yourself to this glorious compilation of essays about real mothering.

Awakening Your Child's Natural Genius, by Thomas Armstrong (Los Angeles: Tarcher, 1991). This book contains more than three hundred practical suggestions showing parents how they can play a pivotal role in helping their children realize their true gifts.

Bringing Out the Best in Your Child, by Cynthia Ulrich Tobias and Carol Funk (Ann Arbor, Mich.: Servant Publications, 1997). This book offers eighty ways to focus on developing your children's unique strengths.

The Challenging Child: Understanding, Raising, and Enjoying the Five "Difficult" Types of Children, by Stanley I. Greenspan (Cambridge, Mass.: Perseus, 1995). A renowned child expert provides straightforward, reassuring advice on how to recognize five different kid temperaments and how to raise kids with these different temperaments.

In Their Own Way: Discovering and Encouraging Your Child's Personal Learning Style, by Thomas Armstrong (Los Angeles: Tarcher, 1987). This is an excellent resource to help pinpoint and enhance children's unique learning styles. Also by the same author and highly recommended: *7 Kinds of Smart* (New York: Penguin, 1993).

Know Your Child, by Stella Chess and Alexander Thomas (New York: Basic Books, 1987). The authors' now famous research found that most children can be classified as "easy," "difficult," or "slow to warm up." This book will help you tune up your perception and understand your child's basic temperament. Once you understand it, you'll be able to alter your parenting to fit your child's needs.

Loving Each One Best: A Caring and Practical Approach to Raising Siblings, by Nancy Samalin (New York: Bantam Books, 1997). With warmth and humor, this well-known parenting expert comes to the aid of parents who have entered the sibling minefield. She offers strategies culled from her workshops and seminars and hundreds of questionnaire responses from parents and children.

Siblings Without Rivalry: How to Help Your Children Live Together So You Can Live Too, by Adele Faber and Elaine Mazlish (New York: HarperResource, 1998). The central message—avoid comparisons—sounds almost too simple; moms know that's easier said than done. But the authors talk you through dozens of different situations and outcomes to help you teach your brawling offspring a new set of responses. Valuable!

Temperament Talk: A Guide to Understanding Your Child, by Kathy Goodman, Lyndall Shick, Barbara Tyler, and Barbara Zukin (La Grande, Oreg.: Center for Human Development, 1995). This book has good advice to help you understand that kids are different and how to adjust your parenting for those differences.

Understanding Your Child's Temperament, by William B. Carey (Old Tappan, N.J.: Macmillan, 1997). This reference helps parents understand the nine temperamental traits inborn in every child and how to work with them from infancy through adolescence.

A Mother Who Encourages Independence Cultivates Self-Reliance

What Real Mothers Know: Let Go of Rescuing Your Kids Every Time, So They Can Thrive Without You

What Really Matters for Mothering: Plan for the Future

The Real Benefit for Kids: Self-Reliance and Resourcefulness

The Lesson a Real Mother Teaches: No mother wants her child to suffer heartaches and disappointments. Our basic maternal instinct is to try to protect our kids from frustrations and solve their problems for them. But real moms know that doing so would prevent their children from developing the very skills they'll need to deal with the multitude of issues they'll face in the real world. One of the simplest ways to influence your child's future without you is also the easiest to use: *stop rescuing!* Do not write one more cover-up note to your child's teacher. Do not put out the garbage when your child conveniently disappears. Do not take your kid's overdue library book back and pay the fine. Do not go back and get your kid's forgotten soccer shoes for the umpteenth time. If you really want your child to become self-sufficient and thrive without you, your role must be that of a guider, not a doer. It's another case of doing less, not more—the natural mothering way. That simple twist teaches your children that you expect them to be resourceful by solving their own problems—whatever they may be—and that you believe they are capable of doing so. It's the best way to prepare our kids to face life on their own and help them learn to handle *whatever* problem comes their way.

"She Taught Her Children to Live Without Her"

*The most beautiful sight in the world is a child going confidently
down the road of life after you have shown him the way.*
—Confucius

Anne Leedom always loved waiting in her car to pick up her two daughters, Kasey and Rachel. She couldn't wait to hear them tell her all the details of what went on at school that day. And one afternoon was particularly memorable.

Rachel, her eight-year-old, jumped in the car looking pretty tense. Her usual little happy bounce was missing—her grin was replaced by a grimace. Her shoulders were hunched over, her fists clenched. Obviously something distressing had happened. *But what could it be?* Anne wondered.

She noticed that Rachel was hiding something behind her back as she walked out of school, but couldn't quite make out what. She greeted her daughter with the usual big hug, while trying to sneak a peek at what she was holding. She helped her take off her backpack and asked Rachel the typical "How was school today, Sweetie?" questions to try to find out why she was so upset. Anne finally saw that what her daughter was clenching so tightly was a crumpled up piece of paper. Anne took the paper gently from her hand. Rachel crumpled it. Anne uncrumpled it. Rachel crumpled it. Anne finally won. But when she straightened out the page, she was surprised to see the cause of her daughter's distress: it was the spelling test she'd taken that morning.

Usually Rachel did really well in spelling. Oh sure, sometimes Anne would correct her daughter's homework so that there wouldn't be any mistakes. Why not? She wanted her daughter to do well. Anne would also go over the spelling list with Rachel a few times every Thursday, and by Friday morning she would go off to school ready to take the test with confidence.

"I know all my words, Mom," she would exclaim each week. "I'll ace the test no problem."

Last night, however, Anne had a last-minute call from her girlfriend, who was sick and needed someone to watch her daughter while she went to the emergency room. So this Friday morning, Rachel had gone to school without the usual coaching. When Anne smoothed out her daughter's crumpled test paper, she could see immediately that it didn't look like all the others. In the past, Rachel's teacher would draw a big happy face at the top with her bright red pencil. This time there was no happy face but instead two big checks and corrections for mistakes she had made.

Rachel looked mortified. This had never happened before. She always got happy faces and was proud to show her mother her perfect scores. "See?" she'd say. "I told you I'd get all the words right."

But today was terribly different. Anne was surprised to see how embarrassed and ashamed her daughter was for getting just two out of ten wrong on a routine spelling test.

"It's okay, Rachel. Don't worry, Honey; you'll get a chance next week."

But Rachel didn't buy it and shook her head sadly. "No, Mommy, no . . . I flunked."

Anne began to recite to herself the litany of typical mother guilt: *Did she think I would love her any less if her score wasn't perfect? Have I put too much pressure on grades? How at such a tender young age did she get the idea that making a mistake meant failure?*

Anne looked at the panic on her daughter's face and knew she needed to help Rachel learn from this experience. After all, making mistakes or getting thrown a few curve balls is a part of life, and Rachel's life was just beginning. Anne had never realized how much pressure her daughter placed on herself to succeed and how little, if any, experience she'd had of getting anything but positive scores. If this is how she responds to missing only two spelling words, what would she do in the future when bigger problems came her way? How could she learn to be self-reliant?

It suddenly hit her: *Maybe I've been helping her too much, correcting her mistakes and protecting her from knowing what it's like to be anything less than perfect.*

Anne realized she had to do something different, or Rachel would never survive on her own in the future. She began searching for the right words, words that wouldn't just help in this moment but teach Rachel some skills for the long term. What finally popped out wasn't exactly what she would have said if she'd spent time weighing her words (okay, it was far from it). But she had to start somewhere, right? So she leaned over and gave Rachel her best shot.

"Wasn't it nice that your teacher took the time to put these red check marks on your paper?"

The look on Rachel's face was priceless. Anne could almost hear her thinking, *Is mom crazy? Can't she see I made two mistakes?*

But Anne ignored her skeptical look and kept on. She was on a roll.

"You know it takes a lot of time checking work to let you know which words you missed," Anne said. She then added, "Your teacher must care a lot about you. She takes that time because she really is concerned about your learning," she told her. "What she wants you to do is study the words she's marked so you won't make the same mistakes the next time."

And then Anne went for her grand finale: "Wasn't that nice of her?"

These next seconds were what mothers live for—those precious, rather extraordinary times when you realize you've said or done something that is really getting through to your kid. Anne could tell that her daughter was really contemplating everything she'd said to her, and sizing things up. And then, all of a sudden, she saw the light go on in her daughter's little head.

Rachel nodded, gave Anne a quick hug, and told her assuredly, "OK, Mom, I'm gonna correct these . . . Gotta go."

Then she ran to her room with that predictable little bounce restored and her world back in control. At this point, Anne's expectations were still pretty slim: she was just hoping her child would remember something she'd said by dinner that evening. Let's be real, right?

But apparently something in her little mother-daughter talk had clicked. The "confirming moment" happened two weeks later when Rachel was dashing out of the car to get to school on time, and Anne sat in the driver's seat waiting to say good-bye.

As her daughter gave her a quick good-bye hug, Anne noticed she was holding a small package carefully in one hand. It wasn't hard to miss: the box was wrapped in yellow wrapping paper and bound together with yards and yards of brown masking tape. A bright red bow was attached to the narrow box with a large rubber band.

"What's in the box?" Anne asked.

"Oh, it's a birthday present for my teacher," Rachel said. Then she added with absolute confidence: "Mrs. Diamond's going to be soooooo happy when she sees what's in it. She'll love it!"

She looked to see if her mother could guess what she could possibly be giving her teacher that would please her so. Anne shook her head—she honestly didn't have a clue as to what could be in that box.

"I bought her a red pencil!" she told me excitedly. "Now Mrs. Diamond will always have one so she can mark my mistakes and I can learn to spell all by myself." And then Rachel added a bit sheepishly, "She lets me know she cares about me by marking the ones I miss, you know."

She waved and ran to her classroom. Anne stood in place with her mouth open. Her words really had sunk in.

And then a really staggering thought hit this mom: *What if I hadn't found her crumpled spelling test with the two mistakes? What if I hadn't noticed how distressed she was? And what if I hadn't told my child that it's okay to make a mistake? What kind of future would she have on her own?* As her daughter went to school that day, Anne realized that her job over the next ten years was to prepare her daughter to handle whatever the future brought—*without* having her mom around to always smooth things over.

What Real Moms Can Learn from This Story

Anne Leedom had the best intentions when she polished up her daughter's homework and coached her so hard for every test. But after that Friday, with those big red pencil marks, Anne realized how important it was for Rachel to know she wasn't perfect and never would be. Children cannot learn to persevere unless they recognize how to deal with imperfection and failure. Anne also reminded her daughter that there would be another spelling test next week, so trying again and bouncing back could help her cultivate self-reliance and resourcefulness.

As moms, we must look way down the road. We need to be futurists. Too many of us get caught up in correcting past mistakes and putting out fires. It's as though we're hearing our alarm clocks going off, but we're only punching the snooze button. To respond effectively to our children's daily problems, we need to prepare them to cope on their own. After all, they're not going to live with us forever, and we can't always be there to pick up the pieces. Moms who are trying to do everything for their kids in a white heat of manic frenzy aren't doing them any favors.

Is This Real Mom's Secret Part of **Your** Parenting?

Of course we don't want our kids to fail, and of course we always want them to be successful, but always doing, picking up, or mending fences for our kids sure won't help them learn to bounce back and survive on their own. So here's a little test to see just how well you've been practicing the maternal secret of planning ahead or preparing your child to handle life without you.

1. Start by thinking about how you usually act whenever your child seems frustrated, seeks your help, fails, or isn't doing a task quite up to your standards. Which of these traits would you say most accurately describes your response? Would the rest of your family agree with your verdict?

   ☐ *Enabler:* "I know how hard that is. Let me help you."

   ☐ *Rescuer:* "You're going to be in trouble with your teacher if you can't find your library book. I'll tell her I lost it."

   ☐ *Impatient:* "We're late. I'll tie your shoes, and you can learn how later."

   ☐ *Protector:* "I'll call Brian's mom and tell her how sorry you are."

   ☐ *Guilt-ridden:* "Don't worry about your chores. I've been gone so much this week I'll do them."

   ☐ *Competitive:* "You know Ryan's project is going to be really good. Let's add more pictures."

   ☐ *Egocentric:* "Not now. I don't have time."

   ☐ *Perfectionist:* "You run along, and I'll redo your science project. Those letters you pasted on just don't look right."

   Now that you've thought about how you typically respond, would you say your behavior usually strengthens your child's confidence and independence muscle or takes it down a notch? Is there one thing you're currently doing that might be robbing your child of the chance to figure things out for herself? Is there one thing you might change?

2. Do you usually emphasize your child's failures or his successes? For instance, think of the last time your child brought home his report card. Would you say you usually talk first about his high grades or the low ones? When he shows you his schoolwork or test, do you first point to the positive parts of his work or to his mistakes? How does your child respond to your feedback? Would you say your approach in the long run is helping or hindering his ability to bounce back and become resourceful?

3. Now let's suppose your child makes a mistake or fails: she spills her milk accidentally, flunks a math exam, forgets to tell you your boss phoned, strikes out at bat. How do you typically respond? Are you more likely to (A) encourage your child to give it another try; (B) say, "I told you so" or "I knew that would happen"; (C) ignore it or let it slide; (D) yell, shame, criticize, judge, blame, or ridicule; (E) stay calm and use the opportunity to teach your child what to do the next time so she can learn from it? Is your current response helping your child learn to bounce back? Are you satisfied that your typical response is what's best for your child, or do you think there's a more effective way? If so, what would it be?

4. Are mistakes okay to make in your household? For instance, when your child does fail, how does he typically react? For instance, does he shrug it off, cry, blame himself or someone else, get angry? Now suppose you make a mistake and your child is watching you. Do you admit it, apologize, blame someone, rationalize, make an excuse, lose patience, or explain what you learned from it? Tune in to your behavior over the next few days and ask yourself what your child may

be "catching." Is there anything you might want to change in your behavior so that your child has a better model to copy?

5. What is the one thing you recognize in yourself that you need to change to become a more future-oriented mom who prepares her children to survive and thrive without her? Write it on the lines here. Then get ready to learn the secret and use it with your family. _____

_____

_____

_____

> **REAL MOM ALERT**
>
> ### Beware: The Kids Are Coming Back!
>
> Recent research points out one clear trend among today's twenty-something kids: a large number are moving back home after college. Here are some of the stats:
>
> - The percentage of twenty-six-year-olds living with their parents nearly doubled since 1970.
> - According to the 2002 U.S. Census, nearly four million people between the ages of twenty-five and thirty-four still live with their parents.
> - An online survey reported that 60 percent of college students stated they planned to live at home after graduation—and 21 percent said they planned to remain there for more than a year.
>
> If you really do want to raise a self-reliant child (and feel guiltless about turning her bedroom into your private sanctuary), you may need to do some serious rethinking about how you're raising your kid so she can survive without you. Otherwise, hold off on the new house designs!

The Wake-Up Call to Change

Michelle Price of Calgary, Alberta, was driving her
two boys to school and running late. She checked in
the rearview mirror and noticed a look of panic on her
six-year-old's face. "Could we pleeeeease go back and get
my backpack?" he pleaded. "I forgot my show-and-tell."

Any other day, Michelle would have quickly agreed and
made the U-turn back to the house to retrieve the forgotten
items. In fact, there had been more than a few times she'd
done that, but today there was something different about his
face and response—there was a little too much expectation
that mom would rescue him no matter what.

Something clicked in Michelle's head. She thought to herself, *If I'm always rescuing my kids, they'll just take it for
granted that I'll do it for the rest of their lives.*

So her response this time was different: "Sweetie, I know
you're upset. But we're not going back to the house this time.
I know you can figure out something else for sharing. So let's
brainstorm some ideas, and by the time we drive up you'll
have a plan."

Sure there was a bit of initial panic. And no, her kid wasn't
exactly thrilled by the whole idea. But Mom stuck to her guns,
and by the time they arrived, her son had a plan for not only
his sharing but for borrowing a plastic bag from another
teacher for a makeshift backpack that day. Michelle had
experienced one of those "ah-ha" moments that helped her
kids learn to be more resourceful and less dependent on her.

Six Steps to Helping Your Child Become Self-Reliant

You can't expect your children to become self-reliant and resourceful unless you nurture those traits in them. Here are a
few practices you'll want to adopt in your day-to-day family life
to help them achieve that goal.

**Step One: Identify What Your Child Can Do Alone and Then *Back
Off.*** What tasks might your child be capable of doing on his

own, instead of relying on you? Maybe it's time for him to learn to make his own lunch, do laundry, make his bed, call to make his dentist appointments. Of course, this will depend on your child's age, maturity, and current capabilities. The goal here isn't to overwhelm him by piling on new expectations; gradually introduce one new task at a time.

Step Two: Stop Rescuing. Have you found yourself rescuing your kids a lot lately? "Jake is so tired; I'll do his homework tonight." "Kyla is too busy; I'll do her chores this time." It's an easy habit to get into, but if you want to raise a resilient kid, these are major mother "no-no's." Start by setting this rule: "We have a new policy: no more excuses. You need to take responsibility."

Step Three: Boost Organizational Skills So Your Child Won't Use You as His Palm Pilot. Is your child misplacing library books? Unable to find her sports gear? Losing teacher notes? Chances are, your child's lack of organization is a big reason why you end up rescuing her. So when there's another trauma, instead of bailing her out, ask instead, "What can you do to solve it?" For instance, if your child forgets to return her library book every Wednesday, she might hang up a calendar that marks her due dates as well as the dates of music lessons, field trips, sharing days, and tests. Even little ones can draw "picture" reminders. Learning to organize is a skill your child will need for managing her own life so that she relies less and less on you as time goes by.

Step Four: Teach Brainstorming So Your Child Can Solve Problems Without You. The next time your child has a problem, don't be so quick to offer a solution. Instead, teach him how to brainstorm options. First, say to your child, "Tell me what's bothering you." (You might need to help him find the words: "I can't think of anything to bring for sharing.") Express your faith that he can work things out: "I know you'll come up with a solution for your sharing." Then encourage him to brainstorm ideas. "Don't worry about how silly your idea sounds. Just say it, because it may help your think of things to share." You might even call this "The Solution Game"; just remind your child to use it whenever he encounters a problem. With enough practice, your child will be able to use brainstorming to solve many troubling issues that creep up during the day—and do so *without* your help.

Step Five: Teach How to Negotiate. Do your children constantly expect you to be the negotiator and end their battles? Wrong move if you want your kids to become capable of solving their own problems. Your new tactic? Teach your kids how to negotiate so that when the next war breaks out you can tell your darling cherubs to work it out on their own. Here's how. First, explain the new skill: "You need to learn to negotiate. That's when you agree to work out a deal so that you both are happy."

Next, teach your kids a few oldie-but-goodie "tie breakers," such as "rock, paper, scissors," drawing straws, flipping a coin, or using the rule that "Whoever went first last time goes last this time." Oven timers are also great for reducing squabbles. Just show your kids how to set it, and it can be a great sanity saver. "I'm setting the timer for five minutes, but when it goes off, it's my turn to play."

Finally, don't forget to set clear "negotiation behavior": "You must take turns listening to each other without interrupting, and no put-downs. Only calm voices are allowed." Then start practicing using the skill as a family. Not only will it help your child learn a skill that I guarantee he'll need in every arena of life, but you may also experience greater peace on the home front.

Step Six: Talk About Her Future Regularly. Encourage your kids to think beyond the here and now: going away to camp, changing schools, attending college, living in an apartment, making career choices. Discussing your children's future lives can be part of your dinner table conversations. Of course they can change their minds (and majors), but the goal is to help your child think toward the future and realize someday that she really won't be living with you.

Three Simple Steps to Helping Your Child Handle Mistakes

How we respond to our kids' failures plays a big part in how our kids handle mistakes. If you now realize you've typically responded to your child's mistakes in a critical, judgmental, blaming fashion, try the three-step parent response called TLC (not to be confused with Tender Loving Care). There are three parts to this simple strategy:

T—Talk calmly about the mistake with your child. Try not to criticize or show anger. *Mom:* "Let's talk about your spelling paper. What do you notice?" *Child:* "I missed five of my words."

L—Tell what your child can learn from the mistake. *Mom:* "What can you learn from the test so you won't make the same mistakes next time you take it?" *Child:* "I learned I need to study my words a little every night and not wait until the last minute."

C—Comfort your child by reminding him that everybody makes mistakes. *Mom:* "That sounds like a great plan! Successful people look at their mistakes and figure out what they can learn from them. That's what you're doing!"

REAL MOM ALERT

Teach the Value of Not Giving Up

Stanford professor Lewis Terman studied fifteen hundred gifted kids for several decades and found that high intelligence was a poor predictor of future success when kids were out there in the world on their own. What did those who succeeded have in common? They had all learned the value of perseverance and not giving up, and they had all learned it before they left high school. Who they learned it from was their parents, who modeled perseverance and then expected it from their children. So if you really want your child to make it out there in the world without you, instilling in her a "never give up" attitude is essential, and the best way to do so is by tuning up the maternal secret of nurturing perseverance in yourself.

Making a Promise to Yourself

1. Did you identify with or were you inspired by the story of Rachel and her mom, Anne? What was it about them that seemed so similar to your own family? Is this one of the secrets you want to focus on and tune up in your family? How would planning for the time when your child will be independent benefit your family?

2. How would you apply the six steps to helping your child become self-reliant? Review all the boxes, guides, tips, and stories in this chapter.

3. Go to A Mother's Promise on page 56 and write in the one thing you will do differently over the next 21 days to help your child become more resilient.

A Real Mom's Resource Guide

"I Think I Can, I Know I Can!" by Susan Isaacs and Wendy Ritchey (New York: St. Martin's Press, 1989). This book contains a wealth of practical ways to nurture confidence and resourcefulness in children.

Raising a Thinking Child, by Myrna B. Shure (New York: Henry Holt, 1994). This is a valuable resource full of ideas for teaching problem solving to children three to seven years of age.

Raising Resilient Children: Fostering Strength, Hope, and Optimism in Your Child, by Robert Brooks and Sam Goldstein (New York: Contemporary Books, 2001). Renowned psychologists provide practical parenting strategies and practices to prepare kids for the challenges of today's complicated, ever changing world.

Ready or Not, Here Life Comes, by Mel Levine (New York: Simon & Schuster, 2005). Take my word for it: this one is a must-read. This renowned professor of pediatrics expounds on what he calls the "epidemic of work-life unreadiness" that affects our twenty-something set as they move from school to the working world. We underestimate the difficulties they face, Levine argues, and must prepare our kids for life differently; he shows us how.

Unconditional Parenting: Moving from Rewards and Punishment to Love and Reason, by Alfie Kohn (New York: Atria, 2005). Kids do best when given unconditional love, respect, and opportunities to make their own choices. In the end, says Kohn, we sure don't want docility and short-term obedience. Well said, and a great read.

A Mother Who Applauds Effort Nurtures Perseverance

What Real Mothers Know: It's Not Just Winning But Never Giving Up

What Really Matters for Mothering: Be Affirmative

The Real Benefit for Kids: Internal Motivation and Stick-to-Itiveness

The Lesson a Real Mother Teaches: Real moms can make an immense difference in their children's work ethic by emphasizing that it's not good enough just to start; you have to finish. After all, one of the most important traits our kids must develop is the inner strength and stamina to hang tough through trying times. And our daily encounters offer us so many simple ways to teach the value of not giving up. When you point out again and again, "Don't worry about your mistake. Think about what you will do differently the next time." When you resist the urge to step in when your child experiences frustration. When you help your child cope with mistakes through your example: "Wow, I sure didn't do this right. Next time, I'm going to do it this way instead." Or when you convey the belief to your child, "I know it's hard. But I admire how hard you're trying!" Just think for a minute about the long-term effect that stressing effort could have on our children! They would learn from an early age that there's nothing that can stop them from succeeding if they put their heart and soul into their endeavors. They would learn to acknowledge themselves for a job well done instead of always expecting the big reward. And those are the exact lessons our children must be taught if they are going to be able to cope with those inevitable hard knocks life sometimes gives.

"She Applauded Her Child's Efforts"

Applaud us when we run,
Console us when we fall,
Cheer us when we recover.

—Edmond Burke

Diana James and her eleven-year-old daughter, Kate, had never been in a History Day competition sponsored by the Constitutional Rights Foundation before. Three teams from her middle school had worked hard all year on their research projects and had won at their school, district, and county levels to qualify for the big state competition in Sacramento.

For the past three days, Kate and her two teammates had been through the grueling process of presenting their ten-minute video on Japanese American internment camps, fielding tough questions before a panel of history professors, and enduring the pressure and stress of high-stakes competition. Now they were back on the plane headed home to Southern California along with dozens of other student teams, teachers, and their parents.

Diana was sitting near the back of the plane with several other mothers, some she knew and some she hadn't met who had kids from other schools. She could see her daughter and friends several rows ahead. As the mother looked around the plane, she recognized who'd won or lost from Kate's school but not from the others, and she thought some of the kids were behaving kind of oddly. There were three or four students sitting in the front rows who were obviously elated—laughing, slapping high fives to one another, and talking excitedly. These guys were clearly happy campers. But not everyone shared the same euphoria: seated in the next few rows were students appearing as though they had just come from their best friend's funeral, their faces drained, voices muted, shoulders slumped. One or two were subtly trying to wipe away a tear or two. Talk about polar opposites! Diana thought to herself that you sure didn't need to be a detective to figure out which kids on that flight were the winners and losers.

A few minutes after the plane took off, Diana got up and made her way up the aisle to give Kate her sweater, as it was getting kind of chilly. One of her daughter's friends had gone to use the restroom, so Diana plumped herself down for a moment. Across the aisle were two boys from another middle school, the ones who looked as though they'd just come from a funeral, and she couldn't help but overhear them.

"This whole thing was stupid," one boy said to the other. "What a waste of time!"

"The judges asked such dumb questions."

"For sure! And you know those kids from Central Middle were in this only so it would look good on their résumés."

"Well, me too, dude . . . duh. Why else would you do all that work?"

"Hey, I'll tell you something else—I don't think those judges were fair. I saw one talking with a teacher like they were the best buds. It's probably all rigged anyway."

Diana didn't want to hear any more of this complaining and tried not to listen. She was proud that her daughter wasn't a poor loser. Sure, her team hadn't placed in the top three, but she knew her daughter's group had worked very hard and had really enjoyed the competition. These kids were self-motivated and had a terrific sense of responsibility. They weren't celebrating as hard as the kids up front who looked as though they'd won big-time, but Kate and her friends were still excited to have been in the competition.

"I got the phone numbers from the team from Culver City," Kate told her mom. "They were really nice."

"Lots of kids we met were nice," her teammate next to her said. "Don't you think?"

"Yeah, it was fun," Kate commented. "Hey, do you want to do this again next year? I didn't think I'd like history this much."

Diana listened a bit longer as Kate and her teammate discussed the merits of the competition they'd just been through, and even what they'd (shock, shock) *learned* from participating. Diana wondered why her daughter's team had such a positive take on the event. It was the complete opposite of that of the boys who grumbled about the whole "worthless" experience.

Back at her seat, Diana struck up a conversation with a woman whose kid was from one of the other schools.

"Wasn't this great? Did your kid's team enjoy the competition as much as my daughter's did?" Diana asked.

"No, and I can't believe why they would. Too much work, and the prize was crappy."

"What?" Diana was astonished.

"My kids hated it. The teachers were too strict, and it cost a fortune. I can tell you how much money I had to spend on all those photographs, not to mention all the days I spent putting them into that PowerPoint."

"Really?" Diana said. "Our kids made their own slides."

"Oh . . . then they probably didn't win. And you want to know something else?" The mom leaned over and whispered in Diana's ear, "Those judges were definitely racist." Diana shook her head and buried her nose in a book.

The plane landed an hour later, and everyone made their way down through the terminal. As they approached the baggage claim area, Diana began to hear some rather unusual noises: the unmistakable sounds of cheering, whistling, and clapping. She figured it had to be a group of parents waiting to meet the winning teams, and thought to herself, *How nice!* It took several minutes to get through the maze of doors and down escalators, and that whole time the cheering sounds never stopped. This had to be some celebration. In fact, there was so much noise going on, she assumed that the parents brought a school band to play for the champion team.

But when Diana and her group finally reached the baggage claim area, she was stunned. It wasn't a band making the noise at all, but five middle-aged moms dressed in some ragged-looking cheerleading costumes waving their pom-poms jumping up and down in close approximation to a pep rally routine they must have done on a football field some twenty years ago. Behind them there was a huge handmade sign that said, "Welcome Home! Terrific Job!" It was hilarious. It was wonderful. Diana beamed from ear to ear. She loved it. How great!

At first some of the kids were stunned, but gradually moms and kids ran toward each other and started hugging as the whole bunch of them made their way to the carousel and waited for the bags to come up. Then an amazing thing happened. Diana saw the woman sitting next to her on the plane standing alongside the two boys who'd been sitting across from her daughter and complaining so bitterly about the whole competition. Each of the boys was now wearing a large first-place gold medallion strung around his neck on a red-and-white ribbon.

"*Oh my gosh,*" Diana said to herself, "*those boys weren't the losers—they were the winners!*"

Then she saw the kids still hugging the moms dressed as cheerleaders, and none of them were wearing any medals.

"Kate?"

"Yes, Mom."

"Do you know those kids over there with the cheerleaders?"

"Sure—they're from Glenview Middle School."

"How did they do?"

"They only tell us if we're in the top three, so I know they didn't win. But aren't they fun, Mom?"

Kate's mom put her arm around her daughter and gave her a big kiss. "You're pretty great, Kate. I'm so glad you're mine."

What Real Moms Can Learn from This Story

Diana James assumed on the flight back from the state competition that the kids she overheard complaining were the losers and the ones high-fiving each other were the winners, but in fact the exact opposite was true. Her daughter, Kate, hadn't won either, but still got so much out of the whole experience and had so much fun with her team. They didn't care about the external reward. So what made the difference in the kids' reactions? A big part of that secret is how their mothers acted.

Did you notice that the mother sitting next to Diana had focused on how hard it was on *her*, how great the expense, and how inadequate the prize? She even badmouthed the judges. This mother had no concept of the real value of the entire experience: all she cared about was winning and material status. And her kid had learned this lesson all too well.

As for the cheerleading moms, well, you had to love them. But not only that, they modeled a critically important attitude that will last a lifetime in their children. They were letting their kids know in no uncertain terms that what they admired and were most proud of were the effort, self-discipline, and good attitude their kids had shown, not to mention all the history they had learned.

So don't forget, Mom, that whenever your children make an effort—whether they win or lose—be sure to applaud and affirm the joy of their every endeavor. This maternal secret comes into play more often than you think, especially in today's hypercompetitive, over-trophied, performance anxiety–laden world.

The Importance of Acknowledging Your Child's Efforts–Not Just the End Product

Harold Stevenson, a professor of psychology at the University of Michigan, conducted several intensive cross-national studies to answer a question many Americans ask, "Why do Asian students do better academically than American students?" After hundreds of hours observing students in the United States, China, Taiwan, and Japan and interviewing their teachers, the researchers reached a conclusion: a critical key lies in what parents affirm about their children's learning. Asian parents strongly stress the value of effort with their children and affirm over and over, "Work as hard as you can, and you will be successful." Instead of affirming how much effort their kids put into their learning attempts, American parents emphasize, "So what grade did you get?" or "How many did you miss?" or "Did you win?" The effort a child puts into the process is not nearly as important to the American parent as the end product of the grade or score. And this difference in "affirming style" had a remarkable effect: the researchers found that on the whole, Asian children worked longer and harder than their American counterparts and handled frustrations and failures better overall because they had recognized that their success was based on their effort. What you affirm does make a difference.

So now seriously ask yourself this question, Mom: What do you emphasize: your kids' efforts or the end product of their grade or goal?

Is This Real Mom's Secret Part of Your Parenting?

It's perfectly fine to let your children know how proud you are of their endeavors. But if you always pile on the praise only for their final products (the score, the grade, the results), your children may pick up the wrong message: that all you care about is if they won, how they measured up against the other kids, or whether they took home the grand prize. What gets overlooked is your children's effort, the hard work, or the need for your encouragement when things don't always turn out perfectly. And believe me, those are the very lessons they'll need bouncing back from those inevitable hard knocks of life. So let's start by helping you recognize just how often you use this powerful secret in your family.

1. What are your priorities with your kids? Does overcompetitiveness seem to be a part of your natural temperament? How long have you noticed this in yourself? What about when you were growing up? Did your parents emphasize a competitive, win-lose concept or try to temper your quest to excel at everything? Was it effective?

2. Here are some other things to consider about your behavior. Check ones that might apply to you:

   ☐ Are you using your child to compensate for your own frustrated hopes and dreams?

   ☐ Is the emphasis in your family all on win-win-win?

   ☐ Do you praise, reinforce, and reward victory, and punish defeat?

   ☐ Is your child trying to live up to your expectations? Are those expectations realistic?

   ☐ Are you living in a community that is highly competitive, status oriented, and keenly ambitious?

   ☐ Is your family in a one-down position that makes your kid (or you) feel that he has to be the best at something to get that scholarship and succeed in life?

☐ Would your kids say that winning is the only way to gain your acceptance and approval?

3. Start listening to your interactions with your children. On the whole, would you say you are usually more affirming or negative to your kids? Researchers found that parents typically say eighteen negative comments for every affirming one to their children. How many negative comments do you think you say to your kids each day? Some moms actually track their performance for three to five days by keeping a running total of their daily negative statements. The point is, if you really want to change and become more affirming with your children, you must recognize how positive or critical you are with them right now. Is there one thing you can do to help you remember to acknowledge your child's efforts more? By simply counting your comments each day, you can test how you are doing with this secret and determine if you are improving your behavior. Are you affirming your child's efforts? Write it on the lines here. Then get ready to learn the secret and use it with your family. _____

_____

_____

_____

Five Steps to Building Self-Reliance and a Good Work Ethic

Step One: Develop a New Vocabulary. The kinds of words we say to our children can help them learn the value of effort and get into the habit of completing what they start. So here are a few phrases you can use with your child to stress how much you value her effort: "Don't give up!" "I know you can do it!" "Hang in there. Don't stop!" "It's usually harder at the beginning." "Almost! Try again." "You'll get it. Keep at it!" "The more

Affirming Effort

- *Create a Stick to It Award.* Marilyn Waters,
  a mom of four kids from Seattle, Washington, decided
  to emphasize effort with her four kids. In a spur-of-the-
  moment bit of inspiration, she cut off an old broomstick
  and printed "Stick to It Award" across the dowel with a black
  marking pen. She then told everyone to be on the alert for
  family members showing special persistence for the coming
  month. Each night before bedtime, she held a family gathering to announce the names of family members who didn't
  give up and to print their initials on the stick with marking
  pen. She also made sure to tell the recipients exactly what
  they did to deserve the award. Soon her kids were nominat-
  ing each other's efforts, and they decided to begin a family
  contest to see how long it took to fill the stick with their
  initials. Marilyn said her kids loved counting how often
  their initials appeared on the stick! Best yet, it reminded
  her to look for her kids' efforts and not just to focus on
  how things turned out in the end.

- *Develop a family effort motto.* Jennifer Kapler, a mom of
  three in Jackson Hole, Wyoming, conveyed the message
  about effort to her children so successfully that they spent
  an afternoon together brainstorming family mottoes about
  effort, such as, "Try, try, and try again and then you will win,"
  "In this family, we always do our personal best," and "It's not
  if you win or lose but rather how you play the game." They
  wrote them on index cards, and her kids taped them on their
  bedroom walls. Develop your own family motto as a reminder
  that a critical piece of your family code of behavior is always
  to do your best.

you practice, the easier it will be." "Keep it up—don't stop!" "The harder you try, the more successful you'll be."

Step Two: Recognize Your Current Response—Then Change It! How do you typically react to your kid's failures or shortcomings—you know, those moments when he doesn't meet your expectations or achieve the perfect score or get the goal? Yelling, shaming, criticizing, judging, ridiculing, or saying "I told you so" are especially deadly reactions. Here are three alternative ways you might try using to respond to your kid's shortcomings. Choose one and incorporate it in your behavior:

- Focus on what your kid is trying to achieve: "How did you want this to turn out?"
- Affirm your belief in her: "I know you can do it. Hang in there."
- Support trying again: "Just because it isn't easy doesn't mean you're not good at it."

Step Three: Emphasize Going for Your Personal Best. Take the focus off always trying to win and instead emphasize doing the very best you can. "How did you play?" "Did you do the best *you* could?" "What's the most important thing you learned today?" "Is there anything you wish you had done differently?"

Step Four: Don't Praise the Trophy. Praise your kid's hard work and effort, not his grade or gold star, so that he knows that what matters most in your eyes is his effort. "Earning that score took a lot of work and time. Good for you!" "Hey, you really were concentrating on the rink before you went into that spin; you really put everything you had into it." "Your recital wouldn't have been so wonderful if you hadn't put so much time into practicing that piece."

Step Five: Encourage Internal Praise. Many children have become so dependent on our approval that they don't know how

Instead of saying "I'm really proud of your work," say, "You
must be really proud of your efforts." Switching from "I" to
"you" takes the emphasis off of your approval and puts it
on your child's efforts.

---

to acknowledge themselves. A simple way to help them is by
pointing out what they did that deserved merit and then reminding them to acknowledge themselves internally (to use
"self-talk"). Here's how it works: suppose your son has had difficulty controlling his temper whenever he loses at his soccer
games. This time you noticed that he really made an effort to
use self-control and not blame everyone for the loss. During a
private moment, encourage him to acknowledge his success:
"John, you really made an effort not to say anything negative
about the other team today. You used good self-control. Did
you remember to tell yourself that you did a great job?"

Making a Promise to Yourself

1. How did you like the story of Diana, Kate, and the cheerleader moms? Was there anything about it that inspired you
   to apply this mother's secret of affirmation in your family?
   How would teaching internal motivation and instilling a
   stronger work ethic benefit your child's stick-to-itiveness?

2. How would you apply the five steps to building self-reliance
   and a solid work ethic with your family? Review all the
   boxes, guides, tips, and stories in this chapter.

3. Go to A Mother's Promise on page 56 and write in the one
   thing you will do differently over the next 21 days to help
   your child become more self-reliant and develop a stronger
   work ethic.

Five Instant Ways to Applaud Your Kid's Efforts Even When You're Not There

You left on a business trip. You had a late meeting. Your child fell asleep. Or you just plain forgot to affirm your kid's efforts today. Well, there are no more excuses—or guilt. Here are a few simple ways to acknowledge your children's efforts even when you're miles away or they're asleep.

1. *Lunch bag memo.* Write a little note on a paper napkin and put it in her lunch bag: "Selena, good luck today at your game. Remember, it's not if you win that matters, it's how you play the game. See you at dinner. Love, Mom."

2. *Kitchen notes.* Keep a set of magnets on your refrigerator to attach short notes: "Alex, Grandma loved your picture because she knew how much time you put into it. Love, Mom."

3. *Post-it message.* Keep a set of self-adhesive notes handy to stick brief messages to your child everywhere! "Your room looks great. You put a lot of time into straightening out that closet. Kudos to you! Love, Mommy."

4. *PillowGram.* Slip a message under your child's pillow: "Ben, I loved looking at your schoolwork today. I know the math is hard, but I saw how hard you tried. Sleep tight! Love, Mother."

5. *Photograph note.* Want a great way to use that new digital or cell phone camera? Take a shot of your child's effort: the bed finally made or his practicing shooting hoops or piano, and hang it on your refrigerator with a brief affirming note: "Saw you practicing out there. You're getting better with every shot!" Even a toddler will appreciate the photo and can see that you appreciate her efforts.

A Real Mom's Resource Guide

The Learning Gap, by Harold W. Stevenson and James W. Stigler (New York: Simon & Schuster, 1992). This is just plain fascinating reading about a longitudinal study conducted at the University of Michigan to try to determine why some students hang in there longer and handle frustration better than others. The results may surprise you: it's all about what parents emphasize to their kids. Here's the big clue: affirming your child's effort is more important than praising her end result.

The Magic of Encouragement: Nurturing Your Child's Self-Esteem, by Stephanie Marston (New York: Morrow, 1990). "Kitchen-tested" tools to enhance your child's self-esteem and positively affirm his strengths and efforts.

My Kid's an Honor Student, Your Kid's a Loser: The Pushy Parent's Guide to Raising a Perfect Child, by Ralph Schoenstein (Cambridge, Mass.: Perseus, 2003). Sharp observations, spun out in a humorous style, about today's parents obsessed with creating Superkids.

Positive Pushing: How to Raise a Successful and Happy Child, by Jim Taylor (New York: Hyperion, 2002). The author contrasts the old style of parental pushing that's overinvested in kids' grades and soccer scores with the positive pushing of parents who invite children to gain joy from their achievements.

Punished by Rewards: The Trouble with Gold Stars, Incentive Plans, A's, Praise, and Other Bribes, by Alfie Kohn (Boston: Houghton Mifflin, 1999). A stirring (and convincing) argument that affirmation must not be laced with the carrot-and-stick approach of rewarding kids' efforts but be deserved and oriented toward instilling internal joy instead.

Raising Confident Boys: 100 Tips for Parents and Teachers, by Elizabeth Hartley-Brewer (Cambridge, Mass.: Fisher Books, 2001). A wonderful compilation of practical ideas to help bolster a boy's self-image. Also by the same author: *Raising Confident Girls: 100 Tips for Parents and Teachers* (Cambridge, Mass.: Fisher Books, 2001).

Toilet Trained for Yale: Adventures in 21st Century Parenting, by Ralph Schoenstein (New York: Perseus, 2002). A humorous yet scathing look at parenting in overdrive and the effect it's having on our kids. Interesting reading!

Unconditional Parenting: Moving from Rewards and Punishment to Love and Reason, by Alfie Kohn (New York: Atria, 2005). Kids do best when given unconditional love, respect, and opportunities to make their own choices. In the end, says Kohn, we sure don't want docility and short-term obedience. Well said, and a great read.

A Mother Who Accepts Her Children's Shortcomings Nurtures Resilience

What Real Mothers Know: Support Your Children's Natural Abilities and Don't Stress Their Weaknesses

What Really Matters for Mothering: Be Accepting

The Real Benefit for Kids: Optimism and a Bounce-Back Attitude

The Lesson a Real Mother Teaches: Probably the one thing every woman wants most is a healthy child. We pray our kids will be blessed with good health, but we also desperately hope life will bring them happiness. Unfortunately, all too many children aren't dealt easy "life sentences." The array of difficulties might include autism spectrum disorders, learning disabilities, chronic illness, depression, or hearing impairments. But whatever the issue, real mothers know that some things can be changed and some can't. And real moms realize that accepting what can't be changed is a big secret to helping their children cope with their challenges and get on with their lives. And so these moms focus on ways to cultivate their children's natural strengths, skills, and talents and don't stress their weaknesses. The lesson their acceptance teaches their kids is the kind of powerful influence that nurtures a bounce-back attitude, hopefulness, and positive self-esteem. And they are the exact same traits *any* child needs to handle life with confidence and optimism.

"She Accepted Her Child as He Was"

> As a mother, my job is to take care of what is possible, and trust God with the impossible.
>
> —Ruth Bell Graham

At the end of his first week of kindergarten, my five-year-old son, Adam, came home very excited and declared to us all that he'd just met the "greatest new kid."

"His name is Max Englund, and he's my new best friend," he exclaimed. "Can he please come over, Mom?" he pleaded. "Pleeease?"

"How great you found a new friend, Adam." Curious as to what he found so appealing about this boy, I asked, "What do you like about him?"

"He's just so fun to be around. He always makes me laugh. We do everything together and like *all* the same stuff," Adam explained. "Can he please come and play?" he asked again.

"Of course Max can come over. I can't wait to meet him," I said in all honesty.

It's always interesting to meet your children's friends and see what attracts them. This boy sounded like a perfect companion for my son, who loved to have a good time. I didn't have to wait long.

The following week was my turn to carpool. I arrived at school a bit early, hoping to find Max's mom. Most moms were chatting while waiting eagerly by the kindergarten door for their children, but one was standing off by herself as though she didn't know anybody yet. I wondered if that could be her.

"Hi," I greeted her. "I'm Adam's mom."

"Oh, I'm so glad to meet you," she replied in this great Southern accent. She was drop-dead gorgeous. "I'm Bonnie Englund, Max's mom. He's been talking about Adam all week."

"The same goes for Adam. It's so great that the boys seem to be getting along so well."

"Let's plan to get them together some time this week," she said.

Just then the classroom door swung open. I quickly scanned a mass of five-year-old heads for Adam—and heard him before I saw him. His giggle is unmistakable, and he was laughing with another boy who I figured must be his famous "new best friend" whom I couldn't wait to meet. But I must admit that when I finally saw Max I was taken aback.

First, Max was darling: big blue eyes, a head full of blonde tassels, a sweet little cherub face, and a huge infectious Cheshire Cat grin that seemed to go from ear to ear: the kid was just plain adorable. What I wasn't prepared for was that Max was in a wheelchair and severely disabled. His legs were clearly immobile, and he kept his hands on the arms of the chair so that he could work the buttons on the electric motor. In all of Adam's conversations, that little fact had never come up. But my son was clearly oblivious to that detail: his only interest right then was making sure I met his buddy. And to achieve that goal he was hanging on to the back of Max's motorized wheelchair as his new pal drove him to me while both boys laughed the whole short way.

"Mommm!" yelled Adam. "Meet my friend, Max!"

Without missing a beat, Max waved at me happily. "Hi, Mrs. Borba!" he said. "Can Adam come over? We like the same stuff."

Within seconds I knew why Adam was drawn to this child. Max had all those attractive qualities kids (as well as their parents) like: he was fun, polite, kind, genuine, and "just plain nice." No doubt about it: this was the all-around great kid—exactly the type of friend a parent hopes for her child. His classmates obviously recognized those traits—each went out of his or her way to say good-bye to him. As I watched those kindergartners that day, one thing became very apparent: Max was a kid whose company they clearly enjoyed.

From the moment Max's doctors told his parents their son would never walk, they vowed to raise their child as normally as they could. And so Max did everything—almost everything—that "normal" kids his age did: there were swim lessons, Boy Scouts, sleepovers, field trips. Though Max had to undergo several painful surgeries and faced countless obstacles, his parents never excused him from anything nor made him dependent on them. That was how they felt Max would be able to "fit in" and live life to his fullest. His parents' standards would apply to any child: Max was expected to be polite, responsible, respectful, and cheerful.

The basic parenting philosophy they conveyed to Max was, "Yes, it's tragic that you're handicapped, but it can't be changed. So let's focus on the wonderful qualities you do have, what you *are* capable of doing, and the things you are fortunate to have." There weren't any special favors or treats because Max had a "rough night" (which he sometimes did); he was never let off the hook from homework or chores because he was confined to a wheelchair; and a "woe is me" attitude just wasn't allowed.

Adam's introduction to Max that week was the beginning of a close friendship between these two boys. I can't begin to describe all the fun times these kids shared, and the amazing thing was that Max's being in a wheelchair was never a problem. Thanks to his inherent cheerful personality and the great attitude of his parents, we all just loved Max for what he was. When he'd come over for a play date; he'd ask to be taken out of his chair, and I'd prop him up on the floor with some pillows behind him so and he and Adam could build Legos. And whenever he slid down or flopped over on his side by accident, he'd just smile and say in this darling little kidding tone, "Ah, Michele, can you put me up again?" And we would.

On Adam's sixth birthday he wanted a swim party with all the kids at the pool, and of course Max was at the top of his invite list. I was concerned. How could Max feel like he was part of the party when all the kids were swimming?

"Don't worry, Mom. Max can swim no problem."

Sure enough, as soon as Max arrived with his mom, Bonnie slid him into the water, where he floated face down. Whenever he wanted some air, he'd shake his head back and forth and someone nearby would flip him over.

"Oh, thanks," he'd say matter-of-factly. "I was almost out of breath." Then he'd float on his back awhile. The point for him was to be in the pool with all his friends, and to be sure that he could, Bonnie had taught him how to float.

The next year, when the big "in-crowd" kid craze was to decorate the spokes of your bicycle with bright, colorful plastic reflectors, Bonnie did the same for Max's wheelchair. So he zipped around the neighborhood and schoolyard as flashy and shiny as everyone else.

For most of us, Max's wheelchair really became invisible. Patty Service, Bonnie's neighbor, recalled how her five-year-old, Pat, came running into their house after school one day frantically looking for her. "I just heard a terrible thing about Max," her son cried. "Some kids in my school said he's handicapped!" Then Pat added, "He's my friend, Mom. We play together every day. Why didn't anybody tell me he was handicapped?"

Those years created cherished memories for me, and that's because your children's best friends often hold such a special place in your heart. Everyone in our family loved Max: we'd always tell him (half kidding, of course) that any time his parents wanted to get rid of him, we'd adopt him. No chance on that one though; his parents adored him.

Of course, life wasn't always so easy for Max. He made regular visits to the doctor and was hospitalized several times. He also endured a few painful surgeries. I'm sure there were even more difficulties that we never even heard about. But none of this burden ever dampened his spirit, optimism, or positive outlook on life.

Don't get me wrong: Max wasn't a little angel with a permanent halo. Max was a regular kid, and his mom wouldn't let him get away with anything. I remember one time his little brother, Graves, made some crack that upset Max, and he tried to run Graves over with his wheelchair.

"Max Englund," his mother said firmly. "Stop that immediately and apologize to your brother." Which of course Max did right away. Bonnie had high expectations for courtesy and behavior, and there were no excuses.

As time went by and Max felt more comfortable, he shared some of his disappointments with us. His secret dream, he once told me, was to walk: "Sometimes I dream I can fly," he'd say. "Then I'll be like the other kids." But of course he knew that this was one dream that could never come true.

What made Max different from many kids is that he was able to handle his frustrations when he couldn't do things other kids could. He had a glorious sense of resiliency: even when the going got really rough, Max could bounce back and always seemed to keep a positive outlook about life.

All the fun, carefree days of a fond friendship between Adam and Max continued through the years. Their times at Katherine Finchy Elementary School were soon over: the boys were older, and now it was "big stuff," so they were off to Raymond Cree Middle School. Then one terrible afternoon in February when the boys were in sixth grade, I got a phone call that jarred our lives.

Bonnie's friend, Judy Baggott, was sobbing so hard I could barely make out her words. "Max passed away unexpectedly this morning," she said. "His lungs just finally gave out. They couldn't save him." Max was only eleven years old.

I can still remember that exact moment when I heard the news—it was as though all the air was sucked out of me. I was hit with such overwhelming sadness, it took a minute or two until I could breathe. Adam was devastated—at first he couldn't say anything and then he walked around the house in a daze for three days. I noticed when I went into his bedroom that he'd pinned up a photograph of him and Max when they were in kindergarten, dressed in their Tiger Cub outfits—orange and white T-shirts, bright orange baseball caps, a tiger cub patch on the crown—arms around each other and those big, big grins of theirs.

But none of us could even begin to fathom how Max's parents could deal with such a loss—the obvious depth of their grief was just beyond comprehension.

It's been almost twelve years since Max passed away; this would have been the year he graduated from college. I was going through my son's old school scrapbook recently and found photos of Adam with Max that seem like they were taken only yesterday: that special kindergarten class and that very first time I met him (I can still hear Adam say, "Mom, meet my friend, Max!"), their Lego building extravaganzas, all those great birthday parties they attended. How could that have been so long ago? One picture took me back: there was Max with his infectious great smile eating his favorite chocolate ice cream that he loved so much. As usual, chocolate was smeared all over his little face. ("Do you have any chocolate ice cream, Michele?" he'd ask me in that kidding tone. He knew I always had some in the freezer saved just for him.) I wiped away the tears that always come when I think of this child.

I swear that Max came to our lives as a gift. So I can now honestly say that the more I think about this child today, the more I know how blessed we were to have known him. I know I'm not alone in that feeling.

I remembered a conversation I once had with Bonnie about Max. "If you could give a parent one piece of advice, Bonnie, what would it be?"

"I know exactly what I'd say," Bonnie said. "I'd tell parents that when your child is given a life sentence, you make sure you live each day you spend together as though it's your last one. That's what we always tried to do with Max."

So here's to you, Max. What a treasure you were in our lives.

A plaque on the wall of Raymond Cree Middle School reads:

In Memory of Our Friend, Max Englund
July 1, 1982–Feb 18, 1994
And all children who have left us before their time
Dedicated June 9, 1994, by the RC Class of 1996

What Real Moms Can Learn from This Story

Bonnie Englund is an extraordinary mother, but, knowing her, when she reads this she'll probably say, "No, I'm not. It was Max. He was our gift from God." I can't disagree, but nevertheless we can all learn something from how she and her husband raised their son.

Max was born with special needs that gave him only eleven short years of life. But his parents accepted his weaknesses and made sure that they never got in the way of his potential for friendship, fun, education, activities, joy, humor, human love and acceptance, warmth and connection. Max was a well-adjusted child who truly fulfilled his potential as much as possible.

Not all of our kids have special needs, but certainly all of them have weaknesses. And it's our role as moms to accept our kids' inherent shortcomings, acknowledge what can and can't be changed, then support their resilience in fulfilling their many strengths. Too many mothers react to the human reality of their children—which always includes something they're not good at—by overreacting and mounting a campaign against every single potential weakness. What they must come to grips with is the plain and simple truth that there are some things we can change and some things we cannot. A key secret of a real mother is that she focuses on her children's strengths and accepts their weaknesses. Heaven knows we all have them.

The Law of Compensation

Victor and Mildred Goertzel studied the childhoods of four hundred creatively gifted and talented individuals, including such names as Einstein, Schweitzer, Gandhi, Roosevelt, Churchill, and Edison. The researchers were startled to discover that three-fourths of these prominently gifted individuals had tremendous handicaps in their lives, including troubled childhoods, emotionally fragile or alcoholic parents, and serious learning problems. What helped them compensate for their handicaps and become so successful? From an early age, each individual had a "significant someone" help him recognize a hidden talent he possessed and then encouraged its development.

Stresses and handicaps are facts of life. Though we cannot eliminate childhood pressures, we can *minimize* their impact by nurturing our children's talents and strengths.

Now think about your child: What stresses, handicaps, or limitations does she have? What existing talents and strengths can you nurture to help minimize her weaker areas?

Is This Real Mom's Secret Part of Your Parenting?

To support your children's natural talents and abilities and not stress their weaknesses, the first thing you need to identify is where they're strong and where they're not. Your goal is to answer the question, *What makes my child special and unique?*

1. The checklist here provides one hundred strengths and qualities you can review to get you started. Check off those

you feel best describe your child's innate skills or talents. *Make sure these strengths are already present in your child and not ones you wish were there.* When you've identified your child's positive qualities, write them down. Keep the list handy; you'll use it throughout this chapter. As you discover new attributes, add them to your list.

Visual Talents

☐ drawing
☐ photography
☐ recall for details
☐ painting
☐ active imagination
☐ visualizes
☐ map skills
☐ directionality
☐ daydreams

Logical/Thinking

☐ computer skills
☐ organized
☐ problem solver
☐ abstract thinking
☐ math and numbers
☐ thinking games
☐ deciphers codes
☐ common sense
☐ science
☐ quick thinker
☐ learns quickly
☐ keen memory
☐ knowledgeable
☐ intelligent

Bodily Kinesthetic and Physical Strengths

☐ role playing
☐ acting
☐ creative movement
☐ dancing
☐ dramatics
☐ specific sports
☐ running
☐ athletic
☐ strength
☐ graceful
☐ endurance
☐ balance
☐ dexterity
☐ coordinated

Musical Talents

☐ instrument
☐ singing
☐ rhythm
☐ remembers tunes
☐ composes music
☐ reads music
☐ responds to music

Personality Traits

- ☐ creative
- ☐ initiative
- ☐ follows through
- ☐ trustworthy
- ☐ patient
- ☐ reliable
- ☐ sensitive
- ☐ courageous
- ☐ caring
- ☐ hardworking
- ☐ adaptable
- ☐ easygoing
- ☐ responsible
- ☐ generous
- ☐ confident
- ☐ independent
- ☐ neat
- ☐ determined
- ☐ truthful
- ☐ insightful
- ☐ gentle
- ☐ mature
- ☐ happy
- ☐ open
- ☐ prompt
- ☐ optimistic
- ☐ loyal
- ☐ serious
- ☐ honest
- ☐ disciplined
- ☐ affectionate
- ☐ strong character
- ☐ faithful

Social Skills

- ☐ friendly
- ☐ leader
- ☐ helpful
- ☐ good natured
- ☐ sportsmanlike
- ☐ courteous
- ☐ fair
- ☐ takes turns
- ☐ team player
- ☐ cooperates
- ☐ shares
- ☐ empathic
- ☐ understanding
- ☐ peacemaker
- ☐ fun
- ☐ charming
- ☐ encouraging
- ☐ humorous
- ☐ good listener
- ☐ likable

Linguistic Talents

- ☐ reading
- ☐ vocabulary
- ☐ speaking
- ☐ remembers facts

- [ ] creative writing
- [ ] poetry
- [ ] debate
- [ ] joke telling and humor
- [ ] storytelling

Physical Appearance

- [ ] neat
- [ ] attractive
- [ ] good posture
- [ ] special feature

Nature and Outdoor Abilities

- [ ] observer
- [ ] loves animals
- [ ] curious
- [ ] hiking
- [ ] science collections

2. Next, consider your child's existing limitations. Some things you can change, but some are what I call "givens." They're part of the Russian roulette of the gene pool—that shyer, quiet disposition; the short, gawky physique. Sure, you can help your shyer, introverted kid feel more comfortable in a group, but chances are slim she'll become Miss Social Butterfly; you can help your tense and anxious child learn to relax, but chances are that he'll never turn into the laid-back kid you hoped for; you might have had dreams that your child would be in a choir—like you—but he's tone deaf; Harvard was your dream for your child, but considering that your happy kid is struggling with learning disabilities, despite all the tutors in the world, an Ivy League scholarship is highly unlikely. Jot down any revelations you may have just realized. Doing so will help you keep your expectations for your child more realistic.

3. What are the hot-button issues you're having trouble accepting in your child? Be brutally honest: we all have some. Put as asterisk by those areas you recognize are ones you can't change in your kid—they're *your* problems. Recognize that your child's strengths or weaknesses may lie in areas

that don't reflect your personal preferences, upbringing, or personality. This may take some real honesty, so take a pledge to look deep within yourself. These areas may be ones that cause friction between your and your child.

4. Now dig deeper and uncover the "why." Next, reread your notes and review your checkmarks. This may take some real soul searching, but the key is that you can't change unless you know what's at the base of your belief. What's driving the attitude that is causing you to be less than accepting of your child? Take an inventory of your needs, perceptions, and expectations. Here are a few things that can stand in a mom's way of fully accepting her child. Check ones that may be your "hooks"—ones that are pulling you away from being satisfied with who your child really is:

- ☐ **An Achilles heel.** Did you have particular limitations or weaknesses as a kid?

- ☐ **Unfulfilled or squashed dreams.** Had you always fantasized that your daughter would become a star gymnast?

- ☐ **Past traumas.** Did your mother always stress grace, but you ended up with a gawky kid?

- ☐ **Unmet needs for approval, recognition, or perfection.** You're hoping to bask in your children's glory.

- ☐ **Old feelings of insecurity and low self-esteem.** Perhaps you had these problems when you were growing up (you weren't popular, or people called you funny names), and you don't want the same thing to happen to your child.

- ☐ **Desire for social status.** You fear that a less than perfect kid will diminish your status with other moms.

- ☐ **Guilt.** Your child's shortcomings and limitations mean you're less than perfect as a mom.

- ☐ **Fallen expectations.** You expected your kid to go to an Ivy League school. Now your child is receiving less than perfect grades and scores.

5. How are your views affecting your child? This one is going to be tough, but the answer may well give you the "ah-ha" moment that shakes you up and pushes you to change. Look at your final list of strengths and weaknesses. Make this profound—write from child's view—"I wish my mom . . ." What's going to help you be satisfied with who your child really is? Good enough just as he is, thank you? A child's feeling of self-worth starts with her knowing that she is fully accepted for all that she is. What are the one or two things you recognize need changing in yourself right now so you accept your child for his strengths as well as his limitations?

6. What will *you* need to do to start the change process so you are satisfied with your child for who she really is? Write down exactly what you plan to do to start accepting your whole child for the unique person he or she is. The next section will show you how to use this ninth essential secret with your family. _____

_____

_____

_____

Three Steps to Unlocking Your Child's Strengths

Here are the three keys to unlocking children's awareness of their personal talents and areas of excellence that will help your child compensate for his shortcomings. Call them your child's unique "Pathways to Competence."

Step One: Choose One to Three Positive Qualities to Strengthen.

Look at your list of your child's strengths and positive traits. Choose one or two attributes you want your child to recognize about herself right away. Make sure the strengths are really present in your child and not ones you just wish were true about her. Jot down the terms you'll use you point out the strengths to your child. Use the same term every time you praise the quality.

Step Two: Find Opportunities to Acknowledge the Strength Frequently. At the beginning you can give one "strength message" a day; gradually work your way up to two to four strength reminders. Flooding your child with too many compliments a day is not valuable. They begin to lose their effectiveness and become too predictable. Be specific in your praise so that your child knows exactly what he did to deserve recognition. It usually takes at least three weeks for a new image to develop, so keep praising your child's strengths for at least 21 days. Here are a few examples:

"You are so graceful when you dance. Your hands and body move so smoothly to the music."

"You're very artistic; your drawings always have such great details and color combinations."

"You are so caring. I noticed how you stopped to ask that older woman if she needed help crossing the street."

Also let your child overhear your praise. Just acknowledge your child's talents to someone else while your child "eavesdrops" on the conversation. "Wait until you see Kisha's drawings today! She's so artistic. You'll love looking at her new pictures."

Step Three: Find Ways to Cultivate the Talent. Talents and strengths rarely develop by chance, but instead are cultivated and nurtured. Here are a few ways to cultivate your child's *natural* talents.

- Find classes, camps, or lessons related to the talent. Teachers, park and recreation programs, camp directories, and the Yellow Pages are possible resources. Offer this opportunity to your child.

- Seek out experts for advice on ways to nurture the strength.
- Find a mentor in your community who is proficient in the skill who can encourage your child's talent.
- Subscribe to a magazine that features the talent. Use your library and the Internet to find Web sites, videos, and books about the talent. Query experts by email. Ask the librarian for ideas and resources.
- Find opportunities to show off the strength. "Mr. Jones called to ask if you could please help the younger scouts with their drawings at the next meeting."

Two Quick Ways to Acknowledge Your Child's Strengths ⊘ REAL MOM WISDOM

1. *Frame the image.* Take a photograph of your child's special strengths in action. If your child is athletic, a good friend, and reliable, the photos might be of your child hitting a baseball, playing with friends, and taking care of her pets. Frame the snapshots and put them around your child's room, on the refrigerator, or right in the middle of your coffee table. Just be sure you describe her strength when you explain why you framed the photograph. Even if you forget to remind her of the talent each day, she'll see the image.

2. *Hold a strength talk.* Remind your child each night by having a one-minute strength talk. Hold your child's hand in yours and let each of her fingers be a reminder of one of her unique strengths: "You are good at so many things: you're artistic, kind, responsible, a hard worker, and have such a wonderful smile." One mom told me the "strength talk" became an evening ritual her kids loved so much that they begged her to write their special strengths on each of their fingers. She did—but used a permanent marker instead of a watercolor pen. It didn't bother her kids at all. They just went to school the next day and explained to the teacher why they had words all over their hands.

The Value of a Support System

Anamaria Jerald is a mom of three in Southern California. She and her husband, Jim, adopted two brothers, Johnny, four-and-a-half, and Joe, three-and-a-half, who had been in nine foster care placements over the past two-and-a-half years. Their biological parents were incarcerated. These boys had been locked for long periods of time in dark rooms, suffering from severe physical and emotional neglect.

Anamaria knew that parenting these boys would be very difficult, but wasn't prepared for their constant need to be held; the daily violent, loud, and frequent temper tantrums from their emotional pain; and the nightmare of bedtime. Anamaria felt she was making progress with Johnny, but continued to have a difficult time with Joe's behavior.

One day Anamaria was at soccer practice with her older daughter, Rachel, and reading *Endangered Minds*, a parenting book by Jane Healy. Peggy, another mom, noticed the book, which she had read, and started a conversation. After a brief discussion about the trials and tribulations of raising the boys, Peggy asked if she could help.

"We've been talking every other Wednesday since for the last ten months," Anamaria explained. "I tell Peggy what's happening with the boys, and what I thought I needed to do. She makes suggestions. And then we brainstorm and work on a plan for me to try with Joe. Peggy has kept me focused and real about the progress I was making and gives me perspective to see the changes, as small as they were."

If you're feeling overwhelmed in your parenting, you may want to consider getting yourself a support system: someone you can trust and talk to regularly to offer alternatives and a fresh perspective or just to be there for you. It could be a girlfriend, a grandparent, a teacher, or a parent coach. As Anamaria said, "Moms shouldn't be doing this alone."

Making a Promise to Yourself

1. Did anything strike an emotional chord for you in the story about Bonnie and her son, Max? Is this one of the secrets you want to focus on and tune up in your family? How would applying what matters most about boosting acceptance and focusing on strengths benefit your child?

2. Check out the three steps to unlocking your child's strengths. How would you apply them in your family? Review all the boxes, guides, tips, and stories in this chapter.

3. Go to A Mother's Promise on page 56 and write in the one thing you'll do differently over the next 21 days to cultivate your child's natural strengths and talents. Doing so is one way you can give your child the glorious gift of resilience.

A Real Mom's Resource Guide

Awakening Your Child's Natural Genius, by Thomas Armstrong (New York: Putnam, 1993). This book includes more than three hundred practical suggestions showing parents how they can play a pivotal role in helping their children realize their true gifts.

Bringing Out the Best in Your Child, by Cynthia Ulrich Tobias and Carol Funk (Ann Arbor, Mich.: Servant Publications, 1997). The authors describe eighty ways to focus on developing your children's unique strengths.

From the Heart: On Being the Mother of a Child with Special Needs, by Jayne D. B. Marsh (Bethesda, Md.: Woodbine House, 1995). In eye-opening narratives developed from their parent support group meetings, nine mothers explore the intense, sometimes painful emotional terrain of raising children with special needs.

The Good Enough Child: How to Have an Imperfect Family and Be Perfectly Satisfied, by Brad E. Sachs (New York: HarperCollins,

2001). If you've discovered that your child has turned out quite different from the kid of your dreams, these hands-on exercises, strategies, and anecdotes just might be what you need to become more accepting.

In Their Own Way: Discovering and Encouraging Your Child's Personal Learning Style, by Thomas Armstrong (Los Angeles: Tarcher, 1987). This is an excellent resource for helping you pinpoint and enhance your children's unique learning styles.

Nobody's Perfect: Living and Growing with Children Who Have Special Needs, by Nancy B. Miller and J. C. Dieterle (Baltimore: Brookes, 1994). There are tools in this book that are valuable to all of us, whether our struggle is parenting a child with special needs or handling an illness or crisis of any type. The opening stories by "the Moms" (four mothers who have children with special needs) about how they cope are especially wonderful.

Special Children, Challenged Parents: The Struggles and Rewards of Raising a Child with a Disability, by Robert A. Naseef (Baltimore: Brookes, 2001). Naseef, a psychologist in Philadelphia and the father of an autistic child, has written a guide to help the parents and siblings of children with disabilities learn what to expect and how to cope with the challenge, particularly its emotional aspects. Strong and personal.

You Will Dream New Dreams: Inspiring Personal Stories by Parents of Children with Disabilities, by Stanley D. Klein and Kim Schive (New York: Kensington, 2001). Compiled by a clinical psychologist and a former editor of *Exceptional Parent* magazine, this book offers emotional support to the families of children with disabilities and should help educators and health care professionals better understand these parents' perspectives.

A Mother Who Takes Time for Her Children Helps Them Build Strong Relationships

What Real Mothers Know: Do Whatever It Takes to Maintain a Connection with Your Children

What Really Matters for Mothering: Stay Engaged

The Real Benefit for Kids: Healthy and Loving Attachments

The Real Lesson a Mother Teaches: Real moms know that long after you've cut that umbilical cord, you're still always attached to your kids. In fact, one of the miracles of mothering is that regardless of whether or not our kids are physically with us, they are still part of our every waking moment and always in our hearts. A real mother knows *how* to be involved—but not too involved—so that her relationship with her kids is healthy and strong, not smothering or micromanaged. A real mom knows *how* to allow her kids their own space and room to grow and also *when* she should be more involved. That's because she's tuned into her kids and understands those subtle signs that usually only a mother knows. She also realizes there may be times when that precious mother-child bond isn't as strong as she would hope it to be, and that it may even be temporarily severed. That's when she does everything possible to maintain a positive influence on her child and rebuild her relationship. The lesson it teaches her child is powerful: "My mother loves me no matter what and will never give up on our relationship."

"She Never Gave Up!"

The best thing to spend on children is your time.
—Joseph Addison

Greg Mattlin's parents were divorced when he was fourteen years old. His mother, Sara, worked as producer for a talk radio show in the Midwest. I want to tell their story myself because Sara told it to me personally, and it touched me so deeply.

Regardless of where we live, how many kids we have, or whether we're a married mom, single mom, stepparent, or foster mom, all we parents share one common wish: a happy, loving family. Deep down, we also share similar dreams. You know the ones: the nighttime scene in which our family is seated around the dinner table talking, laughing, and enjoying one other; the weekend outings in which our kids can't wait to be with us and drop everything so they can; the evening chats where our children gather lovingly around us and share their deepest thoughts and secrets. But of course, family life is far from always being so picture-perfect.

So let's be honest: life with the kiddies isn't always a bowl of cherries. In some cases, family life is not only difficult but heartbreaking. Regardless of the reason, parent-child interactions can sometimes be stressful and strained. In the worse cases, the relationship can shut down entirely. And that's the exact type of situation I was discussing on a radio talk show one day.

I love doing guest spots for radio: I sit at home, phone in one hand, coffee cup in the other, and discuss a variety of parenting topics. The producer usually calls me a few minutes before the show airs, tells me where the show is based (which could be anywhere in North America), and the name of the host. Next, I'm put on hold a few minutes until the host comes on the line and then—depending the show—I'm on the air talking about parenting for ten minutes to an hour.

My favorite time is when the parents call the station to ask for advice. And by the large volume of listeners who called the station that day wanting help, I realized that a substantial number of parents were dealing with some very tough family issues. Their stories were always troubling and often quite heartbreaking, but regardless of their situation, each and every caller always had the same wish: to find a way to restore her relationship with her child so that they could be a whole and happy family once again.

That day I talked to several callers and offered suggestions; then it was time for the station's news break. Usually that's the time the show's producer comes on the line and tells me she's going to put me on hold until the break is over—about five minutes or so. This time things were a bit different: the producer did come on, but instead of putting me on hold, she began talking while the news aired. She said her name was Sara Mattlin, and she wanted to let me know how much she was enjoying the segment and hearing my advice.

It was obvious that Sara had something she wanted to share, so I waited a bit and then it came. She explained that she had a story that might help these callers. She didn't feel comfortable telling it on the air, but maybe I could relay it somehow to them? So I listened to what Sara had to say, and by the time the news break was over I had goose bumps from her story.

This mom said she identified with so many of the parents calling in that day because she also had had a really tough time with her son. She and her husband had gone through a difficult divorce, and things turned nasty. Though Sara was elated to be given custody of Greg, her then fourteen-year-old son, he had quite different feelings. Greg blamed Sara for the divorce and for "destroying his father." He also was quite adamant about one thing, Sara said: "My son didn't want anything to do with me. He'd live with me only because the judge said he had to, but it didn't mean he had to love me anymore or even talk to me."

Sara had obviously gone through a heart-wrenching ordeal and could barely get through her story. Just recalling the time was like reopening her emotional wounds. She'd really tried to work things out with her husband. They'd tried counseling and even reconciled a few times, but just couldn't live together. But the last thing she wanted was her relationship with her son to suffer—she loved him so—but the boy couldn't understand why his parents couldn't be together. Despite all his mother's repeated attempts to explain, the boy refused to talk to her.

"I just didn't know what to do," Sara explained. "I tried everything I could think of, but my son wouldn't even acknowledge my presence. But I couldn't let him think I didn't love him. He's everything to me—he's my life! So one day I made up my mind that I had to do something to let him know I wasn't giving up on him. I decided to write him a note every day—not a long one—just a short little message jotted on a Post-it," Sara told me.

"One day I might tell him good luck on his soccer game, or another day I'd encourage him to bring his friends over. Sometimes I'd just write and say I missed talking to him. I don't think I ever wrote more than I few sentences, but I'd always end with 'I love you always, Mom.'"

"I must have written dozens of those notes," she said. "I'd tape them to his bathroom mirror every evening, but Greg never said anything about them." Sara paused a second, then softly added more to herself than to me, "That was okay. I just wanted him to know I was always there for him, and would never stop loving him—no matter what."

The mother said that she continued writing the notes each day for weeks, until one day something happened. "I was late for work," she explained, "and couldn't find the garage remote. I was searching frantically everywhere. I had a really important meeting I had to make, and the only place I hadn't looked was my son's bedroom. Greg had already left for school, and I never go in his room without asking him. In fact, I hadn't been in his room in weeks. Sometimes my kid borrows the remote when he forgets his house key, so I assumed that maybe Greg had it. It was worth checking out, anyway.

"I walked in—I remember thinking that the room looked like it had been hit by a hurricane. CDs were all over the floor, dirty laundry piled high on the bed, books and papers scattered everywhere. I quickly looked in his closet, pulled open a few drawers, searched the floor, but wasn't having any luck. I was running out of time, and the only place I hadn't checked was under his bed. So I bent down and pulled up the bedspread, and that's when I saw an old cigar box. I think my heart actually stopped for a second—the air sort of went out of me. All sorts of horrible thoughts passed though my head: I was certain I'd open the box and find drug paraphernalia, alcohol, pornography—you name it.

"I really don't know how long it took me to finally get the guts to open the darn lid, but I know I sat there awhile. Finally I just lifted the lid—and I gotta tell you, I almost died. Inside that box was every note I'd ever written. Can you imagine? Greg had saved every single Post-it. I figured he'd thrown them all away: he'd never said anything about them. But oh no, he had them all piled neatly inside that cigar box. I remember holding that box tightly to my chest and just sobbing."

I have to tell you: at this point I was crying with Sara. "So how are things between you and your son now?" I asked hesitantly. And through the phone I could almost see this mom smile.

"Just great!" she said. And then added quickly: "Oh, it took a little while to work things through, but I decided to let Greg know I'd found his cigar box. I was afraid that he'd accuse me of trespassing, but I'm so glad I did anyway. I waited for him to come home that day and then at the right moment, I showed him the box. Greg turned completely white, and then the strangest thing happened: he started crying.

"I couldn't figure for the life of me why he was so upset until it finally came out, and he confided what had been going on with him those weeks. Turns out that my kid thought he was the one who caused our divorce. All this time Greg was blaming himself for our marital problems. His father and I were always arguing, you see, and my son thought we were arguing about him. He says to me, 'I made you guys break up. Don't hate me, Mom! I'm so sorry!'

"Can you believe it?" Sara said. "All this time, Greg wasn't talking to me because he thought I blamed him for our divorce." Then she paused and quietly added: "Thank God I wrote those notes. What if I didn't have a healthy relationship with my son?"

Just then, the news break was over, and the host came back on the line to tell me the switchboard was flooded with callers. The last words I heard from Sara were, "You just tell those parents to never give up. Five seconds to air."

And that's exactly what I did.

What Real Moms Can Learn from This Story

My radio producer friend, Sara, taught me how important it is to hang in there no matter how bad things seem to be going with our kids. Being a mother is not for the faint of heart. As much as we'd wish, there will be times when our relationship with our children may take a dip, suffer, or even shut down.

When confronted with a daunting obstacle like this, some mothers panic. They try to find convenient alternatives, comb the books, seek out experts, and if things don't work immediately, they throw in the towel. But sometimes it's just a matter of patience, time, and perseverance. A little dogged determination never hurts. This is what real mothering is all about.

Just remember: it's *never too late* to restore a loving relationship with a child. And there's nothing more important for a child to have. It will be the basis for all his future relationships. No, it's not easy. In fact, at times it may be discouraging and heartbreaking, and the final outcome may not always fit your dreams. But not to try would be an even greater tragedy. So don't give up, and do whatever it takes to stay involved and permanently engaged in your child's life.

REAL MOM ALERT

Why You Should Stay Involved: What the Research Shows

Swedish psychologists Mary Margaret Kerr and Hakan Stattin studied over a thousand fourteen-year-olds and their parents. What they found was that the more the parents knew about what their kids did, the better adjusted the kids: they were less delinquent, had fewer school problems, less depression, more positive expectations of life, more positive peers, and better relations with parents. The researchers discovered that it was those "spontaneous little disclosures"—those unplanned little nuggets of information that kids blurt out to their parents—that explained more of what was really happening in kids' lives than all the efforts parents made to monitor their kids or pry information out of them. And the more involved the parents were in their kids' lives, the more likely the kids were to share. The bottom line: not only does staying involved produce better-adjusted kids, but the very relationship keeps kids out of trouble. In fact, kids who feel that their parents are trying to control them by constantly monitoring their every move have worse relationships with their parents than kids who feel their parents trust them. In other words, Kerr and Stattin explain, "It is not so much what parents do, but what their kids tell them about" that makes the real difference. And that's what real mothering is.

Is This Real Mom's Secret Part of Your Parenting?

Let's get something straight: relationships are always tough. And any mom with more than one child will admit that some kids are just easier to raise than others. But that's not what this is about—mothering is going to be tough, especially when one of our children is more challenging. Mothering is a life sentence, and of course we love our children and hurt when they're hurting. So let's dig a little deeper; let's explore what could be causing the pain or the rift in your relationship; and most important, let's find a way to restore your relationship with your child. The first part is going to mean that you'll have to reflect honestly about what's going on and then promise yourself that when you finish this section you'll commit to making one little change in *yourself* to start the change in your child. Ready?

1. How would you describe your present relationship with your child? Is this an all-out war, a once-a-week battle, just subtle friction—or have you two stopped the relationship altogether? I'm only asking these questions to help you get some perspective on things.

2. So what's the problem? If you could think back on the last few battles, are they generally about the same things? Can you predict, for instance, what will cause the next confrontation?

3. When did the friction or breakdown in your relationship first begin? Is there any pattern to the problem? Can it be attributed to a certain event: a divorce, a move, an illness, a loss, a job change, stress in you, a problem with a friend? Is there anything that triggered it? Is there anything that you can change to help matters? And are you aware of which things you can change and which you can't?

4. Now let's think a bit more about your child: What behaviors concern you? What is he doing (if anything) that worries

you? Are there noticeable changes happening? What might the cause be? Here are a few possibilities: hormones are kicking in, substance abuse, troubles with friends (copying), illness, frustration at school, too much pressure, fatigue, stress, exhaustion, troubles with another adult, a major disappointment, lenient parenting. What is your best guess as to the cause? Is there anything you could do to minimize the problem? (For instance, you could hire a tutor to help him with the math class, arrange for a physical to ensure he's not anemic or depressed, eliminate extra activities that are adding to the stress.) What one thing could you do?

5. What about your behavior toward your child? Is there one thing he does that really rubs you the wrong way, irritates you, or is sure to cause your temper to flare? Are you aware of it? How can you stop yourself? How are you currently responding when your child exhibits that behavior? Do you roll your eyes, criticize, blame, shame, yell? When is the last time you were positive or said something nonjudgmental about him? Is there one thing you might do to respond differently so that the behavior doesn't cause such friction?

6. How well do you know your child—really know her? To let your child know you care, you need to take an interest in her life. For instance, how well can you answer these questions?

- **What's happening at school?** Her classes, her activity schedule, her teachers' names, what she ate for lunch yesterday?
- **Who are her friends?** Who does she eat with at lunch? Who does she hang out with after school?
- **What are her favorites?** Music group, TV show, movie star, sports team, hobby, DVD, song, meal, dessert, ice cream flavor, teacher, friend, jacket, place to go after school . . .
- **How much are you a part of her world, and how much do you let her know you are interested in**

her life? When is the last time you plugged into *her* world or walked onto *her* turf? For instance, when did you last sit and watch her favorite TV show *with* her? (You don't have to say a thing—just appear interested.) Have you ever asked her why she likes a certain CD or movie so much? Have you gone to her games or school events?

If you don't know about your child's life and had a difficult time answering some of these questions, what is an easy way you could get to know your child better? What is one simple thing you could do to let your child know you really are interested in her life?

7. So have you learned anything new about your child and yourself? What is the one thing you recognize in yourself that you need to change to be a more involved and caring parent? Write it on the lines here. Then get ready to learn the secret and use it with your family. _____

_____

_____

Four Steps to Restoring a Healthy and Loving Relationship with Your Child

Here are a few ideas to help you get started in making a healthy and loving relationship become a reality. Your goal is to reestablish a relationship with your child. Eventually you can dream of spending a happy weekend together. At the present you want to reopen your relationship and get him to open up for a minute or two longer. So think brief—no lectures—get real.

Step One: Find the Best Time to Approach Your Child. When is the one time your child is a bit more receptive? Preadolescents and teens, for instance, are almost always in different time zones than adults. I finally realized that trying to have a serious con-

Ongoing Parental Involvement Is Key to Your Child's Healthy Development

Laurence Steinberg is one of the country's most distinguished psychologists, a professor of psychology at Temple University, and author of *The Ten Basic Principles of Good Parenting*. He says, "The strongest and most consistent predictor of children's mental health, adjustment, happiness, and well-being is the level of involvement of their parents in their life. Children with involved parents do better in school, feel better about themselves, are less likely to develop emotional problems, and are less likely to take risks or get into trouble. There is nothing more important to your child's psychological development than your deep and sustained involvement. This is true whether your child is an infant, a teenager, or at any point in between."

versation with one of my sons before school was just certain to create friction. I swear the kid didn't physically wake up until noon. I also realized that the best time was at 4:30 P.M. in front of the refrigerator. And that's exactly where I placed myself one day, appearing as though I was putting dishes away while really finding time to connect. Identify the *best* (and worst) times to connect with your child.

Step Two: Temper Your Critical Side. What turns kids off very quickly is your being critical and judgmental. No shaming, blaming, or yelling. Watch your body language: no rolling eyes or shrugging shoulders. Make a contest for yourself: What's the longest you can go without judging or being critical? Time yourself and then keep gradually lengthening that time and changing your behavior.

Step Three: Find One Positive Thing. Just one! One of my girlfriends who was going through hell with her son told me she began by telling him he blew great bubbles from his bubble gum. It was the only thing positive she could find in her kid. You're looking for something—anything—that deserves recognition. No sappy, marshmallowy, sugarcoated praise. It doesn't work, and kids see right through it. Be brief and specific: "Thanks for feeding the dog. I appreciate it." (Say it like you mean it, Mom!) "Hey, nice haircut. Looks good." (Then walk on, and don't expect anything in return. Ignore any sarcasm or denials.) She's probably not used to hearing positive comments.

Step Four: Connect with Your Kid's World. Don't be a brontosaurus. I'm not suggesting you get a makeover and start dressing like a fifteen-year-old, but do take an interest in your child's culture. Read the movie reviews (so you can casually mention a new movie in town); look up game scores for his favorite team and drop them into the conversation ("Wow, the Giants sure walloped the Dodgers, didn't they?"); check the TV schedule for shows she likes ("*Gilmore Girls* is on tonight, right? I'll try to make sure dinner is served on time so you can see it."). At first, just gently drop little nuggets of information. Later it may generate a conversation when he sees you're interested in his world. Take an interest in her friends. At least take an interest in finding out who they are. Offer to store favorite kid food in the fridge, save pizza discount coupons, and make your house kid friendly.

Three Signs That You Should Worry and Seek Help

All kids can be irritable, want to be secretive, mope around, sleep through the day, and appear "alien-like." But when should you worry—really worry? Here are a few red flags that tell you it's time to pick up the phone:

1. There is a sudden marked change in your child's normal behavior that lasts longer than a few weeks. The behavior has become intense, persistent, or both and it troubles you. It might be anger; marked anxiety; blatant defiance; crying

and sadness; retreating from you or the family; spending more and more time alone; a change in sleeping or eating habits; changing friends; missing school; using drugs, alcohol, or cough syrup; showing a drop in school performance or having a tougher time concentrating; getting in trouble with school, the law, or adults.

2. Your child becomes preoccupied with death: drawing pictures or writing poems about death, asking questions about the afterlife or funerals, giving away personal belongs, constantly listening to sad songs or ones with lyrics about dying.

3. Your instinct tells you something is wrong. This is the one sign moms don't rely on nearly enough. Use your instinct. If you think something is wrong, chances are that you're right. Pick up the phone and get help. Do it.

Making a Promise to Yourself

1. How did the story of Sara and Greg affect you? Did anything inspire you to strengthen or rekindle your relationship with your child? What benefit will your staying involved and never giving up have for your son or daughter?

2. How would you apply the four steps to restoring a loving relationship with your child? Review all the boxes, guides, tips, and stories in this chapter.

3. Go to A Mother's Promise on page 57 and write in the one thing you'll do differently over the next 21 days to improve and sustain your intimate connection to your child.

Three Ways to Keep Your Relationship Strong

1. *Show you care.* Every so often, make her favorite meal, bake a batch of cookies and leave them waiting for him when he comes home, mark the calendar prominently with her school event, leave a positive note on his pillow or in his lunchbox, frame a favorite picture of her friend or pet and put it in her room. Let your child know you love him, but don't expect him to show his appreciation at first. Kids who are hurting usually can't give back because they're trying to handle their own pain. Give it time, Mom.

2. *Go for a nonjudgmental brief outing.* It has to be something your child enjoys. (Whether or not you enjoy it is a side issue.) It can be brief: a walk to the park, getting an ice cream cone. This is not about spending money and buying your relationship. Don't get tricked into that concept: give your child your time, not stuff. The key to the outing is for you to stay positive. Listen. Appear to genuinely enjoy or look interested in your child's world. Neutral spots are best for tougher talks: the mall, the park, a sports field.

3. *Find activities that you and your child can share.* Is it playing a video game together, going fishing, eating peach ice cream, reading *Harry Potter*, madly waiting for the next Star Wars movie, cheering for the same baseball team? Find something—anything—that you can do with your child that you enjoy doing together. Kids (especially boys) usually open up doing activities, not just sitting down and trying to "have a conversation."

Staying Connected

- *Find some common ground.* Marilyn
  Rouse, a mom from Springfield, Connecticut, was very
  distraught about her thirteen-year-old daughter, Tiffany,
  who was clinically depressed and severely anorexic. Marilyn
  swore she wouldn't give up, but didn't have a clue about
  how to get her daughter to open up. One day she followed
  her daughter on a walk to a nearby park and then sat. The
  mom pulled out a copy of *USA Today* she'd brought with
  her and read out loud a few interesting articles in the Life
  section. Her daughter never commented, but at least listened. For the next few days, Marilyn did the same thing.

  "After a several days, I could see a change in her—it was
  very small—but it was a beginning. Tiffany was interested
  and even seemed to look forward to me reading to her. I
  kept at it for almost two weeks until finally the breakthrough came: my daughter began talking about what I had
  just read. And that was like her clue to me: it was safe for
  us to talk together again. She's physically and emotionally
  fine now. And we also have a great relationship and talk
  about all kinds of things. But I can't tell you how grateful I
  am to *USA Today*. That Life section really did bring life back
  to our relationship."

  What seemed to do the trick for this mom was avoiding
  direct confrontation and finding a nonthreatening and
  neutral way to reestablish communication and bring the
  daughter out of her shell.

- *Read your kid's favorite magazine.* Jeannette Thompson, the
  mom of a middle school-age daughter from Tucson, Arizona,
  found that the best way to understand her daughter's culture
  was to subscribe to a hip preteen or teen magazine. She
  swears it became a great conversation starter to be able just
  to throw in little tidbits of info about Hayden Christensen,
  Lindsay Lite, Coldplay, or X&Y. A few current magazines are
  *Seventeen, American Girl, Sports Illustrated for Kids, Boys
  Life, Thrasher, Teen People, Elle Girl, Teen Vogue, Sweet 16,
  CosmoGirl, Justine, Discovery Girls,* and *Nickelodeon.*

(A word to the wise: do preview it first; a few are a bit on the racy side.)

- **Form a book club together.** Karen Dischner, a mom of two from Portland, Oregon, found a few other moms with daughters around the same age and formed a mother-daughter book club. It was a great opportunity to spend time with her twelve-year-old, Molly. The moms and daughters alternate meetings at one another's homes to discuss the book. Each month a different mom and daughter choose the book club's selection.

- **Start a private family read-along.** Marj Casagrande, a mom of four from Palm Springs, found a way to stay connected with her kids as they got older: she and her child would both read the same book separately and then discuss it together. Great discussions emerged. Here are a few of Marj and her daughter, Marcail's, recommendations of surefire popular book club reads for older elementary and middle school girls: *Are You There God? It's Me, Margaret*, by Judy Blume; *The Agony of Alice*, by Phyllis Reynolds Naylor; *Out of the Dust*, by Karen Hesse; *Shabanu*, by Suzanne Fisher Staples; *A Ring of Endless Light*, by Madeleine L'Engle; and *The Music of Dolphins*, by Karen Hesse. Other book club favorites these days are *Stargirl*, by Jerry Spinelli; *Hoot*, by Carl Hiassen; *Joy School*, by Elizabeth Berg; *Walk Two Moons*, by Sharon Creech; *Odd Girl Speaks Out: Girls Write About Bullies, Cliques, Popularity, and Jealousy*, by Rachel Simmons; and *"I'm Not Mad, I Just Hate You!"* by Roni Cohen-Sandler and Michelle Silver.

A Real Mom's Resource Guide

Hold On to Your Kids: Why Parents Need to Matter More Than Peers, by Gordon Neufeld and Gabor Maté (New York: Ballantine, 2005). The authors, two Canadian doctors, discovered one day that their children had become secretive and unreachable. Why? This is a profound read that lets parents know that the strong adult-kid attachment is getting lost in the shuffle. The authors contend that those play groups, pre-schools, and after-school activities are all grooming our kids to transfer their attachment from us to their peers. Poignant and powerful. Read it.

Is My Child OK? When Behavior Is a Problem, When It's Not, and When to Seek Help, by Henry A. Paul (New York: Dell, 2000). Every parent wonders what is normal behavior and when they should really worry. The author, an expert in children's mental health, offers reassuring words but also concrete ways to spot the differences between normal behavior and a true problem so that parents will know when to pick up the phone and get help. Also by the same author: *Is My Teenager Okay? A Parent's All-in-One Guide to the Emotional Problems of Today's Teen* (New York: Citadel Press, 2004).

Parenting Your Out-of-Control Teenager: 7 Steps to Reestablish Authority and Reclaim Love, by Scott P. Sells (New York: St. Martin's Press, 2001). This book offers comforting advice and solid steps to reclaim your control if you have a defiant kid.

Parents Under Siege: Why You Are the Solution, Not the Problem, in Your Child's Life, by James Garbarino and Claire Bedard (New York: Free Press, 2002). I'm a big fan of Garbarino's work, so I was especially delighted when this long-overdue book was released. Too often parents (and—let's get real—especially moms) are blamed for their children's problems. The truth is, there are some kids who are just born difficult and hard to raise. Garbarino helps you take a step back and examine your child-rearing practices and become more astute observers of your children's public and secret lives.

Teens in Turmoil: A Path to Change for Parents, Adolescents, and Their Families, by Carol Marym and Leslie B. York (New York: Penguin, 2000). If your child's out-of-control behavior is taking control of your family, this book might be the one to help you get everyone back on track. It also includes a valuable list of extensive descriptions of resources and programs to meet the needs of every family.

What It Takes to Pull Me Through: Why Teenagers Get in Trouble and How Four of Them Got Out, by David L. Marcus (Boston: Houghton Mifflin, 2005). Motivated by a personal quest, this Pulitzer Prize–winning author set out to report on four troubled adolescents at a therapeutic boarding school. The account is astonishing, but the transformation is fascinating as they slowly establish trust with their counselors and ultimately rebuild their relationships with their families. The underlying truth Marcus uncovers is really that of applying the habit of never giving up. Parents must stay actively involved and interested in their children's lives. Heed his words, Mom.

When You Worry About the Child You Love: A Reassuring Guide to Solving Your Child's Emotional and Learning Problems, by Edward Hallowell (New York: Fireside, 1997). A practicing child and adult psychiatrist who teaches at Harvard Medical School helps you understand why your child is unhappy or underachieving and when to worry; perhaps most important, this book will help you do what you can and stop blaming yourself. Very comforting.

Why Girls Talk—and What They're Really Saying: A Parent's Survival Guide to Connecting with Your Teen, by Susan Morris Shaffer and Linda Perlman Gordon (New York: McGraw-Hill, 2004). If you're having trouble connecting with your teenage daughter, this book might be helpful. It offers thirteen strategic solutions for the most common relationship challenges and gives you clearly stated lists of dos, don'ts, and try-not-tos. Also by the authors: *Why Boys Don't Talk—and Why It Matters* (New York: McGraw-Hill, 2004).

A Mother Who Laughs Teaches Joy

What Real Mothers Know: Take Time to Enjoy Your Family Life

What Really Matters for Mothering: Be Lighthearted

The Real Benefit for Kids: Happiness and Joy

The Lesson a Real Mother Teaches: Real moms know that a big part of creating a happy family is lightheartedness and genuineness: those simple, joyous, fun moments of just plain laughing and enjoying each other. Sometimes you can plan such moments, but more often they happen spontaneously, and you just have to tune in and go with the flow. And the lesson you teach your children by doing so is that nothing matters more than being filled with joy together. So don't be afraid to unleash your laid-back side, Mom, and let go every once in a while. Let your kids see a more lighthearted, relaxed you. It's what creates those cherished lifelong memories of a happy home filled with love, laughter, and a mom whom your kids remember as being fun. It also teaches your children one of the best lessons of resilience: to laugh and enjoy life.

"She Realized Her Family Needed Time for Fun"

*We should consider every day lost on which we have not
danced at least once. And we should call every truth false,
which was not accompanied by at least one laugh.*
— Frederick Nietzsche

From the moment her pregnancy test came back positive, Ruth Ginsberg sprang into action. Of course, she was overjoyed: she and her husband had been trying for four years, but she was also fraught with anxiety. She had devoured dozens of books about how to be the perfect mother, had interviewed everyone she knew about it, and searched online for the latest studies and trends on optimizing child development.

So first she called her husband, David.

"Quick, Honey, call Rodeph Shalom. We've got to get a slot in the preschool class of 2010 before it's too late."

Then she called her supervisor at Morgan Stanley, where she'd worked in the IT department for the past seven years, to resign.

That evening Ruth and David made a solemn pact to be the best parents, to give their child every possible opportunity to develop to his or her maximum potential, to provide every experience that would improve his or her chances for success in the world, and to spare no expense, time, or energy in pursuit of their child's happiness and achievement. After staying up all night making passionate plans for the future, David slept fitfully for only a few hours, as Ruth insisted they play a tape of Mozart's "Eine Kleine Nachtmusik."

"Don't worry, Honey," Ruth explained. "I've read all the research that says listening to Mozart will make our baby smarter."

After Sarah was born, Ruth was so much in love with her that she was determined to fulfill the pact that she and David had made. She began to write the names of every object around her on Post-it notes, then put them all over the apartment.

When David came home and just wanted to sit down, he'd have to pull the labels off the chair, the lamp, and then the TV set. When Sarah was six months old, Ruth was reading Shakespeare's "As You Like It" and flashing Baby Einstein cards at her.

On the rare occasion when Ruth and her husband were both away from the apartment at the same time, she was sure to hire Lupe from the second floor to baby-sit. She instructed Lupe to speak only in Spanish so Sarah could learn a second language.

All Ruth's efforts were paying off. By the time Sarah was one, a full page in Sarah's baby book was already filled up with words she had learned. By three, thanks to a giant Hooked on Phonics package from Sam's Club, Sarah knew how to read. In addition to starting preschool (at Rodeph Shalom, of course), Sarah was enrolled in art enrichment, Suzuki violin, and pre-gymnastics.

Everything was going according to plan. Sarah was a precocious child and seemed to flourish in the spotlight her parents shined on her. All their friends and family applauded the couple's superhuman efforts to help their child excel. But then Ruth discovered she was pregnant again. She worried about how she would keep up the pace with twice as much to do. David worried about having enough money for all these lessons and special programs and about how working more overtime and freelancing would keep him away from his family.

With Jonathan's birth, the Ginsberg's family life got pretty complicated. Aside from regular school, Sarah had to be taken back and forth to soccer practices and games, violin lessons and recitals, and ballet class. With David away all day and most of the night, Ruth was so busy with both children that she was usually asleep by nine o'clock and exhausted all weekend. There was never any spare time for just sitting down and sharing a leisurely family meal together. Everything was hurried. The only priority was "Is it good for the kids?"

As the kids got older, the situation only got worse.

"Sarah is showing remarkable talent and maturity on the Bach violin partitas," her music teacher reported. "With her musicality and virtuosity, she ought to concertize."

"If Sarah keeps playing so well," her coach told them, "she could easily get an athletic college scholarship for a Division I soccer team."

"Sarah is really an exceptional child," Ruth and David were told by her eighth-grade science teacher. "She definitely has Ivy League potential."

Ruth and David were so proud of what they had accomplished as parents. They had really fulfilled their goals for their children so far. But just when they wished they could ease up a little, the pressures only increased. With the chance for Sarah to get into an Ivy League school, they enrolled her in special after-school classes and private sessions with the coach. They continued in their passionate resolve to spare no expense and do whatever it took to help their kids succeed, even if it caused pressures and stress that led David and Ruth to quarrel about financial strains and give up even occasional family outings.

When Sarah was accepted at Dalton, the exclusive Manhattan prep school, her parents were jubilant, but Sarah went to bed early with yet another migraine headache. David was getting really concerned and suggested to his wife that they take some time together, maybe drive down and spend the weekend in Atlantic City.

"This family hasn't had a vacation together for years, Ruth," David pointed out.

"I know, Honey, but this just isn't the right time. Sarah has an extra soccer practice on Saturday and that big chamber music recital on Sunday."

When Sara was in her junior year, the migraines were coming at least once or twice a month. Nevertheless, she was elected class president and became editor of the yearbook. These extracurricular activities in addition to her music lessons and soccer practices required her to stay after school until at least five o'clock every day; sometimes she didn't get home to start studying until seven or eight at night.

The beginning of senior year was just plain madness. College applications, final SAT preps and tests, touring campuses for interviews, building up her community service hours for her résumé, writing college application essays, and keeping up with her academic, athletic, and music responsibilities devoured every second of Sarah's day. David noticed that she was also losing weight and seemed to have absolutely no social life whatsoever. But the moment Sarah's early acceptance to Harvard arrived, all their sacrifices seemed to have been worth it. That pact had paid off. Ruth wept tears of joy. Their little Sarah was set for life.

Late that night, David and Ruth sat on the old couch drinking a rare glass of wine celebrating the moment and looking through their old box of family photos.

"Here's Sarah with her first blue ribbon in preschool gymnastics," Ruth said to her husband. "She was so good, even then. And look at her holding that plaque for first prize, second-year violin. She was only five years old and what a darling."

"Yeah, yeah. And here she is winning the spelling bee in the sixth grade," said David, shuffling through dozens more pictures of their daughter with all her trophies, accolades, and awards. Suddenly he stopped and looked up with an anguished expression.

"What's the matter, David?" Ruth asked.

"I just noticed something. Look at these pictures, Ruth. Is Sarah ever smiling, is she laughing, does she look happy? Is there ever any joy in her face? No, she looks blank, like she's not even there."

"I know it was a strain, David. It was a strain on her and all of us. But she made it. She got into the top school in the country. Now all we have to worry about for a while is Jonathan."

But it didn't turn out that way. After a summer internship at a local genetic engineering lab, Sarah packed her books and got on the train at Grand Central to leave home for the first time. For a month or so, Ruth and David were relieved to have only Jonathan to focus on. With Sarah gone, they began to realize that Jonathan had a mind of his own. Jonathan resisted joining his high school basketball team, even though he was tall and the coaches had tried recruiting him. He also told his parents that all those service hours working at the homeless shelter his parents wanted him to put in for his résumé were keeping him from hanging out with his friends.

"Hey look, Mom. I've got great grades. I study my brains off, but give me a break. I need some time for myself and don't want to end up like Sarah."

"What does that mean? Sarah's at Harvard, for heaven's sake," Ruth exclaimed. "You should only do so good."

"Yeah, sure, Mom. She weighs less than a hundred pounds, and I can't remember the last time I heard her laugh. Come to think of it, I can't remember the last time I heard anybody in this family laugh. All I can remember about growing up in this family is working, working, working, trying to keep up with that stupid schedule you've made for us."

Ruth dismissed her son's concern, but only a week later there was a long-distance call from Mental Health Services at Harvard University in Cambridge. It was eleven at night, and the voice on the other end sounded serious.

"Mrs. Ginsberg?"

"Yes?"

"This is Dr. Rubicon. I'm sorry to disturb you at this hour, but I really need to talk to you about your daughter."

Ruth had to sit down and pass the phone to her husband. David sat quietly listening to the doctor explain that Sarah's roommate had brought her in earlier that day requesting help. Sarah had been experiencing crushing migraine headaches for the past two weeks, was unable to hold down food, and couldn't sleep. "She's told us she's feeling overwhelmed, cries all the time, and says it's impossible for her to study."

"This could be just typical freshman-itis, Mr. Ginsberg, but I'm concerned about depression and potential health problems brought on by her not eating for so long. I want to hold her for a couple of days and make sure that at least she gets some water and food in her."

Ruth could hear everything the doctor was saying and suddenly piped in, "But she can't miss class; it could ruin her whole semester!"

David looked aghast at his wife. The doctor quickly responded, "Mrs. Ginsberg, there are more important things than a semester at college. Your daughter's future health and happiness are at stake, and that has to be our priority."

There was dead silence in the room after David hung up the phone. He'd been haunted by those joyless photographs of his daughter for almost a year. Ruth kept hearing Jonathan's words over and over in her head.

"I can't remember the last time I heard anybody in this family laugh."

"What?" David said. "What are you talking about?"

"Jonathan told me that last week, and he was right."

That night, for the first time in eighteen years, Ruth and David revised their Big Pact.

A week later, they drove up to Cambridge with Jonathan and took Sarah, just released from Dr. Rubicon's care, out for a milkshake and a movie. As they were walking back to her dorm arm in arm, Jonathan noticed the orange and black decorations and pumpkins all over town.

"Halloween is coming up. Hey, let's go buy some masks."

Any other time before today, Ruth and David would have nixed such a frivolous waste of time. But today was different— they nodded knowingly at each other and followed Jonathan into a costume store. Jonathan was the first to pick—Spider-man, his childhood hero. David jumped in with a Richard Nixon lookalike. After going through the big bin slowly and carefully, Sarah chose Cinderella. Then the threesome looked at Ruth, curious as to her next move.

Finally, after much hemming and hawing, Ruth started walking around the store and picked out a big red nose and a large, curly multicolored wig.

"What are you going to be, Mom?" her children asked.

Slowly Ruth put the bright red ball on her nose and placed the big crazy wig on her head, and smiled.

"I'm a clown. I love you so much, and I know now that a big part of my job is to make all of us laugh, enjoy each other, and have fun. Don't you think it's about time?"

It was. They had fun, and for the first time they could remember, they all laughed together. There was joy in their family again, and Ruth vowed to keep it that way.

What Real Moms Can Learn from This Story

Ruth Ginsberg and her husband, David, were very hardworking, dedicated parents who obviously loved their kids enormously. They wanted their children to have more experiences and opportunities to succeed than their own parents had provided for them. So it's not surprising that they went all-out, making a pact that required huge sacrifices and ultimately led to their giving up a lot of the fun and pleasures of everyday life. They never gave Sarah a chance to be bored, to have an unstructured or unsupervised time for herself, to just be alone and wonder. Over the years, their whole family life became void of fun, frivolity, and laughter.

Of course, their first child, Sarah, fulfilled all their wildest dreams and expectations. She not only succeeded but excelled at every task she was given. But clearly she paid a heavy price. Her parents didn't see it at first, but Jonathan realized all along that her migraine headaches and joylessness were making life difficult for her. Sarah had been so focused and structured by her parents that she didn't know who she really was and couldn't cope without them.

It wasn't until Sarah left home and struggled to survive on her own that Ruth realized the full extent of her role as mother. She'd done well in many ways. Her daughter was on a good path and would likely have a hugely successful career. But Ruth needed to give Sarah something else and maybe something even more important: a sense of joy and memories of fun together as a family, of laughter, of silliness, and of just enjoying one another. In the end, for this family, love had to be translated less into work and achievement and more into laughter and enjoyment.

Is This Real Mom's Secret Part of **Your** Parenting?

Sometimes we get so caught up in our state of endless busyness and frantic schedules and time-paced lives that we forget that what really counts most with our kids are those simple little things we do that make their homes fun, comfortable, and happy places. These questions will help you reflect on how well you're meeting that objective.

1. What would your child say is the best part of living in your home? What are the best traditions you do together that are so fun she'll want to carry them on with her own child? The bottom line: What kind of memories are you creating for your children in your day-to-day existence?

2. What do you think your own kids would say is the one thing they wish they could change about your family? Could you make that change? What's stopping you?

3. When is the last time your family sat and just giggled and laughed? When is the last time you remember your family doing absolutely nothing?

What the Kids Tell Us

Suppose your children were asked what one thing they really wish they could change about your family. That very question was asked of eighty-four thousand students in grades six through twelve who recently completed a *USA Weekend* survey. What do you think most of the kids said? (Chances are it's the same thing your own kids would say, so think hard.)

It turns out that almost two-thirds of kids surveyed said they wished they could spend more time with their parents. In fact, more than two in five kids feel that time with their moms is rushed. What the kids said they wanted was not just *more* time, but more *relaxed* time. The kind of time a kid would consider as just plain "fun." No expectations. No stress. No frantic pace. Just relaxed, good ol' fun. It's the kind of time that creates family togetherness. That relaxed, carefree time is also what our kids crave and need.

4. What is one simple tradition or family routine you want to do to have fun with your family? Write it on the lines here. Then get ready to learn the secret and use it with your family.

_____

_____

_____

Nine Common Family Traditions That Create Happy Family Memories

REAL MOM WISDOM

1. *Nighttime rituals:* read a nighttime story; remind each other of the best part of the day; give hugs and kisses goodnight.
2. *Special greetings and ways to say "I love you":* rub noses for an "Eskimo kiss"; create your own family funny hugs.

3. **Celebration of successes:** hang a flag on the front door when something special has happened to a family member; use a "fancy" plate at the dinner table when a family member has done something to deserve recognition.

4. **Birthday memories:** each family member chooses his or her favorite birthday dinner menu, cake, outing, and song to be piped through the household as a birthday "wake-up" call. Some families even hang the family member's shirt on a flagpole or broomstick stuck in the front lawn to let the world (or at least the neighborhood) know it's that person's special day.

5. **Frivolous fun:** fly kites on Groundhog Day; play practical jokes on April Fool's Day.

6. **Sports and outdoors:** go fishing on Father's Day; be die-hard Giants fans together.

7. **Volunteering and service projects:** bake an extra turkey for Mrs. Jones at Thanksgiving; serve Christmas Eve dinner at the homeless shelter or help out at another, less "popular" time of year. Make a commitment to help a favorite charity as a family once a week or month.

8. **Enjoying each other's company:** spread a rug or towel on your living room floor, gather the troops, put on some upbeat music, and serve simple sandwiches, finger food, and boxed drinks. Who says you have to go somewhere to have a good time together?

9. **Family Game Night:** dust off the Chutes and Ladders, Yahtzee, Monopoly, Candyland, or that old deck of cards. Older kids might like Trouble, Uno, Kerplunk, Risk, or poker. Some families hold Family Game Night once a week for thirty minutes to an hour. Have an assortment of games and let a different family member choose what you play each time.

Research has proven that doing simple rituals enhances our feelings of togetherness and family belonging by almost 20 percent. What's more, those home traditions and customs also increase our kids' social skills and development. So what are you doing to preserve memories of your times together for your kids?

Four Steps to Creating Family Rituals and Increasing the Laughter in Your Family

When I surveyed hundreds of moms about what really matters in good mothering, family rituals and traditions always came up at the top of their lists. Why? Because they don't have to take much time or money, and they create joy and laughter in the family and wonderful memories that last a lifetime. Here are the steps to begin.

Step One: Begin by Making a List of New Traditions You'd Like to Start in Your Home. Let your brain go wild and allow your only rule to be "anything goes" at this stage. The wilder the idea the better. You might want to ask other moms and your kids for ideas. Also think back on your own family traditions when you were growing up and include any you're fond of. You might also refer to the ideas in the previous box to help jump-start your brain.

Step Two: Now Choose One Idea You Want to Begin With. It's best to begin with the simplest idea. One mom said she got into the habit of always putting on her makeup with her four-year-old daughter next to her. Another mom makes a tradition of taking her son out for hot cocoa after school every Wednesday. It really doesn't matter what the ritual is, as long as it's one your family enjoys doing together.

Step Three: Write Down the Tradition—Ink It. Put it in your Palm Pilot or include it on your weekly calendar. Tell your family. Saying and writing it add commitment. (You'll also have someone to remind you to do it.) Also, think through exactly what you need (if anything) to make the tradition work. Set a starting date. When is the first time you'll begin using it? Research has shown that the sooner you begin (suggestion: within twenty-four hours), the greater the likelihood that you'll stick to it.

Step Four: Plan It, Do It! Celebrate success. And keep at it. You're on the road to creating family memories. Please remember: the family tradition you create isn't something you take away from your child because he broke one of your family rules or didn't finish his weekly chore. Don't use withholding the tradition as a punishment: "If you don't behave, you're not going to be able to do Family Game Night with us." Traditions are sacred and must be consistently honored, whether it is every night, week, or month, or once a year. This is the stuff that is meant to bond your family and make you closer.

Simple Traditions Real Moms Use to Create Happy Family Memories

- *Hold a Do Nothing Day.* Julie Kessel, her husband, and two sons, in Houston, Texas, have a special family ritual that's easy and doesn't cost a cent: once a month they hold a "Do Nothing Day"; to celebrate it, they do—you guessed it—absolutely nothing. Well, almost nothing. They might play Yahtzee, watch a favorite family video, hold a leisurely breakfast, or eat favorite snacks. But friends, phone, fix-it projects, housework, and even chores are all on hold. All they do is decide which day it will be, and the whole family sticks to it. Julie explains, "We have one whole day to reconnect. The kids really like it because they have our full attention without any distractions. It's a great feeling."

- *Celebrate with music.* Judy Baggott, a mom of three from Palm Springs, California, uses special songs for specific occasions. Bruce Springsteen reminds their family it's the Fourth of July by singing "Born in the USA"; special carols (including "There Was an Old Lady Who Swallowed a Fly") bring in Christmas; and for birthdays, the whole house wakes to the Beatles singing, "Today is your birthday . . . gonna have a good time." Though her kids no longer live at home, their tradition continues: each family member still wakes up to the birthday tune, but now it's played over the telephone.

- *Upgrade family meals.* Catherine Ayala, her husband, and two daughters from Santa Rosa, California, started a family tradition when her daughters were young; it is a nightly family meal (or as often as possible), but with one little twist. "I had a dinner party one day," the mom explained, "and the girls saw my nice place settings, candles, and flower arrangement and wondered why I didn't do the same for them. They were right: Why should I treat my friends better than my own family? And from that moment on things were different: one girl picks a few flowers and sets the table with place mats, another puts music on in the background and lights the candles. Everything is set in a basket so it's really quick, but it sets a mood that helps us unwind and enjoy the time together." (If there is one tradition for creating family togetherness I heard most from the moms I interviewed, it's establishing regular family meals.)

- *Reconnect at nighttime.* Jane Turner Michaels started a special family routine with her three teens. They have a nightly family dinner and then everyone goes their separate ways for homework, meetings, and projects, and then at 9:30 P.M. the whole family reconvenes in the kitchen for a nighttime snack. "They'll be yours for twenty minutes," Jane explains. "It's also a great way to stay connected." Then everyone gets his goodnight send-off: a kiss, a backrub, and affirm their love for one another and it's off to bed (or in some cases, back to homework).

Nine Fast Ways to Put More Laughter in Your Home and Spruce Up Your Family Fun Factor

So how is your humor quotient, Mom? When is the last time you belted out a good, long belly laugh with your kids? Here are nine ways to bring a little more fun into your home.

1. **Start on a happy note.** How's your morning? The tone you set can make or break the day. So lighten up. Find what's causing the major stress (you can't find the keys, the backpack, the homework, the notes), and get organized: use a

hook in the door for the keys, a basket on the step for back-packs; set out lunch money the night before; plan an easier way to do breakfast—even have one kid set the table the night before.

2. **Hold a nightly giggle (or other fun tradition).** My husband started this tradition when he came home from work each night; our three sons were three, five, and seven then. After their hugs they'd run to the end of a long hallway. My husband would yell "Giggle Monster!" and each boy would run as fast as he could into my husband's arms for huge hugs, tickles, and giggles. Start your own family nighttime ritual.

3. **Read the Sunday comics—together** (or at least the funniest ones). Make a tradition of saving the favorite Sunday comics to read together.

4. **Start a cartoon bulletin board.** Cut out those cartoons, print out those funny emails, and put them up on the refrigerator with magnets. Some moms even slip copies of jokes into their kids' lunch boxes or tape them on bathroom mirrors or on their kids' doors. Fun to come home to!

5. **Change your voice message.** Brighten up that answering machine message. If I'm ever just a tad down, the fastest way to get me smiling is to call my girlfriend Jaynie Neveras, a mom of two teens from Atherton (whose phone number I will leave out); she has the cheeriest message I know. Some folks leave impersonations or humorous misidentifications. Listen to your voice message—does it give people the idea that you're a happy household?

6. **Watch classic comedy at home.** All those violent, dramatic, scary videos can wreak havoc and break down our funny bone. Check out those classic comedies. Pop the popcorn, slip the disc into the DVD player, and laugh together.

7. **Put on plays or skits, or dress silly.** Comedians swear that the best way they learned their trade was by putting on plays at home—funny ones that made the whole family

laugh. Mary Grace Galvin, a mom from Kalispel, Montana, had a hat box. I walked in on Mary Grace and her four kids (ages four to fourteen at the time) and couldn't help laughing: each was wearing a funny hat and giggling madly. She shared that it's sometimes the best medicine for turning a gloomy day around.

8. **Buy a good joke book.** Store it in the car for those long rides (or when you're ready to pull your hair out). One kid can be the joke teller (or "house jester"), and the rest of the family can guess the punch lines. Adam, my middle son, got so good at memorizing jokes that on one long family ride (an hour and a half), he told jokes nonstop that he remembered from his school carpool rides years back. I swear they are also great for boosting memory.

9. **Just do something silly—and not worry about it.** Celebrate the dog's birthday by baking him a cake. Every once in a while do something just plain different and fun: tape a dollar bill to the garbage can (and not say anything about it) to see who will take out the trash; eat dinner in reverse (why *not* have dessert first?); if you don't have pets, put candies from the door to your kid's room so he gets the hint to clean it (and if he doesn't, leave a note at the end of the candy); put an extra treat inside your kid's lunch pail. Just have fun!

Making a Promise to Yourself

1. How did the story of Ruth, David, Sarah, and Jonathan affect you? Do you think your family needs to focus more on having fun and laughing? Why? What would be the benefits of doing so for your children?

2. How would you apply the four steps to creating family rituals and increasing the laughter in your family? Review all the boxes, guides, tips, and stories in this chapter.

3. Go to A Mother's Promise on page 57 and write in the one thing you're committed to doing over the next 21 days to begin increasing joy and happiness in your home.

A Real Mom's Resource Guide

The Book of New Family Traditions: How to Create Great Rituals for Holidays and Everydays, by Meg Cox and Sarah McMenemy (Jackson, Tenn.: Running Press, 2003). Overcoat Day. Welcome Summer Party. Monthly Pizza Blast. Bus Stop Party. This book shows you the simple steps that help families fully cherish all those special moments and milestones, help heal the wounds of trauma and loss, and create the kind of celebrations that lead to everlasting happy memories.

Family Traditions: 289 Things to Do Again and Again, by Caryl Waller Krueger (Nashville, Tenn.: Abingdon Press, 1998). This is a wonderful compilation of simple ways to celebrate family togetherness.

The Intentional Family: Simple Rituals to Strengthen Family Ties, by William J. Doherty (New York: Perennial Currents, 1999). This book is a sensible, well-written guide offering tips that will help families build satisfying and lasting family ties.

The Joy of Family Rituals: Recipes for Everyday Living, by Barbara Biziou (New York: St. Martin's Press, 2000). This warm and inspirational book offers an array of "ritual recipes," from those that acknowledge ordinary routines (mealtimes, baths, bedtimes) to those that commemorate significant life passages (parenthood, new siblings, puberty) and special family occasions (birthdays and anniversaries). It also includes rituals for first times, last times, and hard times (losing a pet).

Little Things Long Remembered: Making Your Children Feel Special Every Day, by Susan Newman (New York: Crown, 1993). This book offers five hundred realistic, simple, and inexpensive ideas for strengthening family ties and fostering traditions that children will remember for a lifetime. Pick and choose from scores of ideas for parents who travel and for special circumstances, such as sick days, holidays, and birthdays.

Making Ordinary Days Extraordinary: Great Ideas for Building Family Fun and Togetherness (Let's Make a Memory Series), by Gloria Gaither and Shirley Dobson (Sisters, Oreg.: Multnomah Gifts, 2004) Complete with heartwarming vignettes about well-known Christian personalities, this charming book includes a wealth of creative memory-building activities.

Raising Emotionally Intelligent Teenagers: Parenting with Love, Laughter and Limits, by Maurice J. Elias, Steven E. Tobias, and Brian S. Friedlander (New York: Harmony, 2000). Especially recommended is the section on how to increase laughter in your home. For younger children, read *Emotionally Intelligent Parenting* (New York: Harmony, 1999) by the same authors.

A Mother Who Takes Care of Herself Holds Together Her Happy Family

What Real Mothers Know: The Best Thing for Your Family Is a Happy, Healthy You

What Really Matters for Mothering: Stay Balanced

The Real Benefit for Kids: Happiness, Optimism, and Security

The Lesson a Real Mother Teaches: Real moms know that they can't lose sight of their own needs. Taking care of those needs is what helps them feel rejuvenated so they have the strength to nurture and guide their children. So they give themselves permission to take time for themselves. Think about it: what your kids really need is a genuine, healthy, and energized woman who enjoys not only her family but also herself. And when you find the time to nourish yourself (whether it be your relationships, soul, body, or mind), your family will be more likely to appreciate the real you: an interesting, evolving, happier woman who loves them and loves life. The simple everyday examples of working in the garden, reading (or writing!) that great American novel, taking a computer class, meditating, writing in your journal, talking with a friend, soaking in the tub, taking an exercise class, dating your husband—they all teach children the importance of finding balance. It's a lesson they will need when they finally leave your nest and forge their own lives.

"She Knew She Had to Find a Better Balance"

Moms who take care of themselves first make the best mothers.
—Kelly E. Nault

"What kind of a mother is she?"

Barbara Kelly was the chairman of the mother-daughter book club that met every Wednesday night at 7:30, and she was really ticked.

"Out with her husband? Doesn't she know how important it is for her and her daughter to be here tonight? We're discussing '*I'm Not Mad, I Just Hate You!*'"

Barbara, Judy, and Patricia were huddled in the kitchen over the coffee pot so that their daughters couldn't hear what they were whispering about Cindy Cutler, their friend and fellow book club member. Barbara and Cindy had been the co-founders of this book club, which they started last year for a few seventh-grade girls and their moms who knew each other really well. The goal wasn't just educational, but more to give the moms and daughters a chance to talk about important issues like peer pressure and values before the girls went to high school and got swept up in the usual overscheduled pace of teenage life.

"Her priorities are really out of touch. Remember when she turned down the nomination for president of the PTA last month? And she was a shoe-in to get it."

"Can you imagine what an advantage to her children that would have been? We're on the board, and look how it's helped our kids."

"I really wonder sometimes about her idea of what a good mother ought to be."

The women were trying to keep their voices down, but didn't notice that their daughters were eavesdropping and hearing every word they said. Next day during third period break, Barbara Kelly's daughter, Meghan, cornered Cindy's daughter, Teresa Cutler.

"You should have heard what they said about your mom last night."

"What are you talking about?"

"When you didn't show up, the ya-ya sisters really nailed your mom for going out with your dad instead of bringing you to the book club."

"Get out! What's the big deal? It was a special occasion for them."

"Well, they thought she was being a bad mom—something about her priorities being messed up."

That night, after Cindy had finished helping her two younger daughters with their homework and tucking them into bed, Teresa found her mother in her studio working on a new Web site design for a freelance client. Ever since Cindy's husband, Brad, had had his hours cut back at the office, she'd been trying to increase her graphic design business. Ordinarily Teresa tried not to disturb her mom while she was working, but this was important.

"Have a minute, Mom?"

"Of course, Honey. What's up?"

"Well, umm . . . Meghan told me the ya-ya moms were badmouthing you last night because we didn't show up."

"Oh, come on."

"Yeah. They said you weren't being a good mom."

"Oh, for Pete's sake. I told them it was a special anniversary for me and Brad."

"What was it actually, Mom? I know it wasn't your wedding anniversary; that was in August."

Cindy sat back in her chair and smiled sheepishly. She even blushed a little.

"Your father and I always celebrate November twelfth."

"Why? What's so special about it?"

"First kiss," she blurted out. "We were under the waterfall out in Palm Canyon. We got drenched. It was hilarious. And we made this pledge to one another that we'd always celebrate that date—no matter what. I didn't know that the book club meant so much to you, Sweetie. You know I love being with you."

"It's no biggie, Mom. I know how it is with you and Dad. I just didn't like what they were saying about you."

"They don't bother me, so don't let it bother you. Give me a hug."

Cindy Cutler knew in her heart that she was a good mom. And for her, a big part of being a good mom was being able to sustain a healthy balance of focus on her children, her relationship with her husband, work, and herself. It wasn't always easy. But she'd seen how many of her girlfriends were going nuts trying to be Supermoms and spending all their time and energy focused only on their kids. So many carpools, tournaments, school events. Monday: scouting. Tuesday: violin and fencing lessons. Wednesday: soccer practice and computer lab. Thursday: jazz. Friday: math tutoring. Saturday: gymnastics and soccer game. Sunday: youth group. In between that were supervising homework, science fair projects, play groups, birthday parties, sleepovers, ice skating, and just trying to survive.

Cindy had tried to keep up with the other moms in their frenzied mania. She too had reached a point early in her experience as a mother where she had absolutely no time for herself or her husband, whom she adored. Not only that, trying to fit in time for her work as a graphic designer seemed totally impossible, though they could sure use the money. And the worst part was that she had been becoming tense and irritable and starting to take it out on her family.

One Sunday morning when her girls were ages six, four, and one, she had found herself in a screaming fit over the dumbest thing.

"DON'T YOU EVER SPILL JUICE ON THE FLOOR AGAIN! WHAT'S WRONG WITH YOU? CAN'T YOU DO ANYTHING RIGHT?"

And this was directed at her one-year-old!

That was the moment Cindy knew things had to change. She'd just seen one of her wannabe Supermom girlfriends yell the exact same way at her daughter, and Cindy swore she'd never become that kind of parent. She could see now that trying to do too much and be so perfect was bound to backfire. It wasn't good for the kids. It made the moms crazy, so the kids suffered too.

Things have to change, she had said to herself after she calmed down and kissed her one-year-old to make up. *From now on, I'm doing what's right for my children by taking care of my whole family. My kids will be best off in a happy, well-balanced home, and they don't need all that extra stress. I'm cutting back on trying to fill every minute of the week.*

From then on, Cindy was very careful about what she committed to for herself or her kids. She always made sure there was enough family time together. Because she knew being a good mom requires energy, strength, and stamina, Cindy led weekend bike excursions for the whole family. She made a new rule that the answering machine would have to pick up any calls from 6:00 to 8:30 each night so as to preserve everyone's sanity at family dinner, homework time, and tuck-into-bed time. And she began to take classes in graphic design when the girls were at school to give her some skills to help out with the finances.

Her new philosophy of motherhood began to pay off. Her girls were thriving, her relationship with her husband was great, and she even began to bring in some money on the side. She felt healthier, more energized, and was confident she'd made the right decision. So what if her girls didn't do every single thing all the other kids did? She didn't need to keep up with any Joneses, and besides, the activities her daughters chose were the very things they cared most about. As a result, each girl had developed skills and accomplishments they could be proud of. Teresa's artistic talents were blossoming, Kara was one of the best softball players in the county, and Noreen was becoming an exceptional dancer.

Every once in a while, another mother would shake her head when Cindy declined to participate in a school event. More than a few times, mothers would ask her why she wasn't enrolling her daughters in some hot new class. But Cindy would just laugh and shrug her shoulders.

The first time Cindy really took some heat was just six months ago, when a grassroots coalition had nominated her for presidency of the PTA. It was an important job, and they all thought she was the best person to do it. Cindy was flattered, but she also knew it was huge commitment of time and energy that would take her away from her family for many hours every week.

"I really appreciate the honor but have to decline," she explained. "My time at home is really my top priority."

Her refusal to serve upset quite a number of the other parents. They accused her of being selfish and even lazy, but Cindy stuck to her guns.

A few weeks after the book club incident, Teresa's class was told that each student had to submit an essay about the person they most admired for the annual PTA Hero of the Year Contest. The teachers would read all the selections and pick the top five entries. Then three members of the PTA board would award a $300 first prize.

Teresa knew immediately who her hero would be, but didn't tell a soul who she was writing about. She wrote and rewrote the essay several times, spending hours to make sure it was as good as she could get it. Two weeks after she turned in her essay, she was notified by Mr. Wingate, her English teacher, that she had made the top five. In one more week the board would announce its decision.

The day the prize was to be awarded at a special school assembly, Teresa was crushed when the principal didn't call her name. Not for first, second, or third prize. How could that be, when Mr. Wingate had told her how great her essay was, and all the teachers thought she was sure to get into at least the top three? Teresa was so upset that as soon as the assembly was over, she immediately ran up to her friend Meghan.

"Oh, Meghan, I wrote the coolest essay about my mom," Teresa cried. "I really wanted to win so I could buy her a new leather portfolio to present her designs."

"You won't believe what my mom told me."

"What?"

"Did you know she was one of the judges, along with Judy and Patricia?"

"Oh, get real . . . are they still ticked about the book club thing?"

"You got it. My mother told me that what you wrote about your mom being so unselfish and hard working wasn't true. She even told me your mom probably wrote it for you."

Now Teresa was really angry. "You know that's not true, Meghan. You know what a good mom she is."

"I know. Your mom is cool. All the kids talk about how great your mom is. But for some reason my mom really has it in for her."

"This isn't fair. Everything I wrote was true. Do you know where your mom is? I want to straighten this out once and for all."

The two girls went straight to Meghan's house to confront Barbara Kelly.

"Mrs. Kelly, do you have a minute? We really need to talk."

"Of course, Teresa. What's up?"

"I want you to know that I wrote every word of that essay about my mother. And it's all true. I know you don't think she's a good enough mom, but you're wrong."

"I understand, Honey. I know you love your mom. But this was an essay about people who are really unselfish and hard-working."

Teresa shook her head in disbelief. "Right. And that's exactly what my mom is. Where did you ever get the idea she was anything but unselfish and hardworking? My mom does everything for us—and always puts what's best for our family first."

"Teresa, that's really sweet. But haven't you noticed how many more experiences and opportunities all the other girls are given by their mothers compared to you? Don't you sometimes feel deprived?"

Suddenly Meghan piped in, "Yeah, right. Like we really like dong all this dumb stuff. Mrs. Cutler's really neat, Mom. Everybody thinks that, and Teresa's family is really a lot happier than ours, I can tell you. Where did you moms ever get the idea that doing all this stuff was good for us and that's what a good mom should do?"

Barbara was speechless. Her daughter had never said anything like this to her before. She stood aghast as the two girls turned on their heels and left the house.

That night Teresa gave her mom a copy of her essay for the first time. Tears came to Cindy's eyes as she read silently. Her daughter's words confirmed the choice she'd made for her family so many years ago.

"I'm sorry I didn't win the contest, Mom. I wanted to buy you that new portfolio you need as a surprise present for you."

"Oh Honey, the best present you could ever give me is reading what you said. You have no idea how much this means to me, especially this part:"

My mom is my hero. She's pretty different from other moms. She's real. She doesn't do things just because everyone else is doing it. She tunes into what we really need. When she listens, it's like I'm the only person. She's so fun to be with and always takes the time for her family. My mom is a hero because she's the most courageous person I know. She sticks up for what she believes in no matter what other people say. I just hope I can be as good a mom as she's been for me.

What Real Moms Can Learn from This Story

By today's standards, Cindy Cutler was an unconventional mother. Compared to the other mothers in her community, she appeared less willing to go along with the usual image and requirement for the "perfect mom." She had tried that route of doing and being it all, but quickly realized that it didn't work and wasn't good for her children. For her the "ah-ha" moment was when she found herself screaming at her one-year-old for spilling her orange juice on the floor. How many of us have done something similar? But have we also been able to change our parenting style as Cindy did?

Cindy was determined to maintain a balance in her life. Of course she loved her children and wanted the best for them. But she knew that her children would suffer if she continued to pressure them with more and more activities and requirements, a high-performance regime dictated largely by external expectations. She also knew that for her to be the best possible mom she could be, it was crucial for her to maintain her own health, strength, and endurance; to have a fulfilling relationship with her husband, Brad; and to develop her own creativity and skills in the workplace.

For her pains, Cindy Cutler was slandered, and her daughter was denied a prize she really deserved. This did annoy her, but despite the slings and arrows from her so-called friends, Cindy stuck to her guns and continued to earn the respect and admiration of her daughter Teresa and her friends, and of all the other members of her family. History has vindicated Cindy. Her principled vision of motherhood has produced wonderful kids and a happy family life.

Don't Forget to Take Care of Yourself

Studies find that those parents who usually experience strong feelings of fatigue are less capable of taking care of their families. In addition, almost one-third of these burned-out, frazzled moms and dads are less likely to think their families are fairing well. It should remind you not to forget to take care of yourself so you can take care of your family—and also enjoy them.

Is This Real Mom's Secret Part of **Your** Parenting?

So just how balanced is your life these days? How often are you taking time out for yourself? Here are a few questions to test just how well you're using this last essential motherhood secret.

- Are you noticing any of these stress symptoms regularly: rapid breathing, pounding heart, sleeplessness, irritability?

- Do you just seem unable to find enough hours in the day? Do you find yourself always behind or always running to keep up?

- Are you complaining that you never have enough time for yourself—or *any* time for yourself—and then feeling guilty if you *do* take the time?

- Have you lost who you are? Is your identity so wrapped up in the role of "mother" that you've forgotten other aspects of self—you know, woman, gourmet, wife, artist, lover, friend, tennis player, marathon runner, seamstress, gardener, writer, daughter, niece?

- How's your love life going? Is it hard to recall the last time (and the time before that) you and your significant other had a quiet, intimate time together—and that would mean without the kids?

- Do you spend enough time with your girlfriends?
- Exercise, health, medical checkups—are you taking care of you?

What is the one thing you are committed to doing differently to start taking better care of you? Write it on the lines here. Then get ready to learn the secret and use it with your family. _____

_____

_____

A Lighthearted Way to Feel in Control

Becoming a mom has been one of the most challenging things I've ever done, and at times my kids made me feel as though my life was out of control. To help myself stay balanced, I decided to focus on just two simple things I could do each day that would make me feel in control and at the same time happy. The two things I chose were making my bed and drinking water. Throughout the day I'd remind herself that I was really in control of my life because my bed was made and I was drinking water. This helped me smile when things were tough.

–Dina Venezky, a geologist mom with two sons, Redwood City, California

P.S. After talking with many of her friends, Dina realized that a lot of them were in the same semi-shocked state of trying to balance their lives and raise healthy children. Dina has created a Web site, http://highmaintenancemom.com, to share parenting experiences and help moms take care of themselves. If you're finding yourself feeling overwhelmed, you might consider using her tip to start regaining control. Just tailor the two sample things to fit your personality.

Eight Steps to Begin Taking Better Care of You

Step One: Check Out That Daily Schedule. Are you feeling like a human to-do list? Are you always going-going-going? Before you can really make a change and create more balance in your life, you must first have an accurate idea of your typical week. So look at that Palm Pilot or Daytimer or calendar and see what is really going on in your life. And if you're not writing down everything you do, start doing it now.

Step Two: Cut Just One Thing. Cutting out just one of your weekly activities may make a tremendous difference in restoring balance and reducing stress. And if removing one works well for you, try eliminating two or three.

Stay committed to trimming your schedule. One way to do this is to establish a "nag partner." Tell your family or at least the one little kid in your household who always takes on the role of your little reminder: "MOMMMmmmm, you weren't supposed to clean up my room for me!" Believe me, they take the reminder role quite seriously and will help you out. Or use an index card to write a reminder not to take on one more new task, and tape it to your phone. Your new rule is "Say no first"— or at least say you'll have to call the person back after you check your schedule. A survey conducted by *Working Mother* found that only 35 percent of moms admitted that they use "No" as a time-saving strategy, but half of those surveyed confessed that it is the one strategy they need to improve or do more of. So a word to the wise: stick to your decision.

Step Three: Start Delegating. Really! Why do all the work yourself? Share the household chores as a family. Besides a less-stressed you, you'll have more time for your family, and here's the real clincher: research actually shows that when the family pitches in together, your family happiness quotient increases by 32 percent (honest!). The key to this one: don't be so darn picky! If your kid doesn't make his bed like a marine, let it go.

Step Four: Exercise. If you really want to take better care of yourself, you know it's essential to have a regular exercise routine. And no more excuses: you can do it alone, with a girlfriend, or with your whole family. For instance, put the toddler in a stroller or the baby in a front back and walk each evening; join a mother-daughter yoga class; or have your girlfriend come over each day, punch in that "Buns of Steel" tape, and go girl. Then keep doing it.

Step Five: Find Time for One New Thing. Decide what's taking a backseat in your family (spirituality, intellectual stimulation, fun, together time, reading the paper, talking), then boost it. For instance, if you want to read more, then do it as a family. Set an evening reading time. Stash books in a basket (and put them back in the basket for the next night) or spread a blanket on the floor for read-alongs. Granted, this is hard when your kids are toddlers, but for school-age kids, it can be wonderful. And you're actually helping your child because you're modeling the joy of reading to your kids. So what do you want to boost?

Step Six: Date Your Significant Other. Get a babysitter once a week (or twice a month) and leave the kiddies at home. If you think going out sounds selfish, tell yourself you're doing it for the good of your kids. Don't put your marriage on the back burner.

Step Seven: Get a Support System. Friends do matter. In addition to everything else they bring to your life, friends can really help in reducing stress and restoring balance. Here are a few suggestions:

- **Create a Mommy and Me group.** When my kids were young, my girlfriend Ginny Lescroart and I connected weekly. She had kids about the same ages as mine, so we'd alternate being the host or choosing outings. One week she might have us all walk to pick blackberries by the creek. The next week I'd suggest we go see a movie together or attend the read-aloud program at the library. Find one mom and plan little outings. This doesn't have to cost you a lot of time or money, and it means healthy company for you as well as your kids.

- **Start a book club.** If you and your kids like to read, why not start a mother-daughter (or mother-son) book club? Instead of reading apart, you can enjoy each other's company.

- **Set up buddy lists.** Online chat groups are so hot these days, why not set up a time for a twenty-minute chat with your girlfriends? It could be a time not only to stay connected without leaving the house but also to give you a healthy menu idea for dinner or ideas to tame the temper tantrum of your two-year-old.

- **Exercise together.** Set up a Pilates group or exercise class in a home or church building. Just invite a girl-friend or two or three to come over with their little ones. Pop in an exercise video, take turns watching the kiddies, and exercise while enjoying each other's company. Or just put your toddler in the stroller and find one other mom to join with you for a short walk each day.

Step Eight: Incorporate Stress Reducers in Your Daily Life. Child development experts warn us that stress is mounting for our kids. They need to learn ways to relax just as much as you do, so why not learn together? Stress is an inevitable part of life for us all, but all of us—kids included—can learn to use some of the techniques that adults use to cope with pressure. And how great if you learn to use these as a family. Not only will balance be restored and stress reduced, but your child will learn techniques he can use to beat stress for the rest of his life. Practice meditation, prayer, relaxation techniques—whatever you fancy—but incorporate that stress reducer into your family's daily routine.

One day I realized that as my kids got older home life was getting tougher than ever to balance. More activities. More schedules. More carpools. And more financial strains. So I finally decided to set a new house rule: only one extra activity per semester, whether it's band, soccer, art, chess, or dance. So every semester I hold individual appointments with each of my children. They choose the one activity they really want to do and pledge to stick with it (and practice) for the coming months. I even make the older ones sign a contract. Some activities are nonnegotiable (such as the youth church group or tutoring if needed).

The change in my family was profound: there was more time and less stress for both my kids and myself. It also taught my kids how to prioritize. They had to really think hard as to what they wanted to do the most. I never realized how reducing just one activity a month—whether it is the kids' or mine—can make a major difference in family life.

—Joan Saunders, a mom of four
from Palm Springs, California

Making a Promise to Yourself

1. Did anything in the Cutler family's story sound even vaguely similar to families in your community? What about for your own family? On a scale of 1 (poor) to 10 (excellent), rate the kind of job you're doing taking care of yourself. Your health? What about how well you're keeping this balanced?

2. How would you apply the eight steps to begin taking better care of you? Review the tips that offer simple things moms do to stay balanced, and all the other boxes, guides, tips, and stories in this chapter.

3. Go to A Mother's Secret on page 57 and write in the one step you will do over the next 21 days to take better care of yourself so you can take better care of your family.

Simple Ways to Stay Balanced

"How do I balance my work, my family, and still have any time for myself?" It's the age-old mother question, but it can be done! The trick is to find your passion—the one thing that you know you need in order to stay a little saner so you can be the best mom you can be. Whether you work outside your home or are a stay-at-home mom, here are a few ways these moms stay more balanced and in control of their lives:

- *Five-minute family pickup brigade.* Susie Morrison, a mom of two from Rancho Mirage, California, uses a simple tip once a week that gets all family members involved and instantly cleans the house. Each family member (Dad included) is assigned a room or area and given a broom, vacuum, or dust rag. Mom sets a buzzer for five minutes, and everyone runs off to clean things "spick and span" before the timer goes off. Susie swears it's the perfect way to quickly put the house back in order before going to bed or if a guest is to arrive.

- *Lock the door.* Shellie Spradlin, a mom of three girls from Kentucky, offers simple advice that works wonders for her: "Every once in a while I go into my bedroom and lock the door." The mom simply switches off the lights, turns on a CD of sounds to drown out the stress (her favorite is "Spring Rain" because it's so calming), and lies on her bed for five minutes. "It's just heaven," she says, "and just those few minutes is enough to get me energized to go back and face whatever awaits me."

- *Exercise with toddlers.* Heather Poropat, mom of a seventeen-month-old, Madeline, from Chesterfield, Missouri, knows that working out keeps her more balanced, but she still felt guilty taking time away from her child. Her solution: she found a few other moms to exercise together with, along with their toddlers. "This way there is no guilt in working out" and being away from your kids. Heather explains, "This is also a great way to meet other moms and get parenting advice." The ladies plop their kids into their strollers, head to the park each morning, and hang on to their strollers to help them keep their balance as they do their daily lunge stretches. Each also carries a CD player with speakers to play as they exercise. And the music selections couldn't be more fitting: nursery rhymes their toddlers love. "Five Little Monkeys" is perfect for doing jumping jacks; "Hickory Dickory Dock" has just the right tempo to accompany their high steps. A great side benefit is that their kids seem to love the daily outings, too. The toddlers smile and sing the songs in their strollers as their moms get in shape.

- *Have a date night.* Elizabeth Wright, mom of three-year-old, Trinity, from Indiana, found herself frazzled trying to juggle home and career. She also knew that what really keeps her balanced is being with her husband, but she just couldn't seem to find truly uninterrupted time for the two of them to be together. So they made a pact that every Saturday night would be "date night." They hire a baby-sitter and go out to dinner or a movie—alone. Elizabeth's husband, Kevin, explains, "When I was growing up, we all sat at the table and ate as a family. That's not always how it is now, so we decided it was important to make that time for us."

A Real Mom's Resource Guide

The Clutter-Busting Handbook: Clean It Up, Clear It Out, and Keep Your Life Clutter Free, by Rita Emmett (Toronto, Ontario: HouseAnchor Canada, 2005). The author of *The Procrastinator's Handbook* offers a wealth of realistic ways to reduce clutter to simplify your life and be less stressed.

How She Really Does It: Secrets of Successful Stay-at-Work Moms, by Wendy Sachs (Cambridge, Mass.: DaCapo LifeLong, 2005). A former *Dateline* producer interviews successful working moms to create a list of the ways they found to balance work and mothering.

How to Simplify Your Life: Seven Practical Steps to Letting Go of Your Burdens and Living a Happier Life, by Tim Kustenmacher (New York: McGraw-Hill, 2004). If stress in your life is partly due to financial concerns, this program may help. The discussions of how to slow down and get out of debt are especially valuable.

It's My Pleasure: A Revolutionary Plan to Free Yourself from Guilt and Create the Life You Want, by Maria Rodale and Maya Rodale (New York: Free Press, 2005). A mother-daughter writing team offers good behavioral practices for reducing guilt and developing a more balanced, less stressed life.

Life Matters: Creating a Dynamic Balance of Work, Family, Time, and Money, by A. Roger Merrill and Rebecca R. Merrill (New York: McGraw-Hill, 2003). This book offers a wealth of strategies to help you balance all the different components in your life.

The Over-Scheduled Child, by Alvin Rosenfeld and Nicole Wise (New York: St. Martin's Griffin, 2001). The authors make a compelling argument against what they consider "hyperparenting" and the impact it has on kids. Put this one on your "must-read" list, Mom.

Perfect Balance: Dr. Robert Greene's Breakthrough Program for Finding the Lifelong Hormonal Health You Deserve, by Robert Greene and Leah Feldon (New York: Clarkson Potter, 2005). If a hormonal imbalance could be contributing to your Motherhood Mania, this book might be your answer.

Putting Family First: Successful Strategies for Reclaiming Family Life in a Hurry-Up World, by William J. Doherty and Barbara Z. Carlson (New York: Owl Books, 2002). These wonderful authors offer sound advice about why it is so critical to take care of yourself and your family.

Who's Pulling Your Strings? How to Break the Cycle of Manipulation and Regain Control of Your Life, by Harriet B. Baiker (New York: McGraw-Hill, 2004). If you recognize that you're constantly being pulled by other people's aspirations and are manipulated by your own fears of failure, this book is for you. The author provides excellent activities to help you identify what's pulling your strings and how to break that destructive cycle.

Worried All the Time: Rediscovering the Joy in Parenthood in an Age of Anxiety, by David Anderegg (New York: Free Press, 2005). Just why do we worry so much, and what the heck do we feel so darn guilty about? Anderegg makes a clear case that we don't need to worry nearly as much as we do, because most of what we worry about just isn't that important to effective parenting in the long run.

the Last word

Do real moms really read parenting books? Of course they do. They've probably read dozens, especially when their first baby was born.

Have those books been helpful? Yes. In some cases the information about child development and medical health issues is very practical and often comforting.

But frankly, reading book after book hasn't reduced the amount of guilt, stress, and mania among mothers around us. In fact it may have increased it. There have been just too many parenting books by too many authors who call themselves experts. The net result has been confusion, and mothers who still doubt themselves and worry that their children aren't thriving.

I hope this is the last parenting book you'll ever read for a long time. The reason is that you already know how to be a real mom. There is nothing in this book that is new. Everything I've included here is based on solid parenting principles that have been around for decades but are all too often forgotten. What I've tried to do is simply remind us all of the basics—what's always been natural, instinctive, and intuitive for real mothering.

Unfortunately, these core secrets of real mothering have been obliterated by the frenzy and mania of commercialized parenting. But now it's time to get back, get real, and restore the simple truth about mothering: that its foundation is the powerful and unconditional love and connection that ultimately lasts for always.

So trust yourself and those maternal instincts. No one knows your child better than you. Don't forget to stick to your Mother's Promises you've written on pages 54–57, relax, enjoy the moment, and remember to laugh.

46 percent of parents said kids' biggest emotional issues were coping with stress and dealing with depression: P. McGraw, *Family First: Your Step-by-Step Plan for Creating a Phenomenal Family* (New York: Free Press, 2004), p. 182.

One-third of adolescents say they "worry a lot," and nearly half say they have trouble sleeping due to stress: poll of 725 adolescents ages nine to twelve, conducted in 1999 by Georgia Witkin, Ph.D., director of the Stress Program at Mount Sinai School of Medicine in New York City; cited in Kiger, "'What's Wrong with This Picture?'" p. 128.

83 percent of kids say they're stressed about homework; 57 percent say parental relationship causes them stress (Mount Sinai Stress Program poll): cited in Kiger, "'What's Wrong with This Picture?'" p. 131.

Suicide rate in teens has increased 30 percent. Cited by a 2001 Department of Health and Human Services report. Also: cited in Kiger, "'What's Wrong with This Picture?'" p. 132.

Suicide rates for children and teens tripled from 1962 to 1995: M. Elias, "Kids and Depression: Are Drugs the Answer?" *USA Today*, Nov. 30, 1999, p. 2A.

National survey shows college students so depressed that it was difficult for them to function: R. D. Kadison and T. F. DiGeronimo, *College of the Overwhelmed: The Campus Mental Health Crisis and What to Do About It* (San Francisco: Jossey-Bass, 2004).

60 percent of youth want more time with parent: Nickelodeon/*Time* poll of 1,172 children ages six to fourteen in twenty-five U.S. cities, interviewed one-on-one without their parents; conducted by Pen, Schoen and Berland Associates. Cited in C. Wallis, "The Kids Are Alright," *Time*, July 5, 1999, p. 58.

Our kids want *relaxed* time with us: E. Galinsky, "Do Working Parents Make the Grade?" *Newsweek*, Aug. 30, 1999, p. 55.

More than two in five kids feel that their time with moms is rushed; calm mothers get a better grade: survey of a representative group of more than one thousand children in grades 3–12 to evaluate their parents who were employed and to evaluate children of working mothers in twelve areas strongly linked to children's healthy development, school readiness, and school success; Galinsky, "Do Working Parents Make the Grade?" pp. 52–56.

Kids appreciate what we do, but want more relaxed time with us: survey of eighty-four thousand students in grades 6–12, conducted in fall 2000 on the *USA Today* Web site or through survey partner Cable in the Classroom; results interpreted by W. Damon, "The Gap Generation," *USA Weekend*, Apr. 27–29, 2001, p. 9.

One in three kids has stress-related ailments: H. Parlapiano, "Stress in Kids," *Parents*, Feb. 2004, pp. 133–135.

Anxiety rates in children: J. S. Dacey and L. B. Fiore, *Your Anxious Child* (San Francisco: Jossey-Bass, 2000), pp. 2–3.

Statistics on homework, unstructured children's activities, family dinners, and vacations cited in A. Rosenfeld, M. F. Small, and R. Coles, "Voice of the People" (letter), *Chicago Tribune* (Online Edition), http://www.chicagotribune.com/, Aug. 21, 2004.

Statistics on decline in free time and playtime: Six Flags, "Today Is the Time for Playtime: The Facts on Today's Family" (press release), www.sixflags.com/press/itsplaytime.asp, Mar. 19, 2004.

Recess abolished: O. S. Jarrett, "Recess in Elementary School: What Does the Research Say?" *ERIC Digest*, http://www.ericdigests.org/2003-2/recess.html, Feb. 2003.

Quotation of parent to Elisabeth Krents at Dalton School: P. Wingert, "Plight of the Preschoolers: How Do They Beat the Odds?" *Newsweek*, May 15, 2000, p. 76.

MetLife survey of U.S. teachers cited in N. Gibbs, "Parents Behaving Badly," *Time*, Feb. 21, 2005, p. 42.

Two-thirds of high school students cheat on exams, yet 93 percent agree it's important to be a person with good character: survey of 24,763 high school students conducted by the Josephson Institute of Ethics, reported in "2004 Report Card: The Ethics of American Youth," www.josephsoninstitute.org/ Survey2004.

Teacher liability insurance has jumped 25 percent in five years: Gibbs, "Parents Behaving Badly," p. 48.

Youth sports programs in 163 cities require pledge of civility from parents: S. Smith, "Is the Choice Sportsmanship or Death?" Knight-Ridder/Tribune Information Services, www .youthdevelopment.org, July 23, 2000. (Also available from IYD, P.O. Box 150, Washington, D.C., 20041.)

70 percent of kids drop out of sports by age thirteen: cited in S. Gaines, "Do We Push Kids Too Hard?" *Better Homes and Gardens*, Mar. 2000, pp. 94–96.

"We need to prepare our kids . . .": D. Kindlon, *Too Much of a Good Thing: Raising Children of Character in an Indulgent World* (New York: Hyperion, 2001), p. 9.

Two out of three parents say kids measure self-worth by possessions: cited in M. Elias, "Ads Targeting Kids," *USA Today*, Mar. 22, 2000, p. D5.

More than 80 percent of people think American kids are spoiled: AOL Time Warner poll cited in N. Gibbs, "Who's in Charge Here?" *Time*, Aug. 6, 2001, pp. 40–49.

Two-thirds of parents admit their kids are spoiled (from survey of 1,078 affluent parents nationwide): Kindlon, *Too Much of a Good Thing*, p. 197.

75 percent of parents say kids do fewer chores: cited in P. Tyre, J. Scelfo, and B. Kantrowitz, "The Power of No," *Newsweek*, Sept. 13, 2004, p. 45.

73 percent of parents say today's kids are too focused on buying and consuming: cited in Tyre, Scelfo, and Kantrowitz, "The Power of No," p. 46.

"The body cannot learn to adapt . . .": D. Kindlon, quoted by Gibbs, "Who's in Charge Here?" p. 46.

Statistics from the Josephson Institute of Ethics regarding cheating, stealing, lying, and satisfaction with character: "2004 Report Card," www.josephsoninstitute.org/Survey2004.

"What these parents don't realize . . .": Kadison and DiGeronimo, *College of the Overwhelmed*, p. 5.

Parents hovering through college: J. Mathews, "Parents Casting a Shadow over College Applicant: Campuses Try Student-Only Tours," *Washington Post*, July 10, 2004, p. A01.

College kids need "parentectomies": H. E. Marano, "The Pressure from Parents," *Psychology Today*, Mar. 2004.

"If your son or daughter is in college . . .": Kadison and DiGeronimo, *College of the Overwhelmed*, p. 1.

Chapter Four: Can Our Kids Make It on Their Own?

Opening quotation: M. Levine, *Ready or Not, Here Life Comes* (New York: Simon & Schuster, 2005).

Half of Americans ages eighteen to twenty-nine talk to their parents every day: *Time* magazine poll cited in L. Grossman, "Grow Up? Not So Fast," *Time*, Jan. 24, 2005, pp. 42–54.

Percentage of twenty-six-year-olds living with parents nearly doubled since 1970: cited by B. Schoeni, professor of economics and public policy at the University of Michigan, cited in Grossman, "Grow Up? Not So Fast," p. 44.

36 percent of graduates admit they're not ready for careers: Levine, *Ready or Not, Here Life Comes.*

"If you bungle raising your children . . .": J. K. Onassis, quoted in K. Rowinski (ed.), *The Quotable Mom* (Guilford, Conn.: Lyons Press, 2002), p. 206.

PART TWO: THE 12 SIMPLE SECRETS OF REAL MOTHERING

Real Mom's Secret 1: A Mother Who Loves Teaches Worth

Story of Sue Summit and her first-grader, William: S. Gaines, "Do We Push Kids Too Hard? *Better Homes and Gardens,* Mar. 2000, pp. 94–98.

Real Mom Alert (unconditional love and self-esteem): S. Coopersmith, *The Antecedents of Self-Esteem* (San Francisco: Freeman, 1967).

Real Mom's Secret 2: A Mother Who Is Firm and Fair Gives Her Children a Moral Code to Live By

"Parents who are afraid to put their foot down . . .": from V. McLellan, *The Complete Book of Practical Proverbs and Wacky Wit* (Wheaton, Ill.: Tyndale House, 1996), p. 181.

Research on three types of parenting: D. Baumrind, "Early Socialization and Adolescent Competence," in S. E. Dragastin and G. H. Elder (eds.), *Adolescence in the Life Cycle* (New York: Wiley, 1975), p. 130.

Real Mom Alert (Steinberg study of twenty thousand adolescents): L. Steinberg, B. Brown, and S. M. Dornbusch, *Beyond the Classroom: Why School Reform Has Failed and What Parents Need to Do* (New York: Simon & Schuster, 1996).

Real Mom Alert quotation: L. Steinberg, *The 10 Basic Principles of Good Parenting* (New York: Simon & Schuster, 2004), p. 87.

Real Mom's Secret 3: A Mother Who Listens Shows Her Children They Matter

Real Mom Alert statistic (35 percent of kids say adults are poor at listening to and understanding teens): cited in E. Portillo, "Teens Give Adults Low Grades on Ruling World," *Desert Sun*, June 18, 2005, p. A17.

Real Mom Wisdom (giving kids wait time): M. B. Rowe, "Wait-Time: Slowing Down May Be a Way of Speeding Up!" *Journal of Teacher Education*, 1986, 31(1), 43–50.

Research on the best places to overhear kid conversations: survey by Harris Interactive for Chrysler; cited in J. Neyman and K. Gelles, "Snapshots: Chatting the Drive Away," *USA Today*, Oct. 11, 2004, p. D1.

Real Mom's Secret 4: A Mother Who Is a Good Role Model Gives Her Children an Example Worth Copying

Real Mom Alert (A. Bandura study with Bobo doll): A. Bandura, D. Ross, and S. A. Ross, "Transmission of Aggression Through Imitation of Aggressive Models," *Journal of Abnormal and Social Psychology*, 1961, 63, 572–582; A. Bandura and R. H. Walters, *Social Learning and Personality Development* (Austin, Tex.: Holt, Rinehart and Winston, 1963).

Real Mom Alert (M. A. Straus study of parental yelling): cited in R. Sobel, "Wounding with Words," *U.S. News & World Report*, Aug. 28, 2000, p. 53.

Real Mom's Secret 5: A Mother Who Teaches Values Inspires Character

Real Mom Alert (positive effects of sticking to what matters): D. Waldrop and J. Weber, "From Grandparent to Caregiver: The Stress and Satisfaction of Raising Grandchildren," *Families in Society*, 2001, 82, 461–467.

Real Mom Alert (doing kind deeds boosts happiness): research by S. Lyubomirsky cited in C. Brown, "The New Science of Happiness," *Time*, Jan. 17, 2005, p. A8.

Real Mom's Secret 6: A Mother Who Supports Her Children's Strengths Builds Their Confidence

"Children are not things to be molded . . .": J. Lair, quoted in K. Rowinski (ed.), *The Quotable Mom* (Guilford, Conn.: Lyons Press, 2002), p. 93.

Real Mom Alert (five types of difficult temperaments): S. I. Greenspan, *The Challenging Child: Understanding, Raising, and Enjoying the Five "Difficult" Types of Children* (Cambridge, Mass.: Perseus, 1995).

Eight multiple intelligences: H. Gardner, *Frames of Mind: The Theory of Multiple Intelligences* (New York: Basic Books, 1983); H. Gardner, "Multiple Lenses on the Mind," paper presented at the ExpoGestation Conference, Bogota, Colombia, May 25, 2005.

Real Mom's Secret 7: A Mother Who Encourages Independence Cultivates Self-Reliance

Percentage of twenty-six-year-olds living with parents doubles since 1970 from 11 percent to 20 percent based on citations from Bob Schoeni, University of Michigan. L. Grossman, "Grow Up? Not so Fast," *Time*, Jan. 24, 2005, p. 44.

Data from 2002 U.S. Census (four million people between twenty-five and thirty-four live with parents) cited in P. Tyre, "Bringing Up Adultolescents," *Newsweek*, Mar. 25, 2002, p. 39.

60 percent of college students plan to live at home after graduation: online survey by MonsterTRAK.com, a job-search firm, cited in Tyre, "Bringing Up Adultolescents."

Real Mom Alert (kids' unreadiness to cope with life): M. Levine, *Ready or Not, Here Life Comes* (New York: Simon & Schuster, 2005).

Real Mom Alert (teaching a never-give-up attitude): L. Terman's study cited in J. N. Shrunken, *Terman's Kids: The Groundbreaking Study of How the Gifted Grow Up* (New York: Little, Brown, 1992).

Real Mom's Secret 8: A Mother Who Applauds Effort Nurtures Perseverance

"Applaud us when we run": E. Burke, quoted in J. Canfield, M. V. Hansen, P. Hansen, and I. Dunlap (eds.), *Chicken Soup for the Kid's Soul: 101 Stories of Courage, Hope and Laughter* (Deerfield Beach, Fla.: Health Communications, 1998), p. 251.

Real Mom Alert (the importance of affirming effort): H. W. Stevenson and J. W. Stigler, *The Learning Gap* (New York: Simon & Schuster, 1992).

Parents typically say eighteen negative comments for every affirming one to their children: National Parent-Teacher Organization, cited in S. Martson, *The Magic of Encouragement* (New York: Morrow, 1990), p. 100.

Real Mom's Secret 9: A Mother Who Accepts Her Children's Shortcomings Nurtures Resilience

"As a mother, my job is . . .": R. B. Graham, quoted in J. Canfield, M. V. Hansen, J. Hawthorne, and M. Shimoff (eds.), *Chicken Soup for the Mother's Soul: 101 Stories to Open the Hearts and Rekindle the Spirits of Mothers* (Deerfield Beach, Fla.: Health Communications, 1997), p. 84.

Real Mom Alert (study of gifted and talented individuals): V. Goertzel and M. G. Goertzel, *Cradles of Eminence: A Provocative Study of the Childhoods of Over 400 Famous Twentieth-Century Men and Women* (New York: Little, Brown, 1962).

Real Mom's Secret 10: A Mother Who Takes Time for Her Children Helps Them Build Strong Relationships

Real Mom Alert (study of over a thousand fourteen-year-olds and their parents): M. Kerr and H. Stattin, "What Parents

Know, How They Know It, and Several Forms of Adolescent Adjustment: Further Support for a Reinterpretation of Monitoring," *Developmental Psychology*, 2000, *36*, 366–380, described in J. Garbarino and C. Bedard, *Parents Under Siege: Why You Are the Solution, Not the Problem, in Your Child's Life* (New York: Free Press, 2001), pp. 106–108.

Real Mom Alert quotation: L. Steinberg, *The 10 Basic Principles of Good Parenting* (New York: Simon & Schuster, 2004), p. 48.

Real Mom's Secret 11: A Mother Who Laughs Teaches Joy

Real Mom Alert (almost two-thirds of kids want more time with parents): survey of eighty-four thousand students in grades 6–12, conducted in fall 2000 on the *USA Today* Web site or through survey partner Cable in the Classroom; results interpreted by W. Damon, "The Gap Generation," *USA Weekend*, Apr. 27–29, 2001, p. 9.

Real Mom Wisdom (observing family rituals increases family closeness and children's social development): D. Eaker and L. Walkers, "Adolescent Satisfaction in Family Rituals and Psychosocial Development: A Developmental Systems Theory Perspective," *Journal of Family Psychology*, 2002, *16*(4), 406–414.

What Four Real Moms Did (Kessel family "Do Nothing Day" and Jane Turner Michaels's nighttime tradition with teens): C. Fiedler, "7 Secrets of Highly Happy Families," *Better Homes and Gardens*, Oct. 2004, p. 178.

Real Mom's Secret 12: A Mother Who Takes Care of Herself Holds Together Her Happy Family

"Moms who take care of themselves first . . .": K. E. Nault, *When You're About to Go off the Deep End, Don't Take Your Kids with You* (West Vancouver, British Columbia: Stepping Stones for Life, 2005), quoted in L. Mitges, "Put Yourself First: How to Save Yourself and Your Kids," *Calgary Herald*, May 9, 2005, p. E3.

Real Mom Alert (parents who usually are fatigued are less capable in handling their families): S. Elek, D. Hudson, and M. Fleck, "Couples' Experiences with Fatigue During the Transition to Parenthood," *Journal of Family Nursing*, 2002, 8, 221–240.

Only 35 percent of moms use "No" as a time-saving technique: the editors of *Working Mother* magazine (L. Bernmenson, editor in chief), *The Working Mother Book of Time: How to Take It, Make It, Save It, and Savor It* (New York: St. Martin's Griffin, 2000), p. 20.

Delegating family chores increases family happiness by 32 percent: D. Niven, *The 100 Simple Secrets of Happy Families* (San Francisco: HarperSanFrancisco, 2004), excerpted in *Parents*, Aug. 2004, p. 137.

What Four Real Moms Did (Heather Poropat, exercising with baby in stroller): A. Bertrand, "Workout with Baby a Guilt-Free Exercise," *Desert Sun*, May 26, 2005, p. F1.

What Four Real Moms Did (Elizabeth Wright, dating her husband): T. J. Banes, "Timeout for Parents," *Indiana Living*, Jan. 13, 2005, p. E1.

about the author

Michele Borba, Ed.D., is an internationally renowned educator who is recognized for her practical, solution-based strategies to strengthen children's behavior and social and moral development. A sought-after motivational speaker, she has presented workshops to over one million participants worldwide and has been an educational consultant to hundreds of schools.

Dr. Borba frequently appears as a guest expert on television and radio, including NPR talk shows, *Today, The Early Show, The View, Fox & Friends*, MSNBC's *Countdown, Canada AM*, and *Talk of the Nation*. She has been interviewed in numerous publications, including *Redbook, Newsweek, U.S. News & World Report*, the *Chicago Tribune*, the *Los Angeles Times*, and the *New York Daily News*. She serves as an advisory board member for *Parents* magazine.

Dr. Borba's numerous awards include the National Educator Award, presented by the National Council of Self-Esteem. She is the award-winning author of twenty books, including, *Nobody Likes Me, Everybody Hates Me; Don't Give Me That Attitude!; No More Misbehavin': 38 Difficult Behaviors and How to Stop Them; Building Moral Intelligence*, cited by *Publisher's Weekly* as "among the most noteworthy of 2001"; *Parents Do Make a Difference*, selected by *Child* magazine as an "Outstanding Parent Book of 1999"; and *Esteem Builders*, used by over 1.5 million students worldwide. Her proposal to end school violence (SB1667) was signed into California law in 2002. She serves as a consultant for the U.S. Office of Education. She lives in Palm Springs, California, with her husband and has three sons.

To contact Dr. Borba regarding her work or her media availability, or to schedule a keynote or workshop for your organization, go to www.behaviormakeovers.com or www. micheleborba.com.

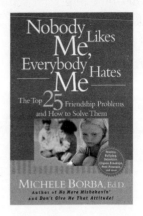

Nobody Likes Me, Everybody Hates Me
The Top 25 Friendship Problems and How to Solve Them
Michele Borba, Ed.D.

Paper
ISBN: 0-7879-7662-8

- Do you wish your kid had more friends or could keep the ones she has?
- Is teasing, gossiping, bullying, or cyber-bulling a problem?
- Is she often left out or rejected by other kids?
- Does he just follow the crowd? Are you concerned about his friends?

Look no further. The resource you need to solve these problems and boost your child's social competence is in your hands. Based on a survey of five thousand teachers and parents, *Nobody Likes Me, Everybody Hates Me* shows how to teach your child the 25 most essential friendship-building skills that kids need to find, make, and keep friends, as well as survive that social pressure from peers.

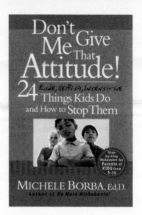

Don't Give Me That Attitude!

24 Rude, Selfish, Insensitive Things Kids Do and How to Stop Them
Michele Borba, Ed.D.

Paper
ISBN: 0-7879-7333-5

- Does your kid never take no for an answer and demand things go his way?

- Do her theatrics leave you drained at the end of the day?

- Are you resorting to bribes and threats to get your kid to do chores?

- Does he cheat, complain, or blame others for his problems?

What happened? You thought you were doing the best for your child and didn't set out to raise a selfish, insensitive, spoiled kid. In her newest book, *Don't Give Me That Attitude!* parenting expert Michele Borba offers you an effective, practical, and hands-on approach to help you work with your child to fix that very annoying but widespread youthful characteristic, attitude. If you have a child who is arrogant, bad-mannered, bad-tempered, a cheat, cruel, demanding, domineering, fresh, greedy, impatient, insensitive, irresponsible, jealous, judgmental, lazy, manipulative, narrow-minded, noncompliant, pessimistic, a poor loser, selfish, uncooperative, ungrateful, or unhelpful, this is the book for you!

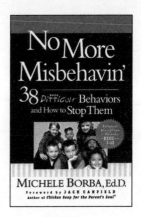

No More Misbehavin'

38 *Difficult Behaviors and*
How to Stop Them
Michele Borba, Ed.D.

Paper
ISBN: 0-7879-6617-7

"Michele Borba offers insightful, realistic, and straightforward advice that is sure to get results."

—Sally Lee, Editor in Chief, *Parents* magazine

Parenting expert Michele Borba tackles the most common bad behaviors that kids ages 3 to 12 repeat over and over—behaviors that drive parents crazy. In this enormously useful, simple-to-use book she shows how to change these behaviors for good. For each negative behavior Dr. Borba offers a series of key tips and guidelines and outlines a step-by-step plan for a customized makeover that really works! Using the steps outlined in *No More Misbehavin'* will give you the help you need to raise your kids with strong values and good character.

Building Moral Intelligence
The Seven Essential Virtues That Teach Kids to Do the Right Thing
Michele Borba, Ed.D.

Cloth
ISBN: 0-7879-6226-0

"No parenting book I know of offers so many practical insights, workable strategies, and inspiring stories, books, videos, and other family-friendly resources for intentionally teaching these crucial character strengths."

—from the Foreword by Thomas Lickona,
author, *Raising Good Children*

Rated one of the top ten notable parenting books by *Publishers Weekly*, this best-selling book provides a way to understanding moral intelligence and a step-by-step program for achieving it. Michele Borba outlines a way to evaluate and inspire our kids with the seven essential virtues that constitute moral intelligence: conscience, empathy, self-control, respect, kindness, tolerance, and fairness. The book is filled with original, hands-on activities designed for kids from 3 to 17.

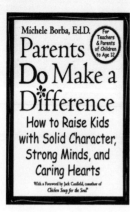

Parents Do Make a Difference

How to Raise Kids with Solid Character, Strong Minds, and Caring Hearts

Michele Borba, Ed.D.

Paper
ISBN: 0-7879-4605-2

"The fact is this may well be the only book you'll ever need on raising great children."

—from the Foreword by Jack Canfield,
coauthor of *Chicken Soup for the Soul*®

Finally, a book that shows you how to teach kids the eight indispensable skills—self-confidence, self-awareness, communication, problem solving, getting along, goal setting, perseverance, and empathy—they'll need for living confident, happy, and productive lives. Filled with step-by-step advice, practical ideas, and real-life examples, *Parents Do Make a Difference* puts field-tested tools into the hands of every parent and teacher who wants their children to succeed.